Challenging Global Finance

International Political Economy Series

General Editor: **Timothy M. Shaw**, Professor and Director, Institute of International Relations, The University of the West Indies, Trinidad & Tobago

Titles include:

Francis Adams, Satya Gupta and Kidane Mengisteab (*editors*)
GLOBALIZATION AND THE DILEMMAS OF THE STATE IN THE SOUTH

Susan Dicklitch
THE ELUSIVE PROMISE OF NGOs IN AFRICA: Lessons from Uganda

Elizabeth Friesen
CHALLENGING GLOBAL FINANCE: Civil Society and Transnational Networks

John Harriss, Kristian Stokke and Olle Törnquist (*editors*)
POLITICISING DEMOCRACY: The New Local Politics of Democratisation

David Hulme and Michael Edwards (*editors*)
NGOs, STATES AND DONORS: Too Close for Comfort?

Gordon Laxer and Sandra Halperin (*editors*)
GLOBAL CIVIL SOCIETY AND ITS LIMITS

Staffan Lindberg and Árni Sverrisson (*editors*)
SOCIAL MOVEMENTS IN DEVELOPMENT: The Challenge of Globalization and Democratization

Laura Macdonald
SUPPORTING CIVIL SOCIETY: The Political Role of Non-Governmental Organizations in Central America

Kurt Mills
HUMAN RIGHTS IN THE EMERGING GLOBAL ORDER: A New Sovereignty

Michael G. Schechter (*editor*)
THE REVIVAL OF CIVIL SOCIETY: Global and Comparative Perspectives

Hans Peter Schmitz
TRANSNATIONAL MOBILIZATION AND DOMESTIC REGIME CHANGE: Africa in Comparative Perspective

J. W. Wright, Jr. (*editor*)
STRUCTURAL FLAWS IN THE MIDDLE EAST PEACE PROCESS: Historical Contexts

---

International Political Economy Series
Series Standing Order ISBN 978–0–333–71708–0 hardcover
Series Standing Order ISBN 978–0–333–71110–1 paperback
(*outside North America only*)

You can receive future titles in this series as they are published by placing a standing order. Please contact your bookseller or, in case of difficulty, write to us at the address below with your name and address, the title of the series and one of the ISBNs quoted above.

Customer Services Department, Macmillan Distribution Ltd, Houndmills, Basingstoke, Hampshire RG21 6XS, England

---

Challenging Global Finance

Civil Society and Transnational Networks

Elizabeth Friesen
Lecturer in Political Science, Carleton University, Canada

palgrave
macmillan

First published 2012 by
PALGRAVE MACMILLAN

Palgrave Macmillan in the UK is an imprint of Macmillan Publishers Limited, registered in England, company number 785998, of Houndmills, Basingstoke, Hampshire RG21 6XS.

Palgrave Macmillan in the US is a division of St Martin's Press LLC, 175 Fifth Avenue, New York, NY 10010.

Palgrave Macmillan is the global academic imprint of the above companies and has companies and representatives throughout the world.

Palgrave® and Macmillan® are registered trademarks in the United States, the United Kingdom, Europe and other countries.

ISBN: 978–0–230–34879–0

This book is printed on paper suitable for recycling and made from fully managed and sustained forest sources. Logging, pulping and manufacturing processes are expected to conform to the environmental regulations of the country of origin.

A catalogue record for this book is available from the British Library.

A catalog record for this book is available from the Library of Congress.

10 9 8 7 6 5 4 3 2 1
21 20 19 18 17 16 15 14 13 12

Printed and bound in the United States of America
by Edwards Brothers, Inc.

Contents

Figures

Abbreviations

AFL–CIO	American Federation of Labor and Congress of Industrial Organizations
AIDS	acquired immune deficiency syndrome
ASEM	Asia Europe Meeting
ATTAC	Association for the Taxation of Financial Transactions and for Citizen's Action or Association pour la taxation des transactions financières et pour l'action citoyenne
BBC	British Broadcasting Corporation
BIS	Bank for International Settlements
CADTM	Committee for the Cancellation of the Third World Debt or Comité pour l'annulation de la Dette du Tiers Monde
CAFOD	Catholic Fund for Overseas Development – later Catholic Agency for Overseas Development
CBC	Canadian Broadcasting Corporation
CCCB	Canadian Conference of Catholic Bishops
CEDETIM	Centre d'études du Tiers Monde
CEJI	Canadian Ecumenical Jubilee Initiative, later Kairos: Canadian Ecumenical Justice Initiative
CIIR	Catholic Institute for International Relations
CoC	Center of Concern
CRID	Centre de Recherche et d'information pour le Développement
CSO	Civil Society Organization
DAC	Development Assistance Committee
DATA	Debt AIDS Trade Africa,
Dette	Dette et Développement
Development GAP	Development Group for Alternative Policies
ESAF	Enhanced Structural Adjustment Facility
EU	European Union
EURODAD	European Network on Debt and Development
FOE	Friends of the Earth
FONDAD	Forum on Debt and Development
G20	Group of Twenty
G-24	Group of Twenty-Four

GCAP	Global Call to Action against Poverty
GCR	Global Competitiveness Report
GLT	Global Leaders for Tomorrow
HI	Halifax Initiative
HIPC	Heavily Indebted Poor Country
HIV	human immunodeficiency virus
ICFfD	International Conference on Financing for Development
IFG	International Forum on Globalization
IFIwatchnet	International Financial Institutions Watchnet
IIE	Institute for International Economics
IIF	Institute of International Finance
IPS	Institute for Policy Studies
IMD	Institute for Management Development
IMF	International Monetary Fund
MAI	Multilateral Agreement on Investment
MDGs	Millennium Development Goals
MDRI	Multilateral Debt Relief Initiative
NAFTA	North American Free Trade Agreement
NEF	New Economics Foundation
NGLS	United Nations Non-Governmental Liaison Service
NGO	nongovernmental organization
NSI	North-South Institute
OAU	Organization of African Unity
OECD	Organization for Economic Cooperation and Development
OSI	Open Society Institute
PGA	Peoples' Global Action
RBWC	Reinventing Bretton Woods Committee
RIFI	Réseau pour la Réforme des Institutions Financières Internationales
SAF	Structural Adjustment Facility
SAP	Structural Adjustment Program
SAPRI	Structural Adjustment Participatory Review Initiative
SAPRIN	Structural Adjustment Participatory Review International Network
TEARfund	The Evangelical Alliance Relief Fund
TOES	The Other Economic Summit
TNI	Transnational Institute
UDN	Uganda Debt Network
UN	United Nations

UNCTAD	United Nations Conference on Trade and Development
UNDP	United Nations Development Program
UNICEF	United Nations Children's Fund
WB	World Bank
WCC	World Council of Churches
WDM	World Development Movement
WCR	World Competitiveness Report
WEA	World Evangelical Alliance
WEED	World Economy, Ecology and Development or Welwirschaft, Okologie & Entwicklung
WEF	World Economic Forum
WSF	World Social Forum
WTO	World Trade Organization

Acknowledgements

This book developed over many years, and I would like to take this opportunity to thank and acknowledge the individuals and organizations that helped make it possible. First I would like to thank all those working in international political economy whose work provides the intellectual foundation on which this book is built. I am grateful to the International Studies Association, the Canadian Political Science Association and the Centre for the Study of Globalisation and Regionalisation, University of Warwick for providing opportunities to me to present my work and receive constructive criticism and feedback on my ideas. I would like to thank the Department of Political Science and the Institute of Political Economy at Carleton University for first making me aware of the many academics and researchers working to make sense of globalization, international finance and global civil society.

Michael Dolan, Randall Germain, Laura Macdonald and Rianne Mahon provided absolutely invaluable support and guidance throughout this process. I am extremely fortunate to have been able to benefit from their advice and expertise. I would also like to take this opportunity to formally acknowledge Rob Aitken, Rick Baker, Isa Bakker, Elizabeth Cobbett, Vincent della Sala, Judit Fabian, Barbara Jenkins, Daniel Pierre-Antoine, Fiona Robinson, Nilgun Onder, Anu Pandey, Andrea Rounce, Arne Ruckert, Herman Schwartz, Devrim Sezer, Miriam Smith and William Walters for their contributions to this effort. Thank you to the Social Sciences and Humanities Research Council of Canada, Ontario Graduate Scholarship Program and Carleton University for their much appreciated financial support. I would also like to thank Tim Shaw and Christina Brian at Palgrave Macmillan for seeing me through the process of publication so efficiently and yet so pleasantly, and I would like to express my sincere gratitude to an anonymous reviewer for a number of excellent suggestions which were a pleasure to incorporate in the final work.

I would also like to acknowledge all those individuals who work in international organizations, civil society organizations, nongovernmental organizations or government who have worked so hard to "make a difference." While they may not always agree and may sometimes work at cross purposes, they are simply admirable. I am especially grateful to all those individuals who formally or informally so generously shared their insights and experiences with me. Finally, I am lucky enough to be part of an extended and diverse community of friends and family whose interest and support has been both a help and an inspiration. In particular, I would like to thank my mother, Kirsten Friesen, my father, the late John Friesen, and my uncle, George Metz. Their life experiences were an important motivation in writing this book. In conclusion, I would like to express a very special thanks to my husband, Bill Metz, and our children, Victoria and Alexander. Without their support, encouragement and patience this book would not have been possible.

1
Introduction

Is politics changing? In the globalizing world it would appear that a network society is taking shape in which powerful institutional structures unhooked from traditional state-centric concepts of government are emerging. Governance is increasingly supplementing government. And, although the extent of its autonomy from state control is debatable, in recent years international finance has developed into an extremely powerful structure of transnational governance. International finance differs from domestic finance in that it is not subject to the clear hierarchical authority of an overarching state. While a number of states undoubtedly continue to play an important role in creating, maintaining and enforcing the rules and practices governing the international financial system, since the demise of the postwar Bretton Woods financial order in 1971, both the public and private organizations and institutions of international finance have grown into extremely powerful structures that challenge conventional national and international channels of authority and accountability. Even in the face of ongoing financial crises and widespread popular outrage it appears far from certain that states will succeed in reining in global finance.

Challenging finance

The rules and practices governing international finance were highly contested throughout the twentieth century. The failure of the gold standard, the rise and decline of the Bretton Woods system and the subsequent "re-emergence of global finance" clearly demonstrate this (Helleiner 1994a). For most of the twentieth century the rules and practices governing international finance were the subject of a highly technical debate conducted primarily by a small community of experts whose primary goal was to create and maintain a financial structure that would both provide financial stability and enhance economic efficiency. In the last decade of the twentieth century, however, a number of civil society organizations (CSOs) and nongovernmental organizations (NGOs) challenged this process as they attempted to make the debate more accessible and to include a wider range of participants and previously excluded points of view. They introduced concepts such as human rights and economic justice into the debate and presented a new vision of the "proper" role of the economy in society. This challenge was based outside the dominant paradigm of neoliberal economics as CSOs and NGOs sought to transform the debate.

By the 1990s the third world debt crisis had become an important catalyst for popular activism with respect to international finance. When the third world debt crisis first started to emerge in the late 1970s it was considered a temporary problem, but, as problems persisted and spread international financial institutions (IFIs) and creditor governments became actively involved in seeking a long-term remedy. At first conventional wisdom held that the discipline of free market relations would lay a solid foundation for economic development in debtor states and the resulting economic growth would, ultimately, provide a permanent way out of the crisis for all concerned. Therefore in the 1980s the International Monetary Fund (IMF) designed and enforced structural adjustment programs (SAPs) in a number of debtor states. Under SAPs debtor states would receive debt relief on the condition that they "adjust" or liberalize the structure of their economies according to the policy prescriptions of the IMF and later the Washington Consensus. These remedies, however, met with little lasting success in resolving the debt crisis.

At the same time SAPs generated negative social outcomes in many debtor states, and this caused a number of CSOs and NGOs within these states to criticize this approach. Many NGOs and CSOs were also based in creditor states, and as CSOs and NGOs within specific debtor states connected with their counterparts in creditor states their demands grew. The demands included calls for economic justice and debt cancellation, as well as a broader critique of the IFIs and the rules and practices governing international finance as a whole. The transnational civil society-based campaign for the cancellation of third world debt was an important product of this challenge.

The idea of debt cancellation

This book explores the origins, tactics and impact of the campaign for the cancellation of third world debt, paying particular attention to the role of moral values and normative ideas in the contestation over the rules and practices governing international finance. It examines how transnational, non-state actors in civil society shaped the rules and practices governing debt cancellation and how the relationship between state actors and CSOs and NGOs played out around these issues. This contestation demonstrates how a shift in discourse or a reframing of the issues can facilitate the progress of demands that were previously off the agenda.

The specific case of the campaign for the cancellation of third world debt provides a way to explore the broader question of how attitudes to economic globalization can be transformed. Understanding this dynamic matters because, not only does it help us to understand how the campaign for third world debt cancellation worked, but it also provides a sense of how their tactics might be adapted to other situations. Therefore this book provides a way into broader questions of international and transnational activism and provides insights that are important for those seeking to understand or participate in the ongoing contest over the rules and practices governing the global political economy. At the moment understanding this dynamic is particularly important in light of the uncertain and sometimes contradictory responses to the ongoing financial and economic crisis.

Although much has been written on both international finance and transnational social movements, little has been written on how these two bodies of literature might be connected. Similarly, there has been little detailed analysis of the origins and interconnections of the debt cancellation movement internationally or transnationally. This book will start to map this level of contestation. Two case studies were selected to explore from two different vantage points how, in this emerging context of transnational civil society-based politics, moral values and normative ideas – ideas about how the world "should" be – are powerful political forces in defining the limits of the possible and shaping the global agenda. The first case study examines the transnational civil society campaign for debt cancellation. This campaign was broad based and far reaching, and although it included an enormous number of organizations, groups and individuals, it became best known through the Jubilee 2000 network. In this campaign, contestation took place in the streets, at high-level international meetings and everywhere in between. The second case study examines the World Economic Forum (WEF) annual meetings at Davos, Switzerland in the period leading up to 2005. Although little work has been done on the WEF, as will be seen, it became an important site of transnational contestation. In contrast to the first case study, the WEF study explores the process of contestation in a contained and exclusive setting within transnational civil society. Although there are a surprising number of interconnections which will become clear in the following chapters, the first case study is situated primarily at the popular level while the WEF case study is primarily at the elite level.

The big question

The fundamental question guiding this study is "How have non-state actors mobilized to change the international financial system and what impact have they had on the rules and practices governing international finance?" Arguably the rules and practices governing international finance are the product of political contestation, and this project explores how NGOs and CSOs can contest the rules and practices governing international finance. This question leads to four hypotheses. First, in the broadest sense normative ideas matter. In other words, in the emerging context of transnational civil society based politics, normative ideas – ideas about how the world *should* be – are a powerful force in shaping change, and this is true even with respect to the opaque, highly technical and, apparently, empirically based system of rules and practices which governs international finance. Second, ideas are influenced by developments in capitalism, and the campaign for debt cancellation can be understood as part of a Polanyian double movement taking place at a transnational level in which the effects of international financial markets have generated a societal backlash (Polanyi 1944/1957). Third, when defining more specific agendas, moral values and normative ideas also matter, and they can be influenced by civil society actors. For example by 2005 CSOs and NGOs had redefined the global agenda with respect to finance and debt and produced a crisis in one elite discursive framework, the Washington Consensus, and a (partial) shift to another discursive framework which incorporated the demands of non-elite actors. Fourth, the relationships suggested by the previous three hypotheses contribute to the fourth and most specific hypothesis that by means of activism and innovative political strategies (by challenging hegemonic ideas) civil society actors can change the process of decision making to include actors and points of view that were previously excluded.

In the last decade of the twentieth century non-state actors such as CSOs and NGOs mobilized to change the international financial system by reshaping the discourse around finance and interjecting concerns about the human impact of financial processes into the ongoing debate regarding international financial reform. While a number of aspects of the organization of international finance were targeted by activists, this process was most visible in the case of the campaign for the cancellation of third world debt. In this campaign CSOs and NGOs accomplished this shift in discourse using a wide range of conventional, as well as innovative, techniques of political contestation at the national, international, and transnational levels. Furthermore, while appeals to material interests are an important part of this process, arguments based on moral values and normative ideas have also been important and sometimes appear to have trumped more conventional understandings of material interests in this contestation. As will be seen NGOs and CSOs reframed the issues around debt, developed a substantial expertise on the subject, and by means of education, lobbying, and moral suasion transformed the way debt was understood at both the popular and elite levels. This, in turn, had an impact on the rules and practices governing international finance with respect to debt cancellation.

While not discounting the explanatory importance of theoretical perspectives which privilege states, markets or class, this book adopts a constructivist perspective in order to bring the power of values and normative ideas in this process into focus. An in-depth analysis of the campaign for debt cancellation requires a study of not only national and international, but also transnational activism. Furthermore, this campaign demonstrates how CSOs and NGOs found a way to contest the substantial power concentrated in the institutions of international finance by means of an appeal to an alternative set of moral values and normative ideas. This conflict, based on competing logics, one largely market based and the other largely based in civil society, can be understood as a transnational variation on the Polanyian double movement. It provides an example of how the tension between socially intolerable market outcomes and a civil society based reaction to these outcomes as suggested in the double movement might provide a means of fine tuning capitalist institutions. Therefore, rather than leading to their destruction, this contestation might be an important step in enhancing the adaptive capacity and resilience of capitalist systems.

This book is a study of a conscious effort to produce a paradigm shift in economics and the part that norms and values play in this. Clearly politics are important to this process and therefore this chapter will now situate this argument in terms of the larger question of "what is politics."

Politics

At its most fundamental level this book is about power and politics in a globalizing world. Harold Lasswell famously defined politics as the study of "who gets what, when, and how?" (Lasswell 1936). This question provides a useful starting point. Embedded in this deceptively simple question are several very complex questions. *Who* decides goals? *How* are these outcomes achieved? On *what basis* are outcomes *accepted*? Throughout history the answers to these questions and the assumptions on which they are based have been highly contested. They vary with time and place. For example political practices that are accepted as legitimate in one era, under different circumstances may be seen as archaic, inappropriate or even a violation of fundamental rights.

Understanding this ongoing process of evolution and contestation, legitimation, and challenge is central to understanding politics. However, like an iceberg, the portion of conflict that appears obvious, the overt political contestation, rests on a larger but also contested set of social and cultural beliefs, assumptions and norms that are less overt but, nonetheless, provide the foundation to politics. Naturalized assumptions set the agenda of political contestation and are a powerful determining factor in who gets what, when and how. These assumptions are central to the authority and legitimacy of political processes and actors.

Politics is contingent and contested and, ultimately, it is based on values and beliefs. Furthermore, a new politics is emerging. At present, aided by technological advances in communication and transportation, changes are taking place in politics in which, not only the state, but also international institutions and social norms have become the target of political activity. Political activity has started to spill out of the boundaries of the state. At the local, all the way through to the global level, attempts are being made to supplement conventional political processes, both democratic and dictatorial, by a bewildering array of actors and organizations such as NGOs and CSOs. In much of this contestation the social and cultural assumptions, the submerged part of the iceberg which underpins political process, have become the target of attempts at a sort of "global consciousness raising" by these groups.

This book draws on theories which put forward a broad encompassing definition of power and, in particular, emphasize the power of ideas (Lukes 1974; Foucault 1977; Gramsci 1971). In this work the importance of norms, values, and frameworks of belief in shaping the very possibilities of action are recognized. As Lukes argues, the capacity to set the agenda, to determine the rules of the game in a given time and place and to have them widely accepted as the most obvious and undisputed choice represents the highest level of power at work (Lukes 1974). For example, within the state specific understandings of the rights and responsibilities of a citizen shape the very possibilities of both political activity and political outcomes. Arguably, this understanding of the power of norms and values can be extended beyond the state and applied to the international and transnational organizations and institutions of the global political economy.

Markets as constructions

In this book capitalism and capitalist markets are understood as specific sets of rules – social and political constructions based on power relations (Polanyi 1944/1957; Bakker 1994; Gibson-Graham 1996; Mouffe 1993; Larner 2000). This challenges the classical liberal and neoliberal understanding of the market mechanism as an impartial and automatic mechanism of efficient economic distribution. Furthermore it challenges the claim that the free market mechanism is above politics, above ideas and interests. Free market processes are neither apolitical nor devoid of power relations (Mouffe 1993; Lindblom 1977). Rather, capitalist economic relations are constructed according to rules produced by a process of political contestation. Some of these rules are visible, but some are so highly naturalized that they have become invisible. While they may seem to reflect a natural order, these rules and practices are subject to challenge and change.

Arguably, the resilience of capitalism lies in its adaptive capacity, and this in turn lies in the dynamic of political contestation which produces change in the rules underlying capitalist relations. In many respects capitalist economic relations work best when they are embedded in a social context (Gramsci 1977; Ruggie 1982). This enhances the stability and sustainability of the system. Unregulated capitalist market processes have a tendency to produce socially intolerable conditions which stimulate a social reaction, which in turn seeks to constrain or regulate their impact (Polanyi 1944/1957). This leads to political contestation and potentially, changes in the rules and practices governing capitalist economic relations. In the case of finance, the rules and institutions governing its relations have been reworked and reconstructed with some frequency.

Furthermore, the rules and practices governing market relations are not completely defined by economic processes. Marxist or economic determinist accounts, which argue that ultimately production and class lie at the base of all power relations, are incomplete (Gramsci 1971; Cox 1983/1993: 61; Lukes 1974). Although these factors are important and their power extends well beyond what might, on the surface, be defined as economic relations, there is something more going on. Arguably moral values and normative ideas can have a life of their own. They need not be determined by relations of production or class but are driven by another logic. As Macdonald (1994: 277) writes,

> The potential long-term impact of actors in global civil society lies not merely in their material resources, but also in their ability to create new identities, to contest established ways of thinking, and to create new linkages between peoples in different parts of the globe.

As will be seen in Chapter 2, in international relations literature as well as in the literature on social movements, there has been a steady movement toward recognizing the importance of norms and values. This has produced more nuanced understandings of power relations (Lukes 1974, 1986; Watson 2005; Foucault 1977; Blyth 2002; J. George 1994; Birchfield 1999). It has produced a body of work which recognizes the importance of society in the construction of the rules and practices which govern economic relations (Ruggie 1982, 1998; Polanyi 1944/1957; Gramsci 1971; Sally 1998; Watson 2005). The social movement literature has similarly recognized the importance of beliefs and values as a driving force in social movements (Keck and Sikkink 1998; McCarthy and Zald 1979; Seidman 2001; Piven and Cloward 1995; Reitan 2007).

There has been a similar move in the literature on international/global finance, and there is a growing and increasingly influential body of literature which addresses the importance of normative ideas and values in international finance (Best 2005; McNamara 1998; Porter 2005; P. Hall 1989; de Goede 2003, 2005; Leyshon and Thrift 1997; Scholte 2002; Abdelal 2007; Germain and Kenny 2005a; O'Brien et al. 2000). Most of the constructivist work in international finance, however, focuses on the role of elite actors, states, or the IFIs at the national or international levels. The case studies presented in this book seek to build on this by introducing insights drawn from the literature on social movements, considering the influence of normative ideas on non-elite actors as well as elite actors, and examining the interaction of CSOs and NGOs at national, international, as well as the transnational level.

The construction of international finance

A particularly interesting case in which the power of moral values and normative ideas has become increasingly apparent is in the debate over the organization of international finance.[1] In the late twentieth century global finance re-emerged as a powerful force in the global political economy (Helleiner 1994) and, while the independence of the international financial system from state control remains debatable, there is little doubt that the rules and practices governing international finance have become an effective means to organize global financial activity as well as coordinate and defend the interests of financial actors. For much of the twentieth century the organization of international finance was a source of conflict and, around the turn of this century there was, once again, widespread concern and dissatisfaction with international finance. At the time the structure of international finance was increasingly referred to as the international financial "architecture." This terminology reinforced the view that the organization of international finance was not an automatic or naturally occurring phenomenon but rather a system based on rules, regulations, and norms, constructed through a process of social and political contestation (Braudel 1979; Arrighi 1994; Helleiner 1994; Cohen 1977).

At the end of the twentieth century international finance was confronted by two significant problems. First, an ongoing series of financial crises culminating in the 1997 Asian financial crisis called into question its capacity to function as a stable and sustainable financial framework for the global economy. Second, the impact of SAPs in the developing world, as well as calls for market discipline, deficit reduction and rolling back the welfare state in the developed world, implicated the international financial system in processes which, in the eyes of a number of civil society actors, appeared to undermine the material welfare of the most vulnerable citizens in debtor states and exacerbated inequality around the world. This led to claims that the existing rules governing the organization of international finance institutionalized "social and economic injustice."

This research explores the CSOs and NGOs which challenged the rules governing international finance, focuses on the campaign for the cancellation of third world debt and analyzes how this campaign provided a means to challenge neoliberal orthodoxy and undermine the push toward international financial liberalization. As discussed above, political contestation has always been central to the construction and reproduction of international finance but, arguably, the nature of this contestation is changing. State actors clearly continue to play an important role; however, it increasingly appears that non-state actors are claiming a part. Since the 1990s an unprecedented number of CSOs and NGOS have sought a voice in determining the rules and practices governing international finance.

State actors continue to be important to the construction and reproduction of international finance. However, international finance represents not only an unprecedented concentration of transnational economic power, but also an important concentration of political power, capable of challenging significant aspects of the autonomy and sovereignty of states in the international system. International financial actors and institutions draw much of their legitimacy from their technical expertise and their ability to function within the complex rules which govern international finance. At the same time, they draw power from the economic impact of financial market processes. Arguably, international finance is an important site of political power cut loose from traditional notions of community and, therefore, free from conventional, territorially based notions of political accountability, legitimacy, and citizenship. In the 1990s, reformers located within this epistemic community tended to advocate for self regulation and informal coordination in international finance. Their calls for reform were based primarily on the technical requirements of a stable and prosperous international financial system but, after the 1997 Asian financial crisis, concerns with values such as economic and social "justice" started to feature more prominently in this debate (Stiglitz 2002: 218; BIS 1999; G20 2001; P. Martin 2001; G7 2002).

At the same time, a number of popular, transnational actors and organizations which sought to challenge the present structure of international finance from the outside became more prominent. While their original mandates often had little to do with international finance, over the years many CSOs and NGOs developed substantial expertise and depth of experience on financial issues. These groups drew much of their legitimacy from secular or faith based norms and values of respect for human rights and dignity. They drew power from their influence on the discourse surrounding financial issues as well as their potential to threaten the social stability necessary for the operation of an orderly international financial system. The networks of interconnected overlapping CSOs and NGOs that participate in this contestation are constantly developing and evolving. In addition to those campaigning for the cancellation of third world debt such as the Jubilee 2000 network, there are organizations that seek to place constraints on international financial market processes. These include those promoting an international financial transactions levy or "Robin Hood tax", groups that campaign against tax havens, others which seek to provide innovative economic solutions to global problems such as micro credit or innovative financing for development, and, finally, groups calling for reform of the organization of international finance in the name of social and economic "justice" (Jubilee Movement International 2002; Halifax Initiative 2002).

In considering this contestation it is very important to remember that many reformers located within the mainstream institutions of international finance, as well as those located in transnational civil society at large, share common ground in their general goal of increasing "welfare." However, they subscribe to very different conceptions of what is meant by welfare and, most importantly, how this might be achieved in practice. In general, while challengers situated in society at large tend to privilege "social justice" based on moral or ethical values, the reformers located within the epistemic community of international finance tend to privilege efficiency and prosperity based on economic measures and technical expertise. Arguably, even the most dogmatic supporter of unfettered free market discipline is no less committed to improving global welfare than the most committed alterglobalization activist. Both seek similar ends. The difference, however, lies in the degree of faith in market logic, the willingness to wait for the "long run" to arrive, and the human toll or collateral damage one is willing to accept in the short term as the cost of progress toward economic efficiency. In liberal economic theory unencumbered market processes will, by definition, ultimately maximize welfare and generate economic justice. From this perspective it is political interference that is seen as a distorting and damaging force to which the market mechanism provides a remedy.

Politics and finance have a long and complex relationship. The charge is often made that civil society campaigners lack political legitimacy, that they have no right to speak for others. Critics ask, who anointed Jubilee 2000 as the representative of the interests of the world's debtors? Yet the same might be said of international finance. The same process of globalization which has allowed CSOs and NGOs to wield power without legitimating it by means of a conventional, territorially based political process has also facilitated the emergence of globally integrated capital markets, increasingly beyond the control of individual states. As Pauly (1997: 3) asks, "Who elected the bankers," This book explores what, in the absence of clear hierarchical ties to a conventionally defined political process, forms the basis of legitimacy and authority for the actors and institutions of international finance as well as for the CSOs and NGOs campaigning for reform.

The international financial system is a particularly interesting target of civil society activism because this contestation involves a popular challenge to a set of highly technical institutions. Until the late 1990s the technical nature of financial issues and the prestige accorded to expert opinion in finance tended to silence popular opposition to financial policies. This, however, appeared to change in the face of a groundswell of popular opinion calling for debt cancellation and invoking moral values and normative ideas as a basis on which to challenge the policies of international financial institutions. In addition, after the Asian financial crisis of 1997, popular dissent appeared to penetrate the financial institutions themselves producing, in many quarters, critical self evaluation and calls for reform from within these institutions.

There is an undeniable tension between the twin goals of economic efficiency and social justice in market relations. From a neoliberal perspective however, it is still possible to make the claim that, in the long run, both will be achieved through the impartial and objective workings of the free market mechanism. Furthermore, it is possible to argue that this can be accomplished without politics, conflict or negotiation and, therefore, the dangers of inefficient, incompetent and possibly corrupt governments can be eliminated by the elegant economic calculus of market relations. However mistaken this view may be in practice, in the case of some economic relations such as international trade this argument is still being made with some degree of success.

In the case of international finance however, events have made this pro-market position much more difficult to support. This has a great deal to do with the characteristics of international finance itself. Historically, finance has been less concerned with social justice than with economic efficiency. Debtors tend to elicit little sympathy. Their condition tends to be attributed to bad judgment or bad character. Furthermore, there tends to be a suspicion of debtors' morals, a sense that debtors deserve the consequences of their actions coupled with a conviction that debts must be repaid and that it is not only inefficient but also immoral *not* to do so (de Goede 2005: 156). To many, finance itself appears a little unwholesome (de Goede 2005; Chernow 1990: 373–377). It remains closely related to gambling and speculation and although it is necessary to modern economic activity, it is prone to "manias, panics and crashes" (Kindleberger 1996). It produces no tangible product. It is dominated by "insiders" working in accordance with increasingly Byzantine calculations and rules. For the initiated it can create fortunes, but it is also capable of drawing even the most experienced into bankruptcy. As de Goede (2005) describes, the history of finance is a history of a search for a means to define certain speculative activities as respectable, but this effort has not been a complete success. Although religious prohibitions on usury have been largely lifted in the developed world, suspicion of financiers and bankers remains an important thread in popular discourse. Perhaps for this reason, in spite of its intimidating technical armour, finance became vulnerable to popular critiques. It is particularly noteworthy that in the campaign for the cancellation of third world debt the critiques which presented the most effective challenges to the rules and practices governing international finance drew on moral values.

Indeed, the earlier efforts to constrain international finance that were an important part of the 1944 Bretton Woods agreement were, in large part, a response to the Great Depression, the financial instability of the interwar period and the subsequent World War (Helleiner 1994b). The desire to avoid a repetition of these events was very much on the minds of those who drafted the Bretton Woods agreement (Skidelsky 2000: 355).[2] Despite the multitude of stresses associated with the postwar reconstruction, Bretton Woods produced a period of relative stability in international finance that only started to unravel in the early 1970s with the demise of the Bretton Woods system, the re-emergence of global finance and a shift away from a Keynesian consensus to what would later come to be known as the Washington Consensus. This illustrates that while material interests of states and non-state actors have played a part in determining the rules and practices governing international finance, changes in values and normative ideas have also contributed to the economic paradigm shifts which underpin the changes in these rules.

The case studies

Values and normative ideas have played and continue to play an important part in shaping the rules and practices which govern global finance.

However, the scale and diversity of this ongoing process is enormous, and to address all aspects of this dynamic is well beyond the scope of this project. Therefore the campaign for the cancellation of third world debt has been selected as the focus of this book. Two case studies are used to explore the importance of normative factors in changing attitudes to debt cancellation and the impact this had on the rules governing international finance. The first case follows the transnational campaign for debt cancellation as it developed in networks of NGOs and CSOs in the 1990s. It explores the emergence of contestation based on a broadly defined concept of human rights in the debate over the reconstruction of the international financial architecture. The catalyst for this activism was the third world debt crisis of the 1980s but, in the period leading up to 2005 social justice and human rights emerged as a powerful basis on which to challenge financial orthodoxy at both popular and elite levels. The second case follows the contestation over the "proper" roles and responsibilities of economic actors which took place at the WEF annual meetings at Davos and the role of this elite organization in shaping the debate on debt cancellation.

Although debt cancellation continues to be a contentious issue, this research takes 2005 as its end point. At the 2005 G8 meeting in Gleneagles, Scotland, debt cancellation was firmly linked to economic justice, ending global poverty, and the Multilateral Debt Relief Initiative (MDRI) was unanimously supported by the creditor states in attendance. This seemed to mark a substantial shift in attitudes to debt cancellation and a turn toward a more critical view of international finance as a whole.

The two case studies were selected to study the process of contestation from two different perspectives – one based largely on the grassroots and popular movements and the other based on an exclusive group drawn from the world business elite. The research identifies the composition and interrelationships of the NGOs and CSOs involved in this contestation, their goals and strategies and how these developed over the period between 1980 and 2005. This allows me to assess how their activities shaped the debate and reframed the issues surrounding debt cancellation, in particular, and the "proper" role of finance in the global political economy, in general. In this analysis, I pay particular attention to the role of moral values and normative ideas in this contestation, how and why they figured in the debate, and their association with shifts in policy with respect to debt and finance.

In this research there is a danger of confusing public relations strategies with real changes in discourse, agenda and policy. And, even if substantial change in policy occurs, the question of how one can be sure that apparent changes are not simply "lip service" or "window dressing" or even part of a larger strategy to co-opt opposition remains. The best answer is perhaps that one cannot be absolutely sure. It is difficult to measure change in attitudes and even more difficult to attribute such change to a specific cause. Furthermore, contestation over the terms of debt cancellation in particular and the rules and practices governing international finance in general is an ongoing process and the outcomes remain to be seen. However, for the purposes of this project attention was paid to four factors in order to separate public relations strategies from real change. First, the shift in discourse over time – a consistent shift in discourse that continued for a sustained period is evidence that the shift is more than window dressing. Second, the number and diversity of those expressing support for an alternative vision – a new consensus on debt cancellation among diverse parties is evidence that the change is more than a public relations strategy. Third, the inclusiveness/exclusiveness of the formal and informal forums at which these issues were debated is an indication of the seriousness with which challenges were taken. Finally, the change in policy outcomes with respect to debt cancellation and the extent to which debt cancellation provisions were complied with is a measure of the commitment to real change.[3]

Conclusion

The following chapters explore the question of how, in the 30-year period leading up to the G8 meeting at Gleneagles, Scotland in 2005, non-state actors mobilized at the national, international and transnational levels to transform attitudes to economic globalization and in this way produced change in the rules and practices governing international finance. I focus on the campaign for the cancellation of third world debt and, using evidence gathered in two case studies, I test the following four hypotheses: first, normative ideas and values, that is, ideas about how the world *should* be were an important part of this campaign; second, Polanyi's concept of the double movement is helpful in understanding this dynamic; third, at both elite and popular levels, campaigning CSOs and NGOs produced a crisis in one elite discursive framework – the Washington Consensus – and achieved a partial shift to another discursive framework which incorporated the demands of non-elite actors; and finally, by means of innovative political strategies CSOs and NGOs successfully challenged the conventional wisdom on debt cancellation and changed the process of decision making to include actors and points of view that were previously excluded.

This book consists of five chapters. Chapter 2 defines the concept of power, as it is used in this research, and discusses the role of power relations and, in particular, the role of values and normative ideas in the construction of economic structures such as market relations. This chapter then turns to the question of how these insights apply in international finance. It surveys the theoretical approaches to analysing the construction of the rules and practices governing international finance and traces the emergence of theoretical approaches which put greater weight on the power of values and ideas in the construction, reproduction and reform of international finance. It then turns to a second body of literature on social movements and contentious politics which examines non-state processes of contestation and change and traces how values and normative ideas have become increasingly important in this literature. Finally, Chapter 2 discusses how these two bodies of literature each provide an important part of the puzzle for understanding changing attitudes to economic globalization and more specifically contestation and change in the rules and practices governing debt cancellation.

Chapter 3 presents the case study on the transnational civil society based campaign for the cancellation of third world debt. It briefly outlines how three factors, the postwar project of international development and modernization, the demise of the Bretton Woods system in the early 1970s and the financial impact of the oil crises contributed not only to the lending which resulted in the third world debt crisis but also provided a foundation for transnational CSO and NGO networking which later became so important in the campaign for debt cancellation. It looks at the roots of the campaign for debt cancellation in civil society, discusses the failed efforts by debtor states to coordinate international resistance to the third world debt crisis during the 1980s and, finally, focuses on the role of civil society, CSOs and NGOs in the campaign for debt cancellation. This analysis is divided into four periods which are associated with five turning points in the campaign: the Mexican crisis in 1982, the fiftieth anniversary of the Bretton Woods institutions in 1994, the Asian financial crisis in 1997, the demonstrations at the World Trade Organization conference in Seattle in 1999, and the adoption of the MDRI at the G8 in 2005. Next the symbiotic relationship between the United Nations (UN) and the CSOs and NGOs campaigning for debt cancellation is considered. Finally, the successes and failures of the campaign are discussed.

Chapter 4 presents the World Economic Forum case study. It focuses on the annual general meeting of the WEF as a site of contestation and the role of the WEF in the contestation over the rules and practices governing economic relations in general and debt cancellation in particular. It traces the origins of the WEF and discusses three areas in which there has been substantial continuity at the annual meeting: leadership, networking and the provision of a meaningful experience for business members of the WEF. Next it considers the WEF as a site of contestation and change. As in the first case study, this chapter is divided into four periods defined by five turning points: the 1971 founding of the European Management Forum (the organization that became the WEF), the fall of the Berlin wall in 1989; the Asian financial crisis in 1997, the demonstrations in Seattle in 1999, and the adoption of the MDRI at the G8 in 2005. Finally, the changes in discourse and policy with respect to debt cancellation and how they are connected with the activities of and participants at the WEF annual meeting are discussed.

In Chapter 5 the two cases are compared and contrasted with respect to the question of how non-state actors have mobilized to change the international financial system and what impact they have had on the rules and practices governing international finance. The discussion is structured around the four hypotheses put forward in this chapter. Next the broader implications of the results of this research are discussed and special attention paid to the lessons that can be drawn from these case studies. Finally I discuss under what conditions this research might be of value in understanding, as well as shaping, the ongoing contestation over the rules, regulations and practices which govern economic globalization.

In conclusion this book examines how conventional wisdom can be challenged, certainty transformed into doubt and how new opportunities for effective political action can be created. By examining the transnational civil society based campaign for the cancellation of third world debt this research traces how the actors involved in this campaign altered the dominant discourse, shifted the agenda and thereby reshaped policy outcomes. I do not claim that these issues were settled in 2005. The contestation continues but, as the question of how to address new debt crises – this time located in the heart of the developed world – and the ongoing financial and economic crisis becomes increasingly urgent, I do argue that the following account has much to offer. Understanding the relative success of the campaign for the cancellation of third world debt is of interest because its relevance is not limited to debt cancellation but can be applied to a variety of other situations including the contestation over the response to the financial crisis that is taking place today. Widespread public anger and indignation characterized the peak of the financial crisis in the fall of 2008 but since then, despite substantial evidence of incompetence and wrongdoing, the popular response remains unfocused. Since the financial crisis peaked in the fall of 2008 there have been renewed calls for financial regulation. At first it seemed that a new era in global finance might be taking shape, and yet civil society actors have not pressed their advantage. In stark contrast to the campaign for the cancellation of third world debt, more recent calls for financial responsibility and social justice are weak and confused. For example, in 2010 during the G8/G20 the demands of campaigning NGOs for a "Robin Hood" tax, an international financial transactions levy, were marginalized and, in the popular press, confused with calls for a "bank tax". The response to the ongoing debt crisis, this time centred in Europe, remains weak and fragmented. In the United States the initial popular anger with Wall Street actors has been defused and transformed into a popular generalized disillusionment with government in general. Therefore at present, as the opportunity to rein in global finance slips away it is particularly worth considering what made the campaign for the cancellation of third world debt relatively effective and what lessons it might provide for future campaigns.

2
Power and Resistance

At its most basic level this book is about power and politics in a globalizing world. More specifically, it is about the transformative potential of moral values and normative ideas in civil society based contestation over the rules and practices of international finance, and how this contestation has contributed to the adaptive capacity of capitalism in the twentieth and early twenty-first centuries. Marx predicted that capitalist economic relations would inexorably lead to their demise and that capitalism contained the seeds of its own destruction. Yet, a century and a half later, despite periodic crises and even after the most recent brush with financial disaster, capitalism appears to be in fairly good health. The resilience and adaptive capacity of capitalist systems are not only the result of its impressive capacity to mobilize technical and material resources through market relations, but are also due to capitalism's relation to social and normative structures that, historically, have supported as well as generated societal limits on market processes (Ruggie 1982, 1998; Polanyi 1944/57; and Gramsci 1971).

Economic structures in general and international finance in particular, are complex systems of rules and practices that are constructed through an ongoing process of contestation and consent. While many of these competing forces are materially based, moral values and normative ideas also play an important part in the contest to shape the rules and practices governing international financial relations. This is of more than theoretical interest. The organization of international finance is a profoundly powerful structure with an impact, for better or worse, on the welfare of almost everyone in the world today. For the past 30 years a number of civil society based actors and organizations have contested the existing rules and practices governing international finance by challenging the conventional wisdom regarding the "proper" role of finance. In these campaigns, human rights, social justice and other normative arguments have been employed in a kind of global "consciousness raising" process. The campaign for the cancellation of third world debt has been the most visible of these campaigns.

This book takes the case of the campaign for the cancellation of third world debt to address three puzzles. First, what produces challengers to a given set of rules and practices or as de Goede (2003: 96) puts it, what produces a "fundamental questioning" of previously accepted orthodoxies in international finance? Second, how does a non-state based challenge produce change? And, finally, what is the importance of moral values and normative ideas, ideas about how the world *should* be, in the case of civil society based politics? In the case of the campaign for the cancellation of third world debt, a number of actors including debtors as well as certain creditors clearly had their material interests served by debt cancellation but, arguably, a number of the actors who were active campaigners for debt cancellation would receive no such benefit. What then motivated these actors?

Power

The first and perhaps most important part of this discussion centers on the concept of power – the power to make the rules, change the rules, maintain the rules and enforce the rules. A broad and flexible definition of power is necessary to understanding the forces at work, not only in obvious conflict situations, but also in hidden and latent conflict situations. The theoretical framework employed in this book draws on theories which put forward a broad encompassing definition of power and, in particular, emphasize the power of ideas. In this work the importance of norms, rules and frameworks of belief in shaping the very possibilities of action are recognized (Lukes 1974, 2005; Foucault 1977; Gramsci 1971; Lipschutz with Rowe 2005; Olesen 2011; Marques and Utting 2010; Moschella 2010; Porter and Ronit 2010a; Kenny and Germain 2005). As Lukes argues, the capacity to set the agenda, to determine the rules of the game in a given time and place and to have them widely accepted as self evident and as the most reasonable choice represents the highest level of power (Lukes 1974: 25).

Lukes' concept of power is particularly useful in understanding processes of contestation and change in a globalizing world. In Lukes' (1974: 25) essay on power he presents three "views" of power. According to him, the "one dimensional view of power" focuses on the power relations inherent in decision making and observable overt conflict. The "two dimensional view of power" expands the concept to focus on decision making as well as non-decision making issues, as well as potential issues, and covert, as well as observable overt conflict. Finally, the "three dimensional view of power" focuses on decision making as well as control of the political agenda including that control which may be achieved without making decisions. It includes observable conflict, either overt or covert, and includes latent conflicts. Therefore Lukes' three-dimensional view of power allows the consideration of more conventional forms of power as well as less easily observable forms of power. It,

> allows for the consideration of the many ways in which potential issues are kept out of politics whether through the operation of social forces and institutional practices or through individual's decisions. This, moreover, can occur in the absence of actual, observable conflict, which may have been successfully averted ... What one may have here is a *latent conflict*, which consists in a contradiction between the interests of those exercising power and the *real interests* of those they exclude [italics in original] (Lukes 1974: 24–25).

This view of power is important in understanding political contestation in international finance. It emphasizes that power relations can be at work, even in the apparent absence of overt conflict. It helps to clarify the immense power inherent in economic structures and the political power that derives from the capacity to determine the rules and practices that govern these structures. Yet Lukes is always aware that the privilege to set the rules is won in a political contest either overt or latent. Writing from the perspective of a trained economist Galbraith (1983: 14–37), like Lukes, divides power into three categories: "condign; compensatory; and conditioned." He argues that conditioned power, based on personality, property and organization is central to the functioning of the modern economy because it conditions people to believe that alternative economic forms are not practical. This kind of power is very similar to the concept of power Lukes proposes.

Both Galbraith and Lukes recognize that power relations may be at work even where harmony appears to reign. Similarly, Foucault argues that power "is not that which makes the difference between those who exclusively possess and retain it and those who do not have it and submit to it." Rather, Foucault (1976/1980: 98) maintains that power is,

> never localised here or there, never in anybody's hands, never appropriated as a commodity or piece of wealth. Power is employed and

> exercised through a net-like organisation. And not only do individuals circulate between its threads; they are always in the position of simultaneously undergoing and exercising this power.

In Foucault's view power can be not only invisible and pervasive but also internalized within the subject herself. This view of power complements that of Lukes and Galbraith suggesting that, not only is setting the limits of what is understood as possible an extremely powerful act but that such limits may well be set within the agent (see also Lukes 2005: 88–107).[1]

In the postwar era realist theories, which subscribed to a one- and two-dimensional view of power, were well suited to addressing questions associated with the balance of terror in a bipolar world, but they have proven to be less useful in addressing the complexities of a globalizing post Cold War world. Over the years international relations theorists have reintroduced norms and values into international relations theory. Theories which address regimes and community values (Keohane and Nye 1977; Ruggie 1982, 1998; Haas 1992), theories which address justice, ethics and morality in international relations (Linklater 1982; Robinson 1999; Held 2004) and theories which address the role of collective understandings and beliefs (Brassett and Higgot 2003; Wendt 1992; Onuf 1989; Steans 1998) have produced a more nuanced view of power which is closer to the three-dimensional view of power put forward by Lukes. In addition, a number of theoretical approaches now seek to bridge the gap between international relations and comparative politics. They examine transnational civil society actors, the role of principled ideas and values in shaping politics at the transnational level and how, in turn, this relates to state actors at the national and international level (Sikkink 1998; Keck and Sikkink 1998; Reitan 2007).

From a Marxist perspective the power of ideas and ideology has always been central; however, within this tradition which holds that the ruling ideas are the ideas of the ruling class, the power of material interests clearly dominates. There have however, been a number of challenges to the base/superstructure view of the relation between economic and ideological processes. The Gramscian concept of hegemony provides a complex understanding of the power of ideas which has been refined and developed by neo-Gramscians (Cox 1986; Gill 1995; Birchfield 1999; Birchfield and Freyberg-Inan 2005; Kenny and Germain 2005). In Gramsci (1971), hegemony is a form of power in which force is complemented by consent; however hegemony is not without the potential for change. There is a dynamic relationship between hegemony and the forces of counter hegemony which challenge it, and intellectuals are an important part of this challenge. They "question the forms of power (both ideational and material) that perpetuate marginalisation" (Birchfield and Freyberg-Inan 2005: 156–157). As will be seen in the following case studies this is an important dynamic in the contest over the rules and practices governing international finance. Cox applies Gramsci's concept of hegemony at the international level. By emphasizing the importance of social forces in both hegemony and counter hegemony Cox provides an explanation of change in hegemonic systems that is based on an understanding of the complex power relations of social forces. Normative ideas, beliefs about how the world *should* be, are important to this process. As Jim George (1994: 178) writes, in Cox's work,

> systemic and hegemonic power is understood as the "temporary universalisation in thought of a particular power structure, conceived not as domination but as the necessary order of nature [Cox, 1982: 38]." In other words, the power of ideology – the power that transforms particular global structures into the "necessary order of nature" – is just as important as politico strategic power, which buttresses the "necessary order".

In addition, although based in a different intellectual tradition, Polanyi's concept of movement and countermovement is a useful complement to the Gramscian concept of hegemony and counter hegemony. The double movement underlines the power of societal norms in changing, as well as maintaining, economic systems (Polanyi 1944/1957; Birchfield 1999). In Polanyi's double movement, society acts to constrain the dynamic of unfettered market processes in an effort to protect itself from potentially "intolerable" outcomes of market processes. Counter movements develop as society seeks to protect itself and adjust the market–society relationship in order to render this relationship sustainable. Blyth (2002: 10–11) builds upon Polanyi's insight by emphasizing the role of economic ideas in institutional change:

> Economic ideas provide agents with an interpretive framework, which describes and accounts for the workings of the economy by defining its constitutive elements and "proper" (and therefore "improper") interrelations. Economic ideas provide agents with both a "scientific" and a "normative" account of the existing economy and polity, and a vision that specifies how these elements should be constructed.

Although both Blyth and Polanyi focus on the national level, these insights can also be applied to the transnational and global levels. Both Gramsci and Polanyi are helpful in understanding change in the rules and practices governing international finance. They emphasize the power of ideas and the importance of consent in hegemonic systems. By conceptualizing consent as an outcome of social forces it becomes possible to consider not only how consent is constructed but also how it is undermined.

Finally, the governmentality approach underlines the power of ideas to shape, not only understanding, but also the very possibilities of action (Foucault 1977; Dean 1999; Lukes 2005). In Foucault, discursive networks are seen as networks of power and, in much of Foucault, there is a sense of being enmeshed and paralyzed by power. But Foucault too has a theory of change. Foucault (1983: 225) argues that every instance of power brings with it an instance of resistance and this resistance may produce change in discursive formations. For example, Escobar (1995: 5–6) describes how the discourse of development "produces certain permissible modes of being and thinking while disqualifying and even making other ideas impossible." At the same time, understanding the historical specificity of a given discourse opens the way to challenge and change:

> [C]hanging the order of discourse is a political question that entails the collective practice of social actors and the restructuring of existing political economies of truth. In the case of development, this may require moving away from development sciences in particular and a partial strategic move away from conventional Western modes of knowing in general in order to make room for other types of knowledge and experience (Escobar 1995: 216–217).

Foucault's emphasis on self discipline and the internalization of power relations provides a complement to neo-Gramscian and Polanyian accounts in highlighting both the potential and pitfalls of individuals as agents of change as well as suggesting the possibility of multiple sites of resistance. De Goede (2005: 152) discusses a number of sites, past and present, where the dominant financial discourse has been contested. She concludes that at these sites "rearticulation and repoliticization" of various aspects of international finance have resulted in the "emergence of new responsibilities in the era of liberalized finance" (2005: 153). This understanding of a multiplicity of sites and forms of contestation is helpful in understanding the campaign for the cancellation of third world debt presented in the following chapters.

Finally, it is important to clarify that, although the understanding of political contestation adopted in this thesis is greatly influenced by Lukes' definition of power, it does diverge from Lukes in one important way. Lukes (1974: 25) argues that what he calls "real interests" exist and even if the excluded "may not express or even be conscious of their interests ... the identification of those interests always rests on empirically supportable and refutable hypotheses" (see also Lukes 2005: 144–151). "Interest" is a good deal more complicated than this, and "interest" is based on a more complex foundation than Lukes suggests. In both political and economic theory there has been a tendency to assume that goals will reflect a calculation of the material interest of the parties involved. This is not always the case. Reitan (2007: 96) describes how "moral responsibility", altruism and identity were all important motivators in the NGO networks campaigning for debt cancellation. As Sikkink (1998) argues, there can be substantial political power inherent in certain normative ideas such as human rights and when norm entrepreneurs succeed in creating a norm cascade this is a powerful force. I follow those who take a nuanced view of the relationship between ideas, interests and action and suggest that, although quantifiable, empirically measurable interests do remain very important, material interests may sometimes conflict with normative interests and it is by no means certain that the materially oriented, interest-maximizing goal will always dominate (Porter and Ronit 2010b; Abdelal et al 2010; Chweiroth 2008; Avant et al 2010a; Germain and Kenny 2005a; Carpenter 2010; Moschella 2010; Marques and Utting 2010; Olesen 2011).

Markets as constructions

Economic institutions and, specifically, markets and the rules and practices that govern economic relations are important expressions of power. Lukes argues that the three-dimensional view of power – the capacity to set the rules of the game and the political agenda without seeming to do so – is the most potent power of all. In capitalist economies, economic structures exert substantial three-dimensional power. Lindblom (1982) wrote about the "automatic and punishing recoil" which market forces present to those who do not conform to market logic or seek to act outside it. He describes how market discipline imprisons policy making and how uncritical enthusiasm for the market as a social institution imprisons our thinking about politics and economics. Building on this, market actors are also similarly imprisoned by market discipline. Market discipline can force market actors to either conform to the logic of market processes or be forced out of the market. This is particularly true in financial markets where, as Lukes' concept of power suggests, the norms and rules governing financial relations shape the very possibilities of action.[2]

When the Washington Consensus, a term coined in 1989, came to dominate the policy of international economic institutions neoliberal economics became a powerful force in shaping the global agenda.[3] The belief took hold that market discipline would eventually provide a lasting way out of the third world debt crisis and other economic difficulties. The dominance of neoliberalism has produced a simplistic understanding of economic relations which undermines the intellectual richness of the liberal tradition (Sally 1998: 2–5), and as Watson (2005: 8–9) writes, "(n)eoclassical economics tends to be ruthlessly ethnocentric in the extent to which it disregards all potential forms of rationality that are inconsistent with the continued reification of the exchange structures of a modern market economy." But privileging the rational actor paradigm excludes important power relations from the analysis.

Adam Smith's *The Wealth of Nations,* which contains his famous description of the automatic and welfare maximizing "invisible hand" of market processes is often presented as evidence that market relations are a natural result of human nature (Smith 1789/1937: 423). This view, however, involves a profound misunderstanding of the social context in which Smith was living and working (see Watson 2005: 119). However, despite its excessive simplification, or perhaps because of the popular appeal of its simplistic approach to complex problems, neoliberal theory became an important justification for a new approach to reshaping the rules and practices governing national and international economic relations after the apparent "failure" of Keynesian liberalism in the early 1970s. Neoliberal discourse proved to be a powerful tool in reshaping the international political economy (Robinson 2004: 77–81; Lipschutz 2010: 243). On the surface adherence to strict market discipline appears to provide a means to avoid the pitfalls of political contestation and replace the messy business of politics with an efficient and rational market-based calculus. This however is an illusion because it simply displaces the political contestation from the distributive decisions to conflict over the rules and practices governing the design of the mechanism of distribution. The power relations remain but they are rendered less visible.

Economic institutions are inevitably constructed through an ongoing process of contestation and consent; free market systems do not emerge naturally from human interaction. Markets are much more than a collection of rational, utility-maximizing individuals content to pursue their narrowly defined economic interests in the conviction that, where markets lead, efficiency, welfare and, ultimately, democracy seamlessly follow. From the embedded liberalism of Ruggie, to the Polanyian double movement and the Gramscian concept of hegemony, society is recognized as having an important role in the processes by which the rules and practices which govern economic relations are reproduced and also how they are challenged. Politics and power relations are inescapable but, rather than being a weakness, this rather messy political process is a source of strength, adaptive capacity and resilience within capitalist economic systems.

The construction of international finance

International finance is a complex system of rules and practices which shape very real material outcomes. It is a combination of understandings, treaties and agreements in combination with a number of enormous and innovative markets which deal with an ever changing array of financial products. While recent work has gone a long way in revealing the contingent and constructed nature of the rules and practices governing international finance, even so the power relations which underpin the system have been rendered largely invisible by its technical complexity as well as the claim by neoclassical economists, neoliberal political theorists and "market fundamentalists" that market logic is, by definition, impartial and objective (Geske 2000; de Goede 2003). The assumptions which underpin market relations are highly naturalized and difficult to challenge or even expose. Money permeates our culture and our decision-making processes. While money can be a means to an end, a help in achieving a given outcome, it can also be a means of *determining* the ends – a form of calculation defined by the rules governing financial relations. The market mechanism is tremendously appealing because it appears to de-politicize distributive decisions. If determined by free market processes, outcomes seem to be fair. Wealth and poverty appear to be based on merit (or the lack thereof) even though these outcomes can only be as fair as the conditions and assumptions on which the rules and practices governing financial relations were constructed.

It is difficult to exaggerate the practical importance of finance in the daily life of people around the world. A financial calculus underpins investment and production decisions, state policy goals and options, and even influences the security agenda. International finance is an example of an invisible, agenda setting, power structure that, for better or worse, has an important impact on individuals, organizations and states around the world. International finance has become so naturalized that the contingency of its foundations and the historical specificity of its various incarnations are easily overlooked however, as economic history demonstrates, the rules and practices governing international finance are contested and contingent. The dynamics of this process of challenge and change are explored in this book.

Construction

How is the international financial order reproduced or reconstructed over time? This question is the first step in understanding how the rules and practices governing international finance might be challenged and changed. Ultimately, money and finance are based on a fiction, an idea, a leap of faith; however, the financial system has become so much a part of daily life that the flimsiness of its foundations is only rarely visible. Recent work has contributed to this awareness by emphasizing the importance of practice and discourse in the construction of international finance (de Goede 2003, 2005; Geske 2000; Abdelal et al 2010; Abdelal 2007; Porter 2005; Germain 2005; Scholte with Schnabel 2002; Moschella 2010; Marques and Utting 2010). This point of view is not completely unprecedented. In the earlier literature, discussions around the possible emergence of a "paper dollar standard" as a replacement for the American dollar backed by gold illustrate the awareness of the "constructedness" of international finance (Triffin 1978). Similarly, the long history of financial bubbles and crises illustrates the contingent and constructed qualities of financial systems in historical context and highlights the importance of confidence, as well as the effect of a loss of confidence, on financial systems (Kindleberger 1996). As the international financial system developed in scale, scope and complexity since the 1970s, there was a corresponding deepening and broadening of the theoretical literature on international finance. Although theoretical perspectives which focus on competing material interests have clearly dominated, this is slowly changing to include approaches which incorporate the role of moral values and normative ideas in both the reproduction and the transformation of the rules and practices governing international finance.

First, there is a large body of work which addresses the construction of the Bretton Woods order and the pivotal shift in the structure of international finance which followed its demise (Helleiner 1994a; Cohen 1996; Pauly 1997; Germain 1997; Strange 1998, 1988). In this literature this transition is primarily understood in terms of international politics and materially oriented definitions of competing interests. Second, there is a body of literature which raises more fundamental questions regarding the role of states in the organization of international finance. Within this second body of work, a number of scholars see states as effective defenders of conventionally defined state interests (Kapstein 1994: 29; Palan 1998: 635; Helleiner and Cameron 2006). Others, however, focus on how state power is challenged by increasingly powerful market actors and processes. They examine the challenges that market actors present to the apparent monopoly of states in shaping the structure of the international financial system (Cohen 1998; Eichengreen 1999; Frieden 1991; Sinclair 1994; Underhill 1997), the challenge international financial markets present to conventional views of state sovereignty (Bienefeld 1996; Gill 1995; Helleiner 1994a; Porter 1993; Martin 1994; Strange 1998) and the impact of international financial market processes on social and human rights at the national, international and global levels (Birchfield 1999; Larner 1997). This second body of literature emphasizes the power of the state in shaping the rules and practices governing international finance but also recognizes the capacity to challenge state power located in financial markets and other financial institutions.

These first two bodies of literature tend to downplay the power of ideas. There is, however, a third body of literature in which the role of normative ideas and values in constructing and reproducing international finance is increasingly addressed. This work, which reflects the rise of constructivism in international relations theory, has opened up a particularly useful direction in understanding change in international finance. It builds on work which emphasizes the longstanding importance of belief and credibility in financial relations (Eichengreen 1995; Simmons 1994; Cohen 1998: 11–12). It explores the power of ideas and beliefs to shape definitions of interest and state preferences (McNamara 1998: 8; Hall 1989: 389; Best 2005: 38). Geske (2000: 302) defines global finance as "more than an international constraint on state behaviour, it also is a set of practices, beliefs and ideas that both affect state interests and policies and the nature of global finance itself." Furthermore de Goede (2003: 79–95) argues that, in order to study international finance, one must consider the discursive practices which bring finance into being and argues that the production of financial knowledge is an important site where power is exercised. De Goede follows work by Thrift and Leyshon (1999) in which finance is conceived as a series of "authoritative and discursive networks"; and she concludes that "particular discourses of financial knowledge and rationality make *real* material distributions and effects possible." Discourse matters even in the case of an international financial system that on the surface appears to be rational and driven by quantifiable interests (see Epstein 2010).

Much of this work focuses on the role of elite actors and especially actors who are part of the epistemic community or mainstream organizations of international finance. Chweiroth (2008, 2010) traces the importance of norm entrepreneurs in changing the World Bank and the IMF from within (see also Weaver 2010). Moschella (2010) examines the power of normative ideas in shaping change at the IMF. Best (2006) considers the IMF's recent adoption of liberal ethical rhetoric to justify its policies. Abdelal (2007) explores the role of the European Union (EU), the Organization for Economic Cooperation and Development (OECD), the IMF and credit agencies. Porter (2005) examines the role of elite private business authority networks in influencing regulatory change (see also Porter and Ronit 2010a). Marques and Utting (2010) examine how business interests interact with state policy. This book moves beyond this work by looking at non-elite and non-state actors and the relationship between elite and non-elite actors. It builds on work which recognizes the role of civil society in the contestation over the rules and practices governing international finance (O'Brien et al. 2000; Scholte with Schnabel 2002; Germain 2005; Porter 2005).

The constructivist approach suggests that ideas are important forces in the ongoing process of construction and transformation in international finance. The transnational civil society based campaign for the cancellation of third world debt is a useful way into this subject. The campaign was of interest to a broad range of civil society activists including those interested in international development, proponents of a tax on international financial transactions, critics of tax havens, those calling for reform of the IFIs and even environmentalist groups concerned about the role of international finance in funding environmentally questionable projects. The campaigners' demands for economic justice and their broad definition of human rights presented an important critique of the neoliberal approach. The subsequent disillusionment with "market fundamentalism" and the successful linkage of debt cancellation to human "dignity" demonstrate the power of civil society to reframe the debate over debt and in this way challenge the rules and practices governing international finance (Stiglitz 2002; Held 2004: 56; Jubilee Movement International 2002; Halifax Initiative 2006a).

States continue to be important. As Helleiner and Pagliari (2011; see also Helleiner and Cameron 2006) argue, the "interstate political context" as well as the "domestic political contest" are important determinants of the rules governing international finance, but states are increasingly constrained by the transnational context in which they must function (Cerny 2009). Similarly, global business interests and private market actors play an important part (Porter 2005; Helleiner and Pagliari 2011; Porter and Ronit 2010b; Robertson 2009; Marques and Utting 2010). However, beyond the impact of business, more broadly defined transnational civil society actors are also important in shaping the rules and practices governing international finance. This book adopts a broad definition of private authority which includes non-elite transnational civil society actors who seek to achieve reform through broad based political mobilization. Furthermore, this kind of campaigning connects the transnational level of contestation and challenge to the domestic level as transnational actors organize to apply effective pressure to key actors within key states.

Finally, any discussion of the construction of international finance is incomplete unless the power of normative ideas is considered but these ideas do not appear in a vacuum. As discussed above power relations constrain, shape and facilitate the outcomes of political contestation, and it is important to understand not only visible and obvious conflict, but also the dynamics of hidden or latent conflict situations which underpin the rules and practices governing international finance. It is simply impossible to remove politics from market relations. While the "invisible hand" of market relations remains an impressive organizing mechanism for economic activity the rules and practices governing markets are neither neutral nor natural. In practice they are highly political, contested constructions and as such subject to challenge and change. De Goede (2003: 96) locates a potential for structural change in agency. She observes that "despite the rigorous training and education financial agents are initiated by, their performances do not flawlessly reproduce previous formulations but may reformulate, rearticulate, transform and even fundamentally question financial orthodoxies." This "fundamental questioning" of financial orthodoxies by influential individuals and groups is an important driving force in challenging the rules and practices governing international finance.

Challenge and change

Gramsci, Polanyi and Foucault all theorize resistance and change, but how does resistance originate and how does it develop into a political force? What produces a sense that previously taken-for-granted and agreed-upon arrangements have somehow become less than satisfactory? What leads to challenge and perhaps change? Changing material circumstances can change interests, and this undoubtedly provides an important part of the explanation of the sources of change in international finance in the twentieth century. However, while materially oriented explanations are important, they are incomplete. There is something more going on.

The work of Polanyi, Gramsci and even Foucault is connected by a recognition of the potential of society as a site of contestation, challenge and change. Whether called a countermovement, counter hegemony or a challenge to governmentality (see Lipschutz with Rowe 2005: 218) social processes are seen as a powerful force. The power of normative ideas to rewrite the agenda and, in this way, redefine the very limits of the possible is substantial. The "climate of opinion" or the "conventional wisdom" vary with time and place and are subject to ongoing processes of contestation and challenge (Best 2005: 38; Hall 1989; McNamara 1998).[4] Kuhn (1970) describes a process where a scientific or technical breakthrough produces a paradigm shift; however I argue that a paradigm shift is not necessarily based on the transformation of a set of beliefs about the material world. It can also be based on a shift in other kinds of ideas and what passes for knowledge including normative ideas about how the world should be organized. Redefining the agenda, reframing issues and generating discursive shifts at the popular (Johnston 2011: 81; Olesen 2011; Avant et al 2010b; Carpenter 2010) as well as the elite level (Chwieroth 2008, 2010; Moschella 2010; Porter and Ronit 2010b; Abdelal 2007; Abdelal et al. 2010) are a vital part of the process of challenge and transformation. Transnational civil society is an important site of contestation over the rules and practices governing international finance (Germain 2005; O'Brien et al. 2000; Scholte with Schnabel 2002).

The impact of CSOs and NGOs is particularly visible in the transnational campaign for the cancellation of third world debt. While the material interests of debtors undoubtedly played a part in motivating resistance, normative ideas and visions of how the world *should* be, were powerful forces in mobilizing transnational support. In this campaign, civil society actors challenged the logic of embracing policies based on market discipline. They put forward a competing logic based on a normative vision, secular or faith based, of what it meant to be human and the rights, as well as the responsibilities, this entailed. The campaigners judged the financial system not by how well it fulfilled narrowly defined financial goals but by how well it met their broader vision of social and economic justice.

The literature on social movements has increasingly addressed the power of norms and values in political contestation. While early work on social movements focused on material benefits to social movement participants as the primary driving force, the emphasis on material benefit as the motivation of social movement activity has been challenged (McCarthy and Zald 1979: 1213; Della Porta and Diani 1999: 195). This work now examines the distinction between "conscience" adherents and "benefit" adherents in social movement organizations (McCarthy and Zald 1979: 1222), the construction of identity as a force that may potentially transcend material interests as a motivating force in social movements (Jenkins 1983: 535; Piven and Cloward 1995: 160; Reitan 2007: 96) and the argument that a "network society", which is characterized by the emergence of social movements, has emerged not only from a restructuring of capitalism – a material change – but also from technological and communications revolutions – a change focused on ideas and identity (Castells 1997: 352–353). The role of normative ideas and values is increasingly important in social movement theory. Della Porta and Diani (1999: 223) argue that it is necessary to take into account the importance of social construction and perception in assessing political opportunities. McAdam et al. (1997: 147) argue that cultural approaches must be integrated into the study of contentious politics. The need to bring in cultural factors follows logically from the recognition of the role subjective factors play in determining any "objective" assessment of political opportunity. The introduction of identity and norms and values as a driving force in social movements has enriched the explanatory capacity of social movement theory and through this insight actions that might previously have been dismissed as irrational, can now be better understood.

The level of analysis and the impact of globalization is another area in which more recent developments in the social movement literature are helpful in understanding transnational civil society based contestation. At first social movement literature was dominated by a focus on the national level but at present there is a growing body of work which addresses transnational processes (Keck and Sikkink 1998; O'Brien et al. 2000; Guidry et al. 2000; Bandy and Smith 2005; Smith and Bandy 2005; Scholte with Schnabel 2002). Just as the technological and communications advances associated with globalization have facilitated the global expansion of international finance beyond the borders of the state, social movements, CSOs and NGOs have expanded beyond state borders and now network in new and innovative ways.

Furthermore, the institution of the state is undergoing changes which create new openings for civil society based contestation. Slaughter (2004) analyses a new world order in which the disaggregated state is replacing the unitary state and a complex web of government networks working across state borders provide an important complement to conventional forms of international relations. Reimann (2006) sees states as important facilitators of the growth of NGO activism arguing that a "pro-NGO norm" among a number of key states is an important part of the recent worldwide growth of NGOs. Castells however (1997: 266–268) argues that citizens around the world realize the limitations of the state in dealing with the "major issues challenging humankind" and this realization provides, on the one hand, an impetus for multilateralism which further undermines the power of individual states and, on the other hand, an impetus for the growth of social movements based in global civil society in order to address these "major issues" by acting outside the formal structures of the state. Germain (2005) identifies the global public sphere as an emerging enabling environment which makes possible the participation of civil society actors in the previously state-centric processes of international financial governance. Macdonald (2005: 36), however, adds a note of caution by emphasizing the practical difficulties of working at the transnational level and reminding us that, rather than representing a level playing field, transnational civil society is "heavily fissured by hierarchies of gender, class, and geography." Similar concerns appear in the literature on private "capture" in which the financial business elite is seen to exert a disproportionate influence on state actors and international financial governance (Porter and Ronit 2010; Helleiner and Pagliari 2011; Marques and Utting 2010; Robertson 2009).

Others however describe a process where it is the civil society actors who strive to "capture" the state and shape the rules and practices governing international finance according to their vision. In this process CSOs and NGOs employ a variety of innovative as well as time tested tactics to exploit the opportunities presented by globalization (Germain 2010; Olesen 2011; Avant et al. 2010a; Gale and Haward 2011; Pigman 2010; O'Brien et al. 2000; Scholte with Schnabel 2002). Material interests, moral values and normative ideas are all important driving forces in this contestation. Keck and Sikkink (1998: 8–9) argue that transnational social movements and civil society organizations increasingly work together in transnational advocacy networks in which,

> committed and knowledgeable actors working in specialized issue areas ... plead the causes of others or defend a cause or proposition.

> Advocacy captures what is unique about these transnational networks: they are organized to promote causes, principled ideas, and norms and they often involve individuals advocating policy changes that cannot be easily linked to a rationalist understanding of their "interests".

Sikkink (1998: 2–3) argues that "transnational moral entrepreneurs" or "norm entrepreneurs" acting individually, as well as through transnational advocacy networks, play a key role in converting others to their ideas through a process of "persuasion", relying on both the "strength of their normative arguments and the power of facts to support and dramatize their argument." Norm entrepreneurs work to reframe issues and use the power of ideas to reshape the definition of interest (see also Brysk 2009: 31–41). Sikkink (1998: 4) argues that there is "something in the intrinsic quality of human rights norms that gives them their force and influence" and that norms involving the prevention of bodily harm for vulnerable or "innocent" groups are particularly powerful both transnationally and cross culturally. Furthermore Keck and Sikkink (1999: 5) argue that because transnational advocacy networks "are not powerful in the traditional sense of the word, they must use the power of their information, ideas and strategies to alter the information and value context within which states make policies." They frame issues to make them comprehensible to target audiences, influence the broader public's understanding and in this way achieve their goals.

Furthermore Sikkink (1998: 4) sees the international system "as an international society made up not only of states, but also of non-state actors that may have transnational identities and overlapping loyalties." She argues that "(i)n such a society, states may make changes in their behaviour not only because of the economic cost of sanctions, but because leaders of countries care about what leaders of other countries think of them." She continues,

> people sometimes follow norms because they want others to think well of them and because they want to think well of themselves. People's ability to think well of themselves is influenced by norms held by a relevant community of actors.

Similarly the lines between "insiders" and outsiders" often blur. Sikkink (1998: 3) observes,

> Although nongovernmental actors have played a particularly important role in the origins of human rights norms, it is often the

collaboration among norms entrepreneurs inside of governments, those within international organizations, and nongovernmental actors that leads to the emergence of human rights norms.

As will be seen in the following case studies the concepts of transnational advocacy network and norm entrepreneur are extremely useful in understanding the campaign for the cancellation of third world debt.

Finally NGOs and CSOs, both national and transnational, can take unconventional paths to influence. Keck and Sikkink propose the concept of "boomerang" politics (see Figure 2.1) to describe an increasingly important pattern in transnational politics. In boomerang politics national civil society actors, finding the path to their goal blocked within their own state (State A), activate transnational civil society and NGO networks to apply pressure within another, more receptive state (i.e. State B). This state, in turn, applies pressure to the reluctant state (State A).[5] In this way popular pressure "boomerangs" back on its target via an indirect route (Keck and Sikkink 1998: 12–13). As will be seen in the case studies, boomerang politics, as well as a number of variations on this proved to be particularly effective strategies in the transnational contestation over the cancellation of third world debt.

Conclusion

In conclusion, addressing the power and influence of transnational NGOs and CSOs is an increasingly important part of understanding continuity, contestation and change in the rules and practices governing international finance. The history of the organization of international finance reflects changing fashions in expert opinion. Much of the financial history of the twentieth century can be summed up in the debate epitomized by Hayek (1976: 108–129) and Keynes (1936/1942: 378) over the proper relationship between states and markets. But in addition to the ongoing debate over the proper role of states and

Figure 2.1 Boomerang politics

markets – in other words the debate over citizenship rights versus economic rights – more recently human rights have become an important part of the debate. Whether based on religious or secular concepts of human rights, the norm of respect for human "dignity" has come to play an increasingly powerful and legitimate part, and this has created an opening for more populist civil society actors in the contestation over the organization of international finance.

What impact have civil society actors had on the rules and practices governing international finance? This book explores this question through the case of the transnational campaign for the cancellation of third world debt. In this campaign innovative political activism was facilitated by the changed role of the state, activist CSOs and NGOs, and new technologies which created unprecedented capacities for communication and transnational networking. By stressing universal human rights and common human responsibilities, transnational activists worked to "raise consciousness" on a global scale, reframe the issue of debt and in this way challenge the rules and practices governing international finance. The campaign for the cancellation of third world debt shifted the focus from the technical details of the way the financial system worked to a broader emphasis on the shortcomings of the financial system measured in human terms. Campaigners permitted themselves to identify a problem without necessarily proposing a plan for its solution. They refused to accept the human toll of structural adjustment as a tragic but necessary cost of "long term" progress and by refusing to defer to expert financial opinion they made the power relations underlying the debt crisis visible. This facilitated popular involvement in these issues in a way that was not possible earlier.

Lukes' (1974) three-dimensional view of power helps us to understand the tremendous power that exists in being able to define a particular set of rules and practices as not only the best but also the only viable option. Lindblom's (1982) view of the "market as prison" provides a sense of some of the limitations of the market model and helps clarify why market discipline cannot provide a satisfactory replacement for political contestation. Polanyi (1944/1957) and Gramsci (1971) contribute to our understanding of challenge and change and how a social backlash can challenge and perhaps change the conventional wisdom. Keck and Sikkink (1999; Sikkink 1998) develop this insight in their work on norm entrepreneurs and transnational advocacy networks as agents of change.

Theories that focus primarily on states or markets do not adequately address emerging actors and new forms of contestation in transnational politics. The considerable and growing number of new sites of political contestation, both real and virtual, the innovative political strategies now available to unconventional political actors and the power of moral values and normative ideas as a driving force in transnational political contestation all point to the importance of developing a better understanding of new actors and motivations. To this end the following chapters explore one small part of this larger process through two case studies on the transnational civil society based campaign for the cancellation of third world debt.

Finally, I do not suggest that a new, more just world order will necessarily emerge from this process of contestation and resistance. It is important to remember that normative ideas can be progressive or regressive. Nor do I imply that, in many instances, more traditional demands based on material interest or national security are still not capable of easily overriding normative claims based on broadly defined human rights. The events of recent years have made this clear. However, I argue that addressing the power of values and normative ideas, the judgments agents internalize about "proper" and "improper" behaviour, and the "things we do because we do them", is necessary to understanding the complex process of contestation over the rules and practices governing global politics, the global economy, in general and international finance in particular.

3

Transnational Civil Society and the Campaign for the Cancellation of Third World Debt

In the period between 1980 and 2005 transnational civil society organizations (CSOs) and nongovernmental organizations (NGOs) challenged the monopoly of economic experts in dictating the rules and practices governing third world debt. This contestation reframed the "proper" role of international finance and shifted the ground on which these issues were debated from a narrow technical basis to one in which the impact of financial policies on human welfare assumed a central role in defining success or failure. Civil society campaigners invoked a broad interpretation of human rights which included economic and social rights, and by this measure international finance was found wanting. As the chronic third world debt crisis and the international response in the form of debt rescheduling coupled with economic restructuring came to exemplify all that was wrong in the organization of financial relations, civil society campaigners insisted that economic and social justice demanded the cancellation of the crippling burden of debt.

How and why did transnational civil society actors mobilize to challenge the rules and practices governing debt cancellation? This case study tests the following hypotheses. First, moral values and normative ideas are a powerful force in shaping challenge and change, even in the case of the opaque and highly technical system of rules and practices which govern international finance. Second, the campaign for debt cancellation can be understood as part of a Polanyian double movement taking place at the transnational level in which the effects of international financial market discipline produced a societal backlash. Third, when defining more specific agendas, normative ideas also matter and they can be influenced by civil society actors. By 2005 CSOs and NGOs had redefined the global agenda with respect to the cancellation of third world debt and produced a crisis in one elite discursive framework, the Washington Consensus, and a partial shift to a different, more inclusive one. Fourth, by means of activism and innovative political strategies in the campaign for the cancellation of third world debt CSOs and NGOs changed the process of decision making to include actors and points of view that were previously excluded.

As discussed above Keck and Sikkink's (1998) concept of transnational advocacy network and their related concept of boomerang politics is useful in understanding the civil society based response to the third world debt crisis. This chapter develops Keck and Sikkink's concept of boomerang politics by exploring how it applies when the dependent variable is not a state and its behaviour but instead the rules and practices of an increasingly transnational institution such as international finance. It explores how transnational advocacy networks reframed the issues, shifted the agenda and transformed the discourse with respect to debt cancellation and how this redefined the limits of the possible. This case study traces the origins of the debt cancellation movement, identifies the key actors and organizations and explores how NGO and CSO actors came to be well respected experts on the technical, as well as the normative, aspects of international finance and debt cancellation.

Background

The campaign for the cancellation of third world debt is closely connected with both international finance and international civil society. The international financial system generated the unserviceable debts which created the chronic debt crisis, and civil society became the foundation on which the campaign for the cancellation of third world debt was constructed. Historically, the rules governing international financial relations are contingent and contested. The Bretton Woods agreement, drafted in 1944, sought to establish a postwar world of free trade and tightly regulated international finance but this approach did not survive beyond the early 1970s. The collapse of the Bretton Woods system, coupled with the oil shocks of 1972–1973, created systemic and seemingly rampant financial instability even as regulators struggled to prop up the system. But, although it came at the cost of increased financial instability, the end of the system generated increased opportunities for international bankers (Kapstein 2006: 5; James 1996: 351; Helleiner 1994a). There was a tremendous push to lend in increasingly profitable international markets and the Keynesian concern with containing the distorting effects of "hot money", which had been so important in the original Bretton Woods order, was eventually replaced by an uncritical faith in the beneficial effects of market discipline.

This sharp increase in the price of oil in the 1970s produced large accumulations of petrodollars seeking new investment opportunities. As a result international lending surged. Total US bank exposure in the third world grew from $110 billion in 1978 to $450 billion at the end of 1982 (George 1988: 31; see also James 1996: 351–352). Commercial banks saw little danger of default and the herd mentality of bankers in search of a "killing" was reinforced by opinion leaders such as Walter Wriston, the chairman of Citicorp, who famously suggested that this lending was by definition secure because "countries don't go bankrupt" (Chernow 1990: 638). For lenders international lending was more profitable than domestic. For borrowers negative real interest rates during the 1970s made borrowing to fund economic development irresistible. In this era of easy money, overconfident bank lending and the paradigm of development economics came together in a kind of financial feeding frenzy. As difficulties were encountered loans were rescheduled and even in the early 1980s, when developing countries found themselves in a "debt trap" caught between escalating debt service costs and plummeting markets for their commodity exports, international bankers continued to voice confidence in the system.

Paradoxically, the goal of modernization and international development contributed to the debt crisis. As Escobar (1995) argues, at the end of the Second World War, the dream of development "was universally embraced by those in power" but at this time this meant replicating the features of the "advanced" societies and large amounts of external investment were believed necessary to achieve economic growth and development. Lending through the World Bank (WB) and the Paris Club took place throughout the 1950s and 1960s. In the late 1960s commercial banks joined in. By the 1970s, due to growing pressure to recycle oil surpluses, international capital markets expanded and private sector lending to developing countries increased exponentially (Cheryl Payer 1991 cited in Escobar 1995: 82; see also Payer 1982: 15–52).

Although efforts to modernize and develop the third world were in part rooted in the geopolitical interests of Western capitalist societies, they were also, at least in part, a reflection of idealistic values. Evidence of the renewed idealism of the postwar era can be found in the civil society organizations of the time such as Oxfam, founded in 1942 to provide relief during the Greek famine, and Christian Reconciliation in Europe, a forerunner of Christian Aid, first established to respond to the needs of refugees in Europe after the Second World War. At the time economic development was linked to fighting poverty as well as securing international peace. In 1951 the Association for World Peace was founded and in 1952 it was renamed War on Want (War on Want 2006). Furthermore, the Universal Declaration of Human Rights (UDHR) adopted by the United Nations (UN) in 1948 asserts that "recognition of the inherent dignity and of the equal and inalienable rights of all members of the human family is the foundation of freedom, justice and peace in the world" (UN 1948). It sets out a broadly defined vision of human rights and, in articles 23 to 25, clearly includes economic rights as basic human rights.

Religious as well as secular groups were active in development. Groups such as the World Council of Churches (WCC), Christian Aid, the Catholic Agency for Overseas Development (CAFOD), the Catholic Institute for International Relations (CIIR) and the Evangelical Alliance Relief Fund (TEARfund) all have roots going back to the 1960s and earlier (WCC 2006; Christian Aid 2006; CIIR 2007; TEARfund 2006). In 1964 liberation theology was born at the Latin American Bishops' conference in Medellīn, Columbia (Escobar 1995: 227 note 2). During the 1970s established NGOs and CSOs started to engage more deeply with the political and economic roots of underdevelopment (War on Want 2006; Oxfam UK, 2006). New NGOs were founded. The World Development Movement (WDM) was founded in 1970 (WDM 2006), the Centre de Recherche et d'information pour le Développement (CRID) was founded in 1978 (CRID 2006) and the Development Group for Alternative Policies, also known as Development GAP, an NGO working at the grassroots level in Africa, Latin America and the US was founded in 1977 (Development GAP 2009).

In the 1970s and 1980s a growing number of NGOs and CSOs took an active role in a variety of international development initiatives and were a natural complement to state-sponsored development efforts. Even though the major economic debates of the time involved the rejection of Keynesian economic policy, as the view that "inefficient" bureaucratic decisions should be replaced by "efficient" market logic became increasingly popular within the international development and financial institutions, NGOs and CSOs remained largely agnostic. At this time challenging the rules and practices governing international economic relations was not on their agenda and, with few exceptions, they were content to leave the baffling workings of international finance to the experts. Although critiques of the negative effects of capitalist economic relations on human welfare were important in academic circles, they do not appear to have been internalized by most of the CSOs and NGOs active in the developed world at this time.

This, of course, changed in the following decades. For many NGOs and CSOs the third world debt crisis became the way into challenging the rules and practices governing international finance. As the burden of debt grew, measures were implemented to protect the interests of creditors. Debt rescheduling became conditional on economic restructuring and the implementation of structural adjustment programs. For a number of NGOs and CSOs working on development projects at the grassroots level or otherwise involved in the third world, the social impact of this restructuring was obvious and unacceptable, and this marked the start of their critical focus on international finance. They became concerned with the root causes of poverty and developed a more political focus. Their first hand experience provided an important foundation for civil society networking and transnational activism.

Continuity in international finance

As recent events have demonstrated, maintaining a stable and effective international financial system is an ongoing challenge, yet a degree of financial stability is necessary for maintaining a healthy economy. Financial instability can have profoundly negative effects on human welfare. However, while financial stability is a necessary precondition of welfare it is not a sufficient condition. Stability does not ensure economic justice. Furthermore, when hard choices have to be made between negative social impacts and long-term financial stability, economists tend to give priority to stability on the basis of the logic that, without stability, achieving economic and social justice is impossible. This conviction was evident in the economic experts who supported economic restructuring as a remedy to the third world debt crisis. Even though SAPs created a measure of "short term pain", in their view this was necessary to achieve the "long term gain" that would allow debtors to put the chronic debt crisis behind them once and for all. In the 1970s there was little popular interest in international finance. Governing finance was seen as an elite activity, a realm of economic experts that was both too technically complex and too important to be left to the uninitiated. Although there were popular protests against IMF policies, at this time protesters focused primarily on specific grievances within individual states. They did not, nor did they expect to, have an impact on the way finance was organized globally.

As creditor states and the IFIs worked together to ensure a sustainable and stable financial system, the power of financial market actors to, in effect, discipline state policy became increasingly apparent. It was not only developing countries that were disciplined, and the British currency crisis of March 1976 provides evidence of the power of financial forces to influence national policy decisions in the developed world. In a series of events which look remarkably like an early structural adjustment program, the IMF forced policy changes on the British government as a condition of providing standby funding (James 1996: 280–282). Similarly, in the developing world a number of debtor states were forced to accept IMF advice on economic restructuring in return for debt rescheduling. Often an initial default and rescheduling led to a second and a third as interest piled on debt, new debt was incurred to service existing debt, while shifting global macro economic conditions made debt repayment ever more unlikely. Yet, as long as debt could be rescheduled and serviced, lending continued.

At the same time the consensus that structural adjustment could remedy the persistent debt problem was starting to grow, and by the late 1970s it was clear that the IMF saw structural reforms, rather than monetary or fiscal fine tuning, as the best means of achieving long-term stability and development. This economic restructuring included policies to achieve free and flexible labor markets and the privatization of public sector enterprises. By 1980 the belief in the benefits of "adjusting" the economies of the developing world in accordance with neoliberal economic theory had taken hold in government and the IFIs. In 1981 President Reagan praised the "magic of the markets" while government intervention was broadly condemned for its "distortional effects" on the economy (Escobar 1995; James 1996: 525).

In the summer of 1982 the Mexican financial crisis brought the debt boom to a sudden end. It became clear that countries could indeed go bankrupt and, in the process, threaten not only the solvency of major international banks but also the stability of the entire global financial system. These events marked the official onset of the "debt crisis" and produced an important shift in the role of the IMF. Since the demise of the Bretton Woods system of fixed currency exchange in the 1970s, the IMF had been without a clear role in the international system. In 1982, during the Mexican bail out, the IMF adopted the role of gatekeeper and stabilizer of international lending and, in this new role, it became the key institution in the battle to preserve international financial stability.

After 1982, private lending virtually stopped, and yet debt continued to grow mainly as the result of rescheduling and financing of debt service payments through the involuntary extension of new official credit (James 1996: 520–521). Short-term debt relief was achieved by rescheduling and rolling over debt but economic restructuring was implemented to provide a long-term solution. Debtor states were required to liberalize trade, remove controls on foreign investment, reduce government involvement in the economy, improve export capacity and generally meet the conditions of the IMF (George, S. 1988: 190). In theory this would allow unencumbered market processes to generate wealth and development, thus allowing debtors to service and eventually pay their debts, end the cycle of financial crisis and default and eliminate this threat to global economic stability and welfare. State-based efforts to resist or modify this approach met with little success. Expert opinion was firmly on the side of what was later to be called the "Washington Consensus", and the capacity of the IMF in its role as international lender of last resort provided an effective means of enforcement. Any state that was unwilling to be totally isolated from the world economy had little option but to conform. In 1986 the IMF created the Structural Adjustment Facility (SAF) and in 1987 the Enhanced Structural Adjustment Facility (ESAF) was introduced "to provide resources to lower income members undertaking strong three year macroeconomic and structural programs to improve their balance of payments and foster growth" (IMF 2006). By turning its considerable institutional expertise to taking on a strengthened role in the surveillance process, the IMF reinvented itself and found a new relevance in the post Bretton Woods financial order.

In this period despite growing popular resistance to structural adjustment, the neoliberal perspective retained its theoretical persuasiveness among expert circles. Poor outcomes were attributed to the incomplete application of economic restructuring policies or difficulties in their implementation. In 1990 John Williamson coined the term "Washington Consensus" to describe these policies which privileged market discipline, liberalization and privatization (Yergin and Stanislaw 1998: 236–237; Williamson 2004). One by one the governments of debtor states fell in line. In 1994 Brazil became the last of the major debtors to agree to the conditions of long-term debt rescheduling (James 1996: 385). The Washington Consensus dominated the Bretton Woods institutions, and it was not until 1997 when the Asian financial crisis blindsided the international financial elite that its tenets started to be re-examined at the elite level.

At the popular level, however, many citizens in the debtor states of the developing world who experienced debt rescheduling and structural adjustment programs came to oppose these programs and the economic paradigm which underpinned them. The third world debt crisis brought into focus, with unique clarity, just what was at stake in the contest over the rules and practices governing international finance. Ironically, both SAPs and the lending that preceded them were intended to promote development and enhance welfare; however, debt rescheduling and economic restructuring came to be associated with negative social impacts, and this contributed to growing resistance in both domestic and international NGOs and CSOs. As will be seen in the following section, the transnational civil society networks which developed around the issue of third world debt radically altered the terms of the debate and in this way challenged the rules and practices governing international finance.

Contestation and challenge

Early challenges

The foundation for the campaign for the cancellation of third world debt was laid in the years after the Second World War. This took two forms: the first involved the construction of a normative intellectual foundation on which the campaign based its human rights claims and the second involved the growth of international and transnational NGOs and CSOs. First, with respect to the intellectual groundwork, the definition of human rights put forward by the UDHR (UN 1948) is very important. The UDHR provided both an idealistic statement of the goals of the postwar order and, through the authority of the fledgling institution of the United Nations, gave legitimacy to these goals.[1] It provided an officially sanctioned reminder that the ultimate goal of security structures and economic relations is to provide and maximize, not just the welfare of citizens of a particular state or members of a particular class, but the welfare of all of humanity. The Declaration opened up an avenue of criticism of the rules and practices of international finance in terms of their effect on human welfare, and it became an important tool in the hands of debt cancellation campaigners.

Furthermore, dependency theorists provided a compelling critique of development arguing that the participation of underdeveloped countries in international economic relations does not necessarily result in their development and may instead result in their "underdevelopment" (Escobar 1995: 80–82). Underdevelopment is not a stage on the road to development but rather an ongoing condition in which the underdeveloped state is integrated into the international economy in a way that serves the material interests of the developed states. In the light of the chronic financial crises in the third world, the dependency critique of the capitalist model of development resonated with events and provided an alternative perspective on the neoliberal development model.

Finally, growing environmental concerns undermined faith in the neoliberal model. Ever since Ricardo argued that clean water and air were "gifts of nature which exist in boundless quantities" liberal economic theory has had a difficult time incorporating the cost of these external factors in the logic of market processes (Heilbroner 1996: 113). By the 1970s, however, environmentalists were starting to see serious problems associated with economic growth and the impact of uncontrolled industrialization (Escobar 1995: 193–197). Many environmental activists were also concerned with social justice and the debt crisis. At first environmental concerns were marginalized but, as the scientific evidence mounted, it became more difficult to dismiss their criticisms. This undermined faith in the capacity of the existing institutions of western capitalism to deal with environmental issues and, by extension, it suggested that capitalist institutions might not be capable of adequately addressing other economic externalities such as social justice.

Second, during and shortly after the Second World War a number of international NGOs and CSOs were established to provide relief and assistance. Many of these organizations subsequently expanded their mandates and became active in international development, and some eventually went on to become important political actors in the campaign for the cancellation of third world debt. As will be seen below, over time the growing NGO–CSO community developed substantial political skills as well as sophisticated policy expertise which was to prove invaluable in the campaign for debt cancellation. This organizational capacity, which built on the intellectual foundation provided by the UDHR, dependency theory and environmentalism, contributed to the success of the campaign in reframing the issue of third world debt cancellation. In the early 1980s however, this state of affairs was still a long way off.

State-based contestation

When debts became unserviceable and lenders negotiated to restructure the required payments, individual debtor states often tried to resist the economic conditions associated with debt restructuring but they met with little success. While some states were happy to have the IMF as an excuse to force economic restructuring on unwilling populations, most were less cooperative (George, S. 1988: 222). In June 1984,

11 Latin American countries met at Cartegena and formulated a charter to promote a general default on external debt. This would have allowed these states to negotiate as a single unit and made their negotiating position stronger but, in the end, states negotiated individually and the effort failed. The Havana Conference on Debt took place in 1985. It was attended by delegates from 37 Latin American and Caribbean countries and included government, religious and labor representatives as well as politicians and intellectuals. Cuba took up a leadership role and President Fidel Castro made it clear that, while he did not recommend "breaking the banks", the debt was both unpayable and uncollectible (George, S. 1988: 215). In 1985 the state was still seen as the primary level at which to address international financial institutions. In the short term little came out of this conference, but it left an important legacy in the form of the ideas that were articulated as a frame for understanding the debt crisis – ideas that were subsequently developed by civil society actors.

In 1985 the G-24 argued that debt relief needed to be associated with debt restructuring. Instead the Baker Plan was adopted (Dávila 1999: 18). At the time there was concern that any general debt reduction would require public sector support for commercial bank write-offs and that this would, in effect, reward commercial banks for their bad financial judgment. Therefore, under the Baker Plan debt relief primarily consisted of rescheduling and rolling over debt in accordance with conditions set by the IMF (George, S. 1988: 207). Despite domestic resistance and reluctance on the part of the governments of many debtor states, no coordinated default strategy was implemented by debtors. Instead, one by one, debtor states seeking IMF help were forced to adjust.

In 1985 Julius Nyerere, President of Tanzania, became a sharp critic of IMF policies in Africa and expressed his regret that the previously excellent relationship between the IMF and African members no longer existed (James 1996: 521, 524). In 1985 in Nigeria General Babangida called the IMF loans a "Trojan Horse", and in 1986 Nigeria tried to resist the policy prescriptions of the IFIs by adopting a self-styled structural adjustment program (James 1996: 542–543). At the Organization of African Unity (OAU) meeting in Addis Ababa in 1987, Burkina Faso's president proposed the creation for an African Coalition for Debt Cancellation. This effort came to an abrupt end when he was assassinated shortly after the meeting and no other African government leader took up the cause (CADTM 2006).

Zambia came to a new standby arrangement and accepted the IMF program in February 1986, but in April the Zambian economic team was replaced by a group fundamentally opposed to the IMF program. In December 1986 there were large scale riots in response to the proposal to withdraw food subsidies and, as a result food subsidies were restored. Fierce political debate followed with more rioting. In May 1987 Zambian President Kenneth Kaunda broke with the international system. In a radio and television address he announced that Zambia had now chosen to "discard the dependency syndrome" and reject the belief that financial institutions can solve Zambia's problems. Instead, he announced Zambia would follow a national alternative to IMF policies which would limit debt service payments to 10% of net foreign exchange earnings. By 1989 Zambia's economy was in a shambles and the IMF suspended foreign credit. In the Zambian election of October 1991 the opposition came to power and quickly began implementing the economic reforms prescribed by the IMF (James 1996: 528, 537; George, S. 1988: 87).

In 1986 Brazil rejected advice from the international financial institutions and began to experiment with the Cruzado plan, aimed at controlling inflation by freezing prices. In 1987 the Brazilian President announced a unilateral moratorium on interest payments. In the end, however, this unilateral default produced no concessions from and did little to harm the international bankers. In 1988 President Sarney observed, "the fact is we (Brazil) cannot destroy the international system... We can scratch it, but it can destroy us" (James 1996: 400). This observation very nicely sums up the dilemma of most of the states caught in the debt crisis. In 1994 when Brazil became the last of the major debtors to come to an agreement, this marked the end of national and international efforts to coordinate state-based resistance and the triumph of the Washington Consensus.

However, 1994 also marked a turning point for a new kind of resistance, this time based on transnational civil society networks. The next section will describe its growth in scope and scale from the 1980s to 2005. As will be seen below, by the end of the century state actors once again came to play an important part but, by this time, the impetus came less from the national level and more from the coordinated pressure of transnational civil society coalitions and campaigns.

Mexican financial crisis to Bretton Wood's fiftieth anniversary, 1982–1994

At the same time as the neoliberal consensus was developing within international financial institutions, a profound skepticism was growing within civil society both in the developing and developed world. Admittedly this skepticism did not emerge out of nowhere. As material conditions for many of the poorest deteriorated, development NGOs were frustrated as they saw their efforts unraveling. For the citizens of debtor states, deteriorating economic conditions produced disappointed expectations while political theories skeptical of capitalism provided an intellectual framework for analyzing these events. The popular reaction, however, went beyond theoretical analysis in the sense that it incorporated a sense of moral outrage. By focusing on the costs of debt and structural adjustment in human terms the effects of the international financial system were translated into a form that was comprehensible, not only to financial experts and academics, but also to the average person. In this way the debt crisis was reframed and the measure of success (and failure) redefined. As will be seen, this was a profoundly unsettling tactic for which the financial mainstream, as represented by the supporters of the Washington Consensus, had no effective answer.

From 1982 to 1994 three developments laid the foundations for future activism on debt cancellation. First, a number of individuals within CSOs and NGOs developed a substantial interest and expertise in finance. Second, the Ethiopian famine and the 1985 Live Aid campaign politicized important celebrity actors and provided a model of how popular culture could be employed in human rights politics. Finally, the AIDS epidemic, which emerged in the 1980s, produced activists and organizations which eventually played an important part in the debt cancellation campaign.

Since 1976 domestic civil societies in debtor states had mobilized to protest the impact of the chronic debt crisis as well as the IMF austerity measures designed to combat the crisis; however, in the period from 1982 to 1994, the civil society response started to take on a transnational character. Faith affiliated groups led the way. Their existing organizational structure provided ready made networks among communities located both in the North and the South. In 1973 GATT-fly, a Canadian faith based CSO, was founded with the goal of understanding and, therefore, ameliorating the disparity between North and South. At first its focus was on trade but this rapidly grew to include an interest in money and finance. Influenced by Cheryl Payer's 1974 book *The Debt Trap* which received wide play in the international CSO community at the time, GATT-fly maintained relations with both faith based and secular groups in the global South and worked in solidarity with the goals of economic justice in the South (Dillon 2008). In 1984 the World Council of Churches (WCC), an organization which includes representatives from North and South, published a critique of the international financial system. They argued that the international financial system is a valid concern for the churches because it affects the lives of all human beings and often affects them adversely (WCC 1985: 79). The Roman Catholic Church and Pope John Paul II also spoke out on economic justice and finance at this time (WCC 1985: 80).

At the same time the growing civil society based expertise on finance and concern with the debt crisis was coupled with an emphasis on popular education (GATT-fly 1985). In 1984 The Other Economic Summit (TOES) was established when a number of individuals and groups concerned with social justice and the environment decided there should be a "Peoples'" response to the G7 summits. Each year TOES forced issues such as international debt onto the agenda of the G7 and G8 summits. Their first conference was held in London in 1984, and the next year TOES sent a delegation to attend a counter conference at the G7 conference in Bonn. In 1986 the New Economics Foundation (NEF), a "think and do tank", was founded by TOES. In 1987 TOES-USA was founded.

In 1983 the Paris-based Centre d'études et d'initiatives de solidarité internationale (CEDETIM), a pioneer organization on debt issues and later a founding member of ATTAC, raised the issue of debt cancellation (CADTM 2006). In 1987 the Forum on Debt and Development (FONDAD) was founded and Jan Joost Teunissen – a fellow of the Transnational Institute – was appointed as its coordinator (TNI 2006). By 1988 the UK-based Debt Crisis Network, "a group of scholars and activists working to change the terms of the present debt debate", had extended its activities to the US and was active in critiquing the Baker Plan (George, S. 1988: 193; New Internationalist 1987).

In 1990 the All African Council of Churches first called for a year of Jubilee to cancel Africa's debts (Jubilee 2000, 2006a). The Center of Concern (CoC), the European Forum on Debt and Development (EURODAD), the Committee for the Cancellation of the Third World Debt or Comité pour l'annulation de la Dette du Tiers Monde (CADTM) and World Economy, Ecology and Development or Welwirschaft, Okologie & Entwicklung (WEED) were founded to co-ordinate civil society networking and promote economic justice (CoC 2006; EURODAD 2006; CADTM 2006; WEED 2006). Throughout the early 1990s a bewildering number of new NGOs were established while existing CSOs and NGOs continued to expand the political aspects of their activities (Thomas 1992). For Oxfam the 1980s had been dominated by a focus on emergency relief and rehabilitation work but by 1991 Oxfam UK started to devote substantial resources to policy, research and campaigning work aimed at addressing the structural causes of poverty in the South.[2] Oxfam Fairtrade grew, the Oxfam campaigning network was formed, and, in 1993, Oxfam launched the "Africa: Make it or Break it" campaign calling for the international community to increase foreign aid and debt relief for Africa's poorest countries (Oxfam UK 2006).

Furthermore, a number of research groups and institutes were founded in this period, and the expertise that developed in these organizations provided an invaluable resource for the campaign for the cancellation of third world debt (Dillon 2008; NSI 2006; CEPR-UK 2006; Global Policy 2006; OSI 2006). One of the most important research institutes in the debate over finance was the Institute for Policy Studies (IPS) founded in Washington DC in 1963. Its stated goal was to strengthen "social movements with independent research, visionary thinking, and links to the grassroots, scholars and elected officials" (IPS 2006). In 1973 the Transnational Institute (TNI), its "sister institution", was founded as the international program of the IPS. The TNI developed into a "worldwide fellowship of committed scholar-activists", and by the late 1970s it was supporting research into the role of multilateral banks in the third world. In 1986 TNI established the Debt Project led by Jan Teunissen, a fellow of TNI (TNI 2006).

In 1988 Susan George, also a fellow of the TNI, wrote the influential book *A Fate Worse than Debt.*[3] In the introduction she cites her concern over the relationship between debt and a lack of food security as an important reason for pursuing this research and expresses the hope that it will encourage others to "take a similar line of enquiry, to worry about what is happening to the real victims, not to Citicorp and the IMF" (George 1988: 1–4). In 1992 George (1992a; 1992b) first used the phrase "debt bondage" to highlight the injustice of the debt crisis and argued that not only was debt cancellation the "right" thing to do, it was also in the interest of the developed world. The work of civil society based research institutes was extremely important in developing an alternative source of technical expertise and in framing the issue of debt cancellation and clearly linking it to human rights claims.

Before 1982 popular protests and demonstrations against the economic reforms associated with debt rescheduling had taken place within many debtor states. The period from 1982 to 1994, however, marked the start of transnationally coordinated popular actions and demonstrations deliberately designed to pressure governments and IFIs for change in the international financial order. In 1985 Bonn was the scene of a counter conference and mass demonstration against the G7 summit (Days of dissent 2006). In 1988 a major demonstration took place at the September meeting of the IMF and WB in West Berlin. Planning for this demonstration started in 1985 and tapped into a political environment rich in activists and radical protest. The demonstrators were divided into two groups: "autonomists" who believed the World Bank and IMF should be attacked and "reformists" who were campaigning for debt relief for the poorest countries and reform of the IMF through the increased involvement of poor countries. At this meeting a successful two-day counter conference was followed by a peaceful street demonstration of between 50,000 and 80,000 people. There were, however, also a number of "actions" of a different kind including arson and damage to property which ended with 1,000 arrests.

The 1988 demonstration in West Berlin is important because it targeted the IFIs directly; because it was the product of a diverse and unlikely coalition; and, finally, because it mobilized so many protesters. Its legacy according to contemporary accounts is twofold. First, it helped "new political perspectives and structures to be developed" especially among the "autonomists" who concluded that their radical approach was less able to mobilize resistance than that of the more moderate groups. Second, it prepared the ground for further activism on debt and finance because protesters both "newcomers" and "old-timers" were left wondering "Where now?" (Days of dissent 2006).

The Ethiopian famine and the international response it generated also contributed to the campaign for debt cancellation. It contributed in two major ways: first, by politicizing actors who would later become important in the movement around debt and debt cancellation and second, by providing a model of how a popular mass movement might work to address broadly defined human rights abuses through transnational activism. Hunger, famine and starvation had been important motivators of public activism since the early days of Oxfam. Arguably, there is something about starvation that throws arguments about economic rationality, efficiency and long-term benefits out the window. Keck and Sikkink note the cross-cultural impact of norms that involve the prevention of bodily harm for the vulnerable or "innocent" (Sikkink 1998: 4). In the mid 1980s, thanks to modern communication technologies, images of suffering and starvation were communicated around the world, arousing feelings of shock, empathy and eventually a desire to "do something".

The response to the mid '80s Ethiopian famine and drought marked the first intersection of celebrity, popular social activism and relief work. In October 1984 the Ethiopian famine hit the television news. As concerned individuals made donations to relief organizations, Bob Geldof, a British rock musician, and Midge Ure wrote the song "Do

They Know It's Christmas?" to raise money to help address the crisis. When Geldof attracted other stars to join in performing the song under the name of Band Aid it raised £8 million for famine relief (BBC 2006). Other similar initiatives around the world such as Tears are not Enough, We are the World and Comic Relief raised additional funds. Oxfam's income more than doubled in one year, and it launched its "Hungry for Change" campaign which "capture(d) public indignation at the obscenity of famine in the Third World alongside mountains of food in the First" (Oxfam UK 2006b).

In early 1985 Bob Geldof toured the famine affected areas and concluded that more aid was required. He therefore conceived "Live Aid", to raise money for famine relief in Africa. The concert took place in Wembley Stadium in front of a crowd of 72,000 people. TV coverage of the concert was broadcast to 160 countries. In the US a simultaneous concert took place in Philadelphia. At first pledges for Live Aid were disappointing, but after images from the famine itself were aired, pledges took off (BBC 2006).[4] Live Aid politicized many who would otherwise not be involved. In Live Aid the human suffering of the Ethiopian famine was conveyed in such a way that the only possible reaction was a desire to "do something". However, in addition to the satisfaction of "doing the right thing", being part of this movement was fun. The tunes were catchy, the concerts impressive. The community supporting the cause was definitely "cool". But as people sought to join this community by donating to the cause they became, at least to some extent, politicized and, therefore, more open to further involvement in social movements in the future.

Finally, the HIV/AIDS epidemic originated in this period and continues to have far reaching consequences around the world. In 1982 however, it was understood primarily as a condition limited to gay men and intravenous drug users. At first it might seem unrelated to questions of debt or finance, but HIV/AIDS subsequently became an important factor in the campaign for debt cancellation. It has had an impact in two ways: first, many activists who were first radicalized in the often bitter campaigns surrounding the HIV/AIDS epidemic developed impressive skill sets in social movement politics and also became supporters of the debt cancellation movement (PBS 2006; Act Up 2006); second, the crisis provided an example of the failure of SAPs because many argued the severity of the epidemic of HIV/AIDS in Africa was related to cutbacks in public healthcare spending associated with the implementation of SAPs in the 1980s (Lewis 2005: 1–17).

From Bretton Woods' fiftieth to the Asian financial crisis 1994–1997

During this period, CSOs and NGOs laid the organizational foundations for the campaign for the cancellation of third world debt. The 1990s was an era of international summits and preparatory meetings for these summits which provided opportunities for civil society activists to meet and to learn to work together (Tomlinson 2008). Transnational activist networks were formalized. As NGOs and CSOs working on international finance became increasingly good sources of information and analysis, their input became increasingly welcome at the elite level. At the grassroots level popular education initiatives continued and developed an increasingly informed and engaged public. At the same time the normative authority for future claims was being strengthened. In 1996 the Development Assistance Committee (DAC) of the OECD adopted a "people centred" approach to development and articulated a series of goals that later became the foundation for the eight UN Millennium Development Goals (MDGs) adopted at the UN Millennium Summit in 2000 (OECD 2006: 26, 45–50).

January 1, 1994 marks a turning point in two important ways. First, January 1, 1994, the start of the North American Free Trade Agreement (NAFTA), was chosen by the Zapatistas to mark the beginning of their uprising (Ayres 2003: 28). The Zapatista rebellion, based in the Mexican state of Chiapas, created solidarity networks across national borders and North–South exchanges of information aided by computer and fax (Johnston 2003: 86). These networking methods and communications technologies later became central to the transnational civil society campaign to support debt cancellation, and the Zapatistas provided a precocious example of the possibilities of these tactics. Second, 1994 marked the fiftieth anniversary of the Bretton Woods Institutions, and this produced a flurry of new civil society committees, projects and forums aimed at critiquing and reforming the WB and the IMF (RBWC 2006; CoC 2006; IFG 2006; CEPR 2006; 50 Years 1994, 2004; CADTM 2006).

In this period CSOs and NGOs continued their efforts to influence the G7. In 1994 the Halifax Initiative (HI) was formed by a group of Canadian NGOs to ensure that demands for fundamental reform of the IFIs were high on the agenda of the G7 scheduled to be held in Halifax in 1995. The HI defined its mission to "fundamentally transform the international financial system, and its institutions, namely the World Bank, the International Monetary Fund, and Export Credit Agencies.

By doing this we hope to achieve poverty eradication, environmental sustainability, and the full realization of human rights." They sought to end the "unsustainable policies and practices of the international financial institutions" and to "contribute to the realization of an alternative agenda for environmentally and socially sustainable development than the Washington Consensus" (Halifax Initiative 2006). In Canada, members of the HI became influential participants in ongoing discussions with Canadian officials including Paul Martin, the Canadian finance minister who, over time, became increasingly supportive of debt cancellation (Mihevc 2008; Foster, P. 2008; Culpeper 2008; Rayfuse 2008; Dillon 2008).

The Halifax Initiative illustrates the transnational and strategic nature of campaigning that was taking shape at this time. The Charles Stewart Mott Foundation, a private foundation based in Michigan, USA, has provided stable funding to the HI since it was founded. This has allowed the HI to be independent and also enabled it to focus on important issues without worrying about the constraints of fundraising (Foster, P. 2008). The Mott Foundation first became interested in international finance through its concern for environmental issues. It became aware that, in order to understand environmental issues associated with a number of controversial WB development projects it was necessary to "follow the money." In the mid 1990s the Mott Foundation decided that, to this end, it needed a strong G7 strategy and therefore focused some of its funding on NGOs campaigning on the IFIs in a number of G7 countries (Smithey 2008).[5]

In June of 1995 a group of NGOs approached the then new president of the WB, James Wolfensohn, with a proposal to engage civil society in an exercise with the Bank to assess jointly the impact of structural adjustment programs. This resulted in the joint launch by the WB and SAPRIN of the Structural Adjustment Participatory Review Initiative in 1997. The idea was to provide Wolfensohn and his managers a fundamentally different perspective on economic policy, to democratize economic policy making and to legitimize a role for organized civil society in this key area of development programming (SAPRIN 2009). In 1995 Focus on the Global South, an NGO which pursued a program of development policy research, analysis and action, was founded (Focus 1999). In February 1996 the first Asia Europe People's Forum took place in Bangkok. It was organized by TNI and Focus on the Global South among others as a counter conference to the Asia Europe Summit (ASEM). From 1996 on the Forum followed the schedule of ASEM and took place every two years (TNI 2007; TNI 1996).

Oxfam continued to extend and politicize its operations. In 1995 the first international launch of an Oxfam campaign took place with the Campaign for Basic Rights and Oxfam's first television ad asking the public to support long-term development programs was broadcast. In 1996 Oxfam went online (Oxfam UK 2006b). In 1996, in its first report on the impact of SAPs in Latin America and the Caribbean, Oxfam International, in an effort to better communicate its findings to the IFIs, deliberately employed the language and style of the IFI policy elites. This marked an important transition, because, even though the findings of the report were condemned by both the IMF and the WB, they took Oxfam's analysis seriously. This marked the beginning of Oxfam's influence on the WB and to a lesser extent the IMF (Fried 2008).

In this period CSOs and NGOs worked to reinforce the belief that there were indeed serious problems with the IFIs and the organization of international finance that needed to be addressed, both in the name of economic stability and economic justice. Faith based, as well as secular groups, and networks which included both, framed economic and social injustice as a violation of human rights and dignity, and in this way developed a powerful critique of international finance that resonated across cultures. The Jubilee campaign is an excellent example of this strategy in action. In the mid 1990s, the Debt Crisis Network organized an around-Britain tour by Kenneth Kaunda of Zambia and Archbishop Makhulu of Central Africa. They spoke to large audiences in London, Manchester, Edinburgh and Glasgow (Jubilee Debt Campaign 2005a). A coalition of aid agencies, trade unions, churches and campaigning groups was involved in this tour, and this raised the profile of debt issues among their own supporters. Jubilee 2000 later concluded that it was primarily this activity that "went towards building an informed and motivated (and angry) mass movement" (Jubilee Debt Campaign 2005b). In the above quote "angry" is a key word. The supporters of the Jubilee 2000 campaign were indeed angry and indignant at the violation of human rights that, in their opinion, was epitomized by the third world debt crisis. They were determined to "do something" to "right the wrong". For many, achieving Jubilee became a matter of conviction and conscience.

At the same time the critiques of development produced in the third world were starting to circulate widely in the West (Escobar 1995: 224). This further undermined the legitimacy of the IMF and the WB, institutions which at the time subscribed primarily to the neoliberal theories of development which were being so harshly critiqued by many third world theorists. These critiques, in the voice of those who were most immediately affected by the policies of the international financial institutions, played an important part in bolstering opposition to the policies of the WB and the IMF among activists in the North as well as the South.

April 1996 saw the official launch of Jubilee 2000 campaign in the UK by the World Development Movement, Christian Aid, CAFOD and TEARfund. In 1997 Jubilee 2000/USA was established (Jubilee USA 2006a). The German Jubilee campaign Erlassjahr was launched in September 1997 and the Scottish campaign launched in October (Jubilee Research 2007). The Canadian Ecumenical Jubilee Initiative (CEJI) was formed in 1998. In the Jubilee movement there is a strong religious element which is used to strengthen the human rights claims of the movement. In the Jubilee Year, as stated in Leviticus, those enslaved because of debts are freed, lands lost because of debt are returned and the community, torn by inequality, is restored. The Jubilee movement argued that international debt had become a new form of slavery (Jubilee USA 2006a). They adopted the slogan "Break the chains of debt." By linking debt service and slavery the Jubilee movement brought moral legitimacy to calls for debt "forgiveness" or cancellation. Over the course of the campaign Jubilee 2000 and its allies successfully shifted the discourse from the conviction that repayment of debts was a moral obligation to the view that it was, on the contrary, immoral to enslave people in the name of debt servicing.

The Jubilee movement was brilliant in this respect. They took advantage of the coming turn of the millennium to provide a rationale for a fresh start. They were a broad-based coalition of secular as well as faith based groups with room for everyone who wanted to further the cause of debt "forgiveness." They constructed and then took the moral high road. Even more important, they did not suggest the precise way in which debt slavery could be ended. Rather they insisted that the system had to change but did not put forward a blueprint of how exactly this change should be accomplished. Change was necessary, change was imperative but the details of this change were going to have to be worked out by the institutions responsible for the mess in the first place. This meant that the Jubilee campaign was not vulnerable to the charges of technical incompetence or economic naiveté that experts in the IFIs could otherwise have leveled. The Jubilee movement had substantial intellectual depth and technical expertise available in member organizations but it chose to fight the campaign on the terrain of human rights. This was not a battle financial experts were well equipped to win, at least not in the eyes of popular opinion. Not only was Jubilee

2000 a transnational advocacy network, it was also a norm entrepreneur that wisely chose to fight its battle on a transnational and cross-culturally resonant issue.

At the same time as Jubilee 2000 was emerging in the developed world a number of debt advocacy networks were active in the South. For example in 1996 the Uganda Debt Network (UDN) was formed (UDN 2006). It was a coalition of local and international NGOs designed to mobilize Ugandan civil society to engage in the national debate on Uganda's debt problem. At this time most Ugandans regarded the issue of external debt as a government problem that was too complex for ordinary citizens to understand. Uganda had first undergone structural adjustment in 1987 and yet the debt burden continued to grow. International NGOs including Oxfam, EURODAD, Bretton Woods Project, Bread for the World, The Africa Faith and Justice Network and Jubilee 2000 UK all supported UDN with funding and capacity building. This boosted the credibility of the UDN in national debates and, eventually, the Ugandan government began to see civil society groups as allies in the effort to accelerate debt relief (Collins et al. 2001: 145).

In September 1996 at the WB and IMF Annual Meeting in Washington DC the Interim and Development Committees endorsed the Heavily Indebted Poor Countries (HIPC) Initiative. This was the first debt relief initiative designed to give a select group of debtors relief on multilateral debt. Not surprisingly, to benefit from this program eligible countries were required to "establish a track record of reform and sound policies through IMF and WB supported programs"(Paris Club 2006). Although this program was associated with increased debt cancellation for a small number of eligible countries, it did not mark a fundamental change in the approach to managing debt at either the IMF or the WB.

Faith in the policy prescriptions of the Washington Consensus remained strong at the WB and the IMF at the same time as civil society organized to challenge them. In 1996 EURODAD took up the challenge of "acting as an information hub on these issues, developing a body of knowledge to be used as a resource by both members and the wider development community" (EURODAD 2006). Similarly, in 1997 the second phase of the Reinventing Bretton Woods Project (RBWP) at the Center of Concern in Washington DC established links with economic and legal professional organizations around the world. Their aim was to strengthen and broaden citizens' networks that were engaged in discussions on the reform of the WB and the IMF (CoC 2006).

There were no major street demonstrations, and this period was marked instead by civil society counter conferences and international meetings. In 1994 when the G7 was held in Naples, TOES held events in Italy as well as in Australia. At the 1995 G7 in Halifax, Canadian NGOs organized the "People's Summit." In 1996 counter summits took place at Lyons and in 1997 TOES USA organized a "People's Summit" in Denver (TOES 2005). At the same time other opportunities for activists to meet and network multiplied. Some were associated with mainstream international organizations: for example, the UN Social Summit in 1995 and UNCTAD IX in 1996. Others were organized by NGOs and CSOs such as the Intercontinental Encounter for Humanity and Against Neoliberalism held in Chiapas in 1996 (Ayres 2003). Organizations like the International Forum on Globalization provided opportunities for Northern and Southern activists to meet discuss and learn to collaborate effectively (IFG 2009).

CSOs and NGOs were learning to apply effective political pressure to state and international officials. Popular education initiatives demystified finance and lay individuals felt empowered to express opinions and lobby decision makers. This helped campaigning CSOs and NGOs to put the moral and normative aspects of the third world debt crisis on the public agenda (Dillon 2008; Tomlinson 2008). Increasingly, CSOs and NGOs learned to speak the language of international policy elites and were respected for their expertise (Rayfuse 2008; Tomlinson 2008). This respect enhanced their access and allowed them to make their case at the highest level. Therefore, in this period activists, NGOs and CSOs were involved in contestation at both the elite and grassroots levels.

Asian Crisis to battle in Seattle 1997–1999

In 1997, however, the Asian financial crisis took the world by surprise. It undermined faith in the Washington Consensus among several highly respected figures within the international financial institutions themselves. In the following months it spread around the world to Brazil and Russia. This crisis was another brush with global financial disaster similar in impact to the Mexican financial crisis of 1982 but, by this time, the IMF was well practiced in dealing with countries experiencing financial crises. This time, however, the steps the IMF took provoked a split in expert opinion. Both Joseph Stiglitz, chief economist at the WB and Jeffrey Sachs, an important and well-respected economist, publicly argued that the IMF policies were pushing the affected economies into a severe recession, that the IMF lacked transparency and that it was invested with too much power (Davis and Wessell 1998; Sachs 1997). Their criticisms resonated with those of the debt cancellation campaigners but this time they originated within the international financial mainstream.

Calls for reform from within the international financial mainstream

After 1997 there were two parallel reform movements at work in international finance. One was located in NGOs and CSOs and had economic justice and debt cancellation as its focus. The other was centered in the elite community of experts and policy makers connected to the IFIs as "reforming the international financial architecture" became a top priority. The Asian Crisis had driven home the highly precarious state of the globalized and deregulated international financial system, and while almost everyone agreed that the international financial system needed to be reformed, just what was required and how this would be accomplished remained open to debate.

For the IFIs the primary goal of reform was achieving financial stability. Arguably there could be no economic security or welfare in the absence of a secure and predictable financial system. At the 1997 APEC meeting in Vancouver leaders announced the establishment, on a temporary basis, of the G22 (later the G20) to advance reform of the architecture of the global financial system. The G22 met in Washington in April 1998. By the time the G8 met in Birmingham in 1998, strengthening the international financial architecture was a prominent theme (G7 Finance Ministers 1998), but at the IMF the vision of the new "architecture" remained very much in line with the priorities of the Washington Consensus.

However, other critics within the mainstream had become critical of the policy prescriptions of the Washington Consensus. Although many of them had previously been involved in the application of the neoliberal economic policies, they had become disillusioned. Their criticisms provided a tremendous boost to the credibility of the debt cancellation campaigners. In January 1998 Joseph Stiglitz, Senior Vice President and Chief Economist of the World Bank gave a lecture in which he was openly critical of the Washington Consensus. He argued that the dogma of liberalization had become an end in itself, not a means to a better financial system. He called for a new "post-Washington Consensus" which would recognize a broader set of development goals including increases in living standards, sustainable development, equitable development and democratic development, not "just increases in measured GDP" (Stiglitz 1998).

In 2002, Stiglitz, by this time a recipient of the Nobel Prize in Economics, renamed the Washington Consensus "market fundamentalism" (Stiglitz

2002: 221). This term had a tremendous impact. In a simple phrase it dispelled neoliberal claims to rationality and highlighted the fundamentally dogmatic and irrational faith in the rules of liberal free market economics that underpinned neoliberal theory. Suddenly, those appealing to moral values or normative ideas could no longer be so easily dismissed as "unrealistic" or out of touch with the painful but necessary choices of the "real" world, choices that neoliberal economists had previously claimed themselves to be better equipped to make. The phrase "market fundamentalism" reframed the contest as one of competing world views, competing belief systems. With the terrain of the debate shifted in this way by such an influential American economist, debt cancellation campaigners gained another advantage.

After 1997 the power of the dominant discourse in finance was increasingly challenged from within as other mainstream figures rejected the simplistic economic prescriptions of the Washington Consensus and sought ways to improve the social and human outcomes associated with the globalizing world economy (Stiglitz 1999; Ragan 1999a; Soros 1998).[6] The fight, however, was far from over. Supporters of the Washington Consensus remained important. Milton Friedman, who had won the Nobel Prize for Economics in 1976, continued to be an outspoken advocate for free markets and free movement of capital. He expressed his hope that globalization would make governments less able to provide social programs and argued that government interference, in the form of IMF actions, was the real cause of the Asian financial crisis (Ragan 1999b). At the IMF, Jack Boorman, a director of policy development and review, wrote that it was a myth that widespread poverty in the HIPCs was due to debt. He argued that the cause was "inappropriate economic policies." He went on to assert that it was also a myth that debt was responsible for insufficient social spending, concluding that "in reality debt does not preclude any of the HIPCs from providing basic social services" and prescribed encouraging private sector led growth as a remedy to what ills did exist (Boorman 1998).

Civil society

In transnational civil society CSOs and NGOs continued to network to increase their capacity to strategize and coordinate. In February 1998 Peoples' Global Action (PGA) was established at a founding conference in Geneva where hundreds of representatives from diverse social movements gathered to create the PGA Network as "a tool for co-ordination and communication between groups, movements, and individuals wanting to organize anti-capitalist resistance" (Dissent 2006).

At the same time the civil society campaign against the Multilateral Agreement on Investment (MAI) took off. Anti-MAI campaigners feared that,

> The MAI, if ratified, will serve as a Charter of Rights and Freedoms for transnational corporations against citizens and the earth, and represents a grave threat to democracy in Canada and around the world (Clarke and Barlow 1997: 8).

In the fall of 1997, 70 labor, environmental and citizens groups had met with MAI negotiators at the OECD headquarters in Paris. They felt that the negotiators had "talked down" to them, and angered by this treatment by representatives of their own governments, they determined to fight the MAI by mobilizing public opinion to create pressure from the outside at the same time as creating dissent within the ranks of government bureaucrats by highlighting the elitist and secretive nature of the negotiations (Barlow and Clarke 2001: 23). A wide variety of NGOs, primarily from North America, Europe and Australia, participated in the international anti-MAI campaign and eventually convinced the already divided OECD delegates to drop the negotiations (Ayres 2003: 29; NGLS 1999a: 4).

The success of the international anti-MAI campaign demonstrated the power of carefully targeted and orchestrated civil society activism, and it provided encouragement for other campaigns of the time. The second Asia Europe People's Forum was held in London in March 1998 (TNI 1998). In November 1998 the regional European NGO Forum was held in Paris. A few days later the Partners for Development Summit, organized by UNCTAD, discussed the possibility of an international tax on financial transactions and the need for trade and investment treaties to be compatible with the legal obligations of states under the international human rights regime (NGLS 1999a: 5).

In 1998 the Jubilee campaign took off. In February, Erlassjahr, the German Jubilee movement, and Christian Aid launched a joint campaign in Germany and the UK. According to Anne Pettifor (1998), a prominent activist, the campaign was,

> aimed at the German protestant churches. Thousands of CA [Christian Aid] postcards were sent, calling on the German people to remember that their debts had been cancelled in 1953. That debt write-off had given German children a future. Could African children be given the same hope?

As part of the same campaign CAFOD dumped fake gold bullion outside the German Embassy (Jubilee 2000 2006a). In April 1998 the Jubilee 2000 Afrika Campaign was launched in Accra, Ghana by activists and delegates from 20 countries of the African continent. They produced the Accra Declaration, which called for unconditional cancellation of Africa's external debts (Jubilee Research 2006a).

At the G8 the TOES/NEF people's summit was transformed into a site of popular protest as the Jubilee 2000 coalition mobilized 70,000 peaceful protesters in the streets of Birmingham. Prior to the summit,

> Christian Aid, CAFOD, WDM, and TEARFUND had campaigned enthusiastically behind the Jubilee 2000 campaign and ensured that almost every available church hall was used to organize a Jubilee 2000 meeting. Their staff and volunteers organized and spoke at meetings, distributed leaflets; wrote articles; mobilized petitions; staffed stalls, and chained themselves to railings! All the while, educating, educating, educating. By the time the big day – 16 May 1998 – arrived, a huge swathe of the British public, and a fair section of the media had been taught the basics of international debt and finance. To the astonishment of politicians and the surprise of the G8, millions had a firm grip on the issues (Jubilee Debt Campaign 2005b).

At the Birmingham G8, Jubilee organizers met with British Prime Minister Tony Blair (Jubilee 2000 2006a). After Birmingham the debt cancellation campaign took off as a large scale transnational campaign. Two years later there were Jubilee collectives in 66 countries. These networks met at seminars, international conferences and demonstrations. From 1998 to 2002 CADTM strengthened its network of activists both in the North and the South (CADTM 2006). In 1998 in France Réformer les Institutions Financières Internationales (RIFI) was founded (RIFI 2006). In December 1998 the international ATTAC movement was created in Paris.

The Jubilee networks were a very important force in the debt cancellation movement at this time. The Jubilee movement draws a great deal of support from those interested in defending human rights from a secular perspective but it also draws a great deal of support from faith groups and organized religion. It is located at an intersection of the religious and the secular, willing to accept support where it can find it and yet unwilling to ally itself with any specific faith perspective. It is indeed a "big tent" but very aware of the organizational benefits of being connected to organized religion. The very concept of Jubilee is religious, and this was key in the success Jubilee 2000 experienced in taking the essentially economic debate around finance and debt to the higher level of human rights. A concern with debt is deeply embedded in many cultures. On the one hand, there is a sense that debts must be paid for moral as well as pragmatic reasons. On the other hand, there is a sense that demanding excessive interest or perhaps any interest at all, is not quite morally acceptable. This ambivalence particularly as it existed in Western culture provided an important target for the reframing efforts of the Jubilee movement.

In September 1998 the Canadian Ecumenical Jubilee Initiative (CEJI), a successor to GATT-fly, was launched (Scarboro Missions 2006; Jubilee Research 2006a). In October Jubilee USA held a national conference and in November the first international Jubilee 2000 conference took place in Rome. Thirty-eight national Jubilee campaigns and 12 international organizations met in Rome to decide a common policy and campaign strategy (Jubilee 2000 2006a). The conference produced a document titled "A Jubilee call for debt cancellation", which called for cancellation, by the year 2000, of unpayable debt, which was defined as debt that cannot be serviced without placing a burden on impoverished people; debt that in real terms has been paid; debt for improperly designed policies and projects; and odious debt, debt incurred by illegitimate regimes in order to oppress people or for personal purposes. A second document, "The Jubilee 2000 international campaigning statement", outlined strategies to target creditor and debtor governments and parliaments, the UN, the IFIs and commercial banks "to build political will and economic commitment in support of the aims of the Jubilee 2000 movement." It called for the education, mobilization and empowerment of civil society actors at the national, regional and international levels. Finally, it called for the sharing of resources and experience between national Jubilee campaigns, both within and between the South and the North (Jubilee Research 2006c).

In France the Jubilee campaign and the Jubilee petition were put forward by the campaign "Pour l'an 2000; annulons la dette" (Dette 2006). In late 1998 Jubilee 2000 Australia was founded when TEAR Australia invited church overseas development agencies, churches, aid agencies and community groups to work together for a "world free of debt for billions of people" (Jubilee Australia 2006). Pope John Paul II voiced support. In a Papal Bull in December 1998 Pope John Paul II announced that wealthy nations should relieve the debts of developing nations in order to remove "the shadow of death." He continued, "Christians will have to raise their voice on behalf of the poor of all the world, proposing

Jubilee as an appropriate time to give thought, among other things, to reducing substantially, if not cancelling outright, the international debt which seriously threatens the future of many nations" (Jubilee 2000 2006b).

In 1998 Sojourners magazine, an American Evangelical publication, published its first three articles in support of the Jubilee movement (Sojourners 2006). In August and October of 1998 heads of the IMF and the WB attended conferences organized by the Anglican and Catholic churches, both major supporters of the Jubilee movement. In December 1998, the World Council of Churches (1998) adopted a policy statement that,

> the assembly encourages member churches and its partners to provide critically needed for discussion with governments and international financial institutions. They should urge governments of the wealthier countries to: (1) increase support for bilateral and multilateral debt cancellation, and (2) under gird efforts to make international financial institutions more democratic, transparent and responsive to the needs of the world's most impoverished.

In January of 1999 the Latin American and Caribbean Jubilee 2000 campaign was launched in Tegucigalpa, Honduras (Jubilee 2000 2006a). In addition to representatives of 16 Latin American countries the launch was attended by representatives from Africa, Europe and North America. Important figures were called upon to provide support. Alberto Esquivel, the 1980 winner of the Nobel Peace Prize, was described as having "taken on the debt issue as his new human rights campaign." Bishop Monseñor Oscar Andres Rodrigues called foreign debt "a tombstone pressing down on us" (Jubilee Research 2006d; Jubilee Research 2006e).

In January of 1999 Pope John Paul II continued to call for urgent debt relief to ensure that the millennium becomes "a time of renewed hope" (Jubilee 2000 2006a). In the Ecclesis in America the Pope expressed the criticism that "if globalization is ruled merely by the laws of the market applied to suit the powerful, the consequences cannot but be negative" (Engler 2005a). On September 23, 1999 Pope John Paul II met with a Jubilee 2000 delegation including Bono, Jeffrey Sachs, Bob Geldof and Ann Pettifor (Jubilee 2000 2006a). In November 1999, Jubilee South was formally constituted in Johannesburg (Jubilee South 2006).

The religious connection helped the debt cancellation movement in several ways. First, it underlined the moral basis on which the campaign to cancel third world debt was framed. Second, the faith group involvement gave the debt cancellation movement access to readymade organizational structures ideally suited to mobilize public opinion and coordinate activism transnationally. Finally, it connected the movement with a number of effective and experienced norm entrepreneurs (Sikkink 1998). This is not to deny that many in the debt cancellation movement had their material interests served by debt cancellation, but there were many others whose immediate material interest was not served by their involvement. Many, who can best be described as "conscience adherents", were drawn to the movement by their values and the conviction that to do nothing would be a betrayal of themselves and their values (McCarthy and Zald 1979). Human rights campaigners as well as faith group adherents fell into this category. The conviction that one was doing the "right" thing became a considerable source of strength.

Third world debt was only one of the issues campaigners used to demonstrate the need to make international finance more accountable to broadly defined human rights values. As NGOs and CSOs devoted substantial resources to research, seminars and education, they worked to achieve a kind of "global consciousness raising" with respect to international finance, targeting both grassroots and elites. The debt cancellation campaign was interconnected and, to a certain extent, located within a larger community of CSOs and NGOs all drawn together by various concerns with the shortcomings of the global economic system and its impact on the most vulnerable around the world.

When the Trade and Development Board of UNCTAD met in Geneva in October 1998, it was preoccupied with the effects of the Asian Crisis and the failure of the Washington Consensus. It determined to make the UNCTAD X meeting a highly inclusive process that would draw on a wide variety of international institutions and civil society actors to "rethink development" and emphasize the connections between economic, social and cultural rights on the eve of the new millennium (NGLS 1999a: 1). In 1999 the CADTM network and ATTAC-France co-organized an international meeting titled "Against the Dictatorship of the Market: another world is possible." In March 1999 a civil society conference on global financial reform called "Economic Sovereignty in a Globalising World: Creating People Centred Economics for the 21st Century" was hosted by Focus on the Global South, Development Alternatives for Women in a New Era (DAWN) and Structural Adjustment Participatory Review International Network (SAPRIN). Three-hundred-and-forty leading thinkers and activists on global financial and trade issues from 40 countries met in Bangkok. Participants from the Jubilee 2000 campaign stressed that the South must play a significant part in debt cancellation (NGLS 1999b). Equitable international taxation systems were also considered and ATTAC-France discussed the Tobin tax and other similar levies (NGLS 1999b: 3).

In this period the participation of NGOs and CSOs campaigning for debt cancellation was increasingly solicited by the IFIs. In September 1998 the head of Jubilee 2000 participated in a World Bank seminar during the WB/IMF Annual meetings. In March 1999 officials of the IMF, WB, G7 finance ministries and the Paris Club attended an all-day meeting in London with representatives of 10 national Jubilee campaigns and discussed the critique of current debt relief and the rough cost of alternative proposals for debt cancellation. In April, the IMF and WB released a 65-page review of critiques of the current Heavily Indebted Poor Countries (HIPC) debt relief initiative, extensively quoting analyses of Jubilee 2000 and other NGO and CSO proponents of debt relief. At the annual meetings of the WB and the IMF in September 1999 the IMF invited Jubilee to respond to a summary of the post Cologne reforms of the HIPC initiative (Collins et al. 2001: 139–140).

Furthermore, in the lead up to the Birmingham G8, a series of meetings between Canadian officials and Canadian NGOs and CSOs opened up the thinking process. In 1999 at the Cologne G8, when the 1996 HIPC debt relief initiative was enhanced, both the Canadian Prime Minister Jean Chrétien and Finance Minister Paul Martin were vocal advocates for debt cancellation. Their support provides evidence of the impact of the efforts of the CSOs and NGOs in advocating on this issue within Canada (WB 1999; Standing Committee on Finance 1999; Canadian Conference of Catholic Bishops 1999a; Finance Canada 2005a; Foster, P. 2008; Rayfuse 2008).

In addition to the education, networking and lobbying activities described above, debt cancellation campaigners launched demonstrations and symbolic actions designed to build solidarity within the movement and attract the attention and support of the public at large. At the May 1998 G8 summit in Birmingham, demonstrators formed a human chain to recall the importance of breaking the chains of debt, and delivered an early version of the Jubilee petition with 1.5 million signatures (Jubilee Research 2006b). Later that year mock voting booths were set up in front of the German embassies in Tokyo, Oslo, London, Edinburgh and Manchester to give people a chance to "vote" for debt relief in the run up to the German election (Jubilee 2000 2006a).

In February 1999 Bono and Muhammad Ali took the stage at the Brit Awards to voice their support for demands that western governments cancel the third world's debt by 2000. As Angela Travis of Jubilee 2000 said, "This is Live Aid grown up ... We are taking the issues that were raised in Live Aid and making something of them in the long term." The strategy of mixing pop music and human rights politics was explained by Marc Marot, managing director of Island Records, as follows: "Savvy pop musicians realize they have a captive market ... They know that while their fans may not be looking for a message, they may well be open to it when it is presented to them. That's what we are hoping will happen in this campaign" (Younge 1999). The next day Bono published an article in support of Jubilee 2000. He argued that both lenders and borrowers are to blame but that,

> the millennium is a key moment in time. We have to grasp that moment. It is not a time for factions, for narrow sects or ideological crusades. Jubilee 2000 is none of those things. Jubilee 2000 is bipartisan. It is broad, inclusive and international. It is emerging as a fresh convergence of differing groups. Including conservative elements, recognising the role of the money lenders has gone too far.

He listed other prominent institutions and individuals who had expressed support for debt cancellation and argued that "nineties people may feel at times disaffected or disenfranchised politically but they are not without a conscience." Finally, Bono compared Jubilee 2000 with the movements that ended slavery and apartheid and concluded that "We must not let it pass us by" (Bono 1999).

In April 1999 about 1,200 people attended the first foreign debt tribunal in Rio, Brazil; later that month Jubilee campaigners in the Philippines formed a human chain around the Asian Development Bank in Manila. In May, Comic Relief launched the Debt Wish campaign. In June Bono went on line in "the world's biggest net chat" to talk about debt; on June 12, 10,000 formed a human chain in Edinburgh and on June 13, 50,000 held hands in London to call on Blair to "drop the debt" (Jubilee 2000 2006a).

On the eve of the G8 summit in Cologne Madeline Bunting (1999) wrote, "(i)n the last year, what was a backroom issue for number-crunching officials has become a mainstream campaign which has succeeded in capturing the public's imagination over an immensely complex economic issue." Canadian NGOs had created a groundswell of popular support within Canada and had also enjoyed the opportunity of in-depth discussions with Canadian officials. By the spring of 1999 the Canadian delegation to the G8 was prepared to be a leading advocate for more generous debt cancellation in the interests of "justice 'and "fairness" (WB 1999; CCCB 1999; Montador 2007; Foster, P. 2008; Mihevc 2008; Fried 2008; Rayfuse 2008).

The TOES event at the 1999 G8 was called "Alliance Cologne 99/ Bundnis Koln 99" and was sponsored by a consortium of German groups (TOES 2005; NGLS 1999b). On the first day of the G8, the Peoples' Global Action (PGA) network coordinated a "days of action" in financial centers around the world (Dissent 2006; CSIS 2000). Jubilee 2000 planned a Global Week of Action on Debt to coincide with the G8 (NGLS 1999b). On June 19, the second day of meetings, 50,000 Jubilee 2000 supporters demonstrated in Cologne to demand the G8 leaders adopt deeper cuts to debt than they had accepted in the Cologne Debt Initiative[7] announced the previous day. A Jubilee 2000 delegation with representatives from each continent, including Bono and the Archbishop Oscar Rodrigues from Honduras, met with the German chancellor Gerhard Schroeder to underscore these demands, and Jubilee 2000 once again presented their petition for debt cancellation. By this time it had 17 million signatures (Jubilee Research 2006b; Kairos 2003b).

Throughout the summer and fall of 1999 popular pressure continued to build in support of debt cancellation. In July, UNICEF published a report revealing the devastating effects of debt on children. In September thousands of Jubilee supporters in the US joined in a fast to highlight the debt crisis. On November 11, 4,000 demonstrators formed a human chain outside the British Treasury to call for 100% debt cancellation. On November 13, thousands took to the streets in over 20 cities in Spain to call for debt cancellation in advance of the Ibero-American Summit (Jubilee 2000 2006a). The main event of the fall, however, was undoubtedly the protests at the WTO meeting in Seattle, Washington. The "battle in Seattle" attracted unprecedented popular attention and became a turning point in the public imagination. In Seattle 30,000 protestors joined in forming a human chain for debt cancellation (Jubilee Research 2006f; Jubilee 2000 2006a). Jubilee was an important part of this but many other NGOs and CSOs participated in the carefully planned Seattle protests. Seattle was a group effort. It was a big tent protest made up, not only of networks, but also networks of networks. While the organizations involved would probably not have been able to agree in detail on any specific policy solution, they were drawn together to protest based on a conviction that "something" was seriously wrong with the impact of the world economic system on human rights and the environment. The organizers of the Seattle event made effective use of modern communications both to organize protests and to publicize the message that not only was "something seriously wrong" but also that "something had to be done."

After Seattle, 2000–2005

The protests at the WTO meeting in Seattle attracted unprecedented public attention, and, in the following year, campaigners worked hard to take advantage of this. On December 31, 2000, the new millennium started and, as previously planned, the Jubilee 2000 Coalition ceased to exist but it was replaced by three successor organizations: Drop the Debt, Jubilee Plus and Jubilee Debt Campaign Network (UK) (Jubilee Research 2006g; WDM 2006). Jubilee USA continued to function after December 2000 (Jubilee USA 2006). Australia Jubilee 2000 rolled over into Jubilee Australia (Jubilee Australia 2006). The French Jubilee campaign "Pour l'an 2000: annulons la dette" became Dette et Développement and joined EURODAD in 2001 (Dette 2006). In 2001 the Canadian Ecumenical Jubilee Initiative (CEJI) joined several other previously independent inter-church coalitions and formed a new ecumenical organization called Kairos: the Canadian Ecumenical Justice Initiative (Kairos) (Kairos 2003a; Kairos 2003b). Jubilee South continued to operate unchanged.

The widely distributed images of the "battle in Seattle" had an important impact. Oxfam believed they had caused the public to "wake up" to injustice (Oxfam UK 2006a). After Seattle the technique of targeting major world meetings to publicize the alterglobalization message continued. On April 16, 2000 street protests, rallies, panels and teach-ins took place at the IMF/WB meetings in Washington. Protesters were heartened by supportive statements from Stiglitz and Sachs as they issued "stinging rebukes" of the IMF and WB (Barlow and Clarke 2001: 33–34). The cycle of international meetings accompanied by large popular protests continued throughout the spring and summer and culminated in the IMF/WB meeting in Prague in the fall of 2000. In the days before the meeting, President Vaclev Havel brought together 300 representatives of the IMF, WB, governments and NGOs in an effort to defuse the protests. However in the end, over 15,000 protesters took part in demonstrations organized by the umbrella organization Initiative against Economic Globalization. There was some violence, closing ceremonies were held a day early, and officials left town by public transportation commandeered for their use when ongoing protests made the streets and highways impassable (Barlow and Clarke 2001: 33–42).

Jubilee 2000 delivered its final petition to the WB/IMF meeting in Prague.[8] By this time it had 24,319,181 signatures from 161 countries (Jubilee Research 2006b). The petition read,

> We, the undersigned, believe that the start of the new millennium should be a time to give fresh hope to the impoverished people of the world. To make a fresh start, we believe it right to put behind us the mistakes made by both lenders and borrowers, and to cancel the backlog of unpayable debts of the most impoverished nations. We call upon the leaders of lending nations to meet in Africa this year and agree to write off these debts by the year 2000. We ask them to take effective steps to prevent such high levels of debt from building up again. We look for a new beginning to celebrate the millennium (Jubilee 2000 2006a).

The Jubilee campaign wove together pragmatic and normative arguments in favor of debt cancellation. However, as Anne Pettifor, a cofounder of Jubilee 2000, argued, although the debt cancellation campaign had secured significant debt reductions its goals remained much broader. In her final assessment of Jubilee 2000 she wrote that "future campaigns will have to tackle the deep structural injustices in international financial relationships" and support "the continuing struggle for justice in international financial arrangements" (Pettifor 2001). For many the campaign for debt cancellation was part of a larger strategy aimed at the underlying structural causes of inequity and exploitation in the global economic system and international finance in particular. Although debt cancellation was the issue that most lent itself to popular activism, the CSOs and NGOs campaigning for the cancellation of third world debt were connected to a broader movement seeking to promote economic and social justice through a diverse series of proposals ranging from renewing Bretton Woods, to eliminating tax havens, implementing taxes on international financial transactions and creating microcredit initiatives (ATTAC 2003; Tax Justice 2006; Yunus 2006).

In 2001 the most important innovation in transnational networking was the World Social Forum (WSF) founded by ATTAC France and the Brazilian Workers Party. In January 2001 the first WSF was held in Porto Alegre, Brazil. The WSF was deliberately designed to be all that the elitist World Economic Forum (WEF) was not. While the WEF was designed to be a meeting place for the global corporate elite, the WSF was conceived as a forum for civil society, and from the start it provided a meeting place for those interested in challenging the rules and practices governing international finance. The WSF's official slogan was "another world is possible." In January the first WSF was attended by 12,000 people, and this event raised the profile of the alterglobalization movement around the world. (CADTM 2003; CoC 2006).

At the same time demonstrations and protests at international meetings continued through the spring and summer of 2001. In April 70,000 took to the streets at the Summit of the Americas in Quebec City (Anti-Capitalist Convergence 2006). There were street protests, teach-ins, workshops and an alternative People's Summit. The Carnival against Capitalism brought a creative flair to the protest. According to contemporary accounts, the security perimeter, defended by 6,000 riot police, appeared to be a serious obstacle to protest but, in the end, it "emerged as a source of unity as the unprecedented level of police repression led several 'moderate' organizations (including the Council of Canadians and several labour unions) to assail the fence in solidarity with more militant activists." In the end this symbolic confrontation built solidarity and radicalized those involved (MacKay 2002).

At the G8 summit in Genoa in July 2001 the counter summit was called the "Genoa Social Forum: the world is not for sale" (Jubilee South 2001). In the lead up to Genoa there had been growing tensions between activists who favored violent protests and those who opposed such measures. In preparation the NEF launched a code of conduct for protesters; however, at Genoa the street protests became the scene of violent confrontations, and on July 20th a protestor was shot dead. Even so, on the next day the protests continued (NEF 2005; Bevanger 2001). At the 2001 G8 in Genoa the first meeting of the South North Working Group on Illegitimate Debt was convened by Jubilee South with the help of the CEJI. Participants discussed strategies and initiatives including plans for a People's Tribunal on Debt to take place at the World Social Forum (WSF) in February 2002.[9]

The following month, in August 2001, Jubilee South and Jubilee South Africa organized a three-day workshop on illegitimate debt at the World Conference Against Racism in Durban, South Africa. At the same time public education continued. Lidy Nacpil from Jubilee South made the case for action at teach-ins in New York and Washington; in Seattle Jubilee South took part in a series of mobilizations and forums called "Voices of the Global South" and, in the same month, Alejandro Bendaña and Lidy Nacpil of Jubilee South toured Canada to generate support for activist events planned around the G20 and the WB/IMF meetings (Jubilee South 2001).

After Seattle the connection between popular activism and financial expertise continued to develop. This was a symbiotic process in which solid research and a growing expertise in NGOs and CSOs, coupled with the capacity to communicate effectively with officials in the IFIs, government representatives as well as the public proved its worth. While the underlying message of the debt cancellation campaigners was based on human rights concerns, technical details were not neglected. NGOs and CSOs benefited from the expertise of "defectors", individuals who had previously worked in finance but who had become disillusioned and migrated to civil society advocacy work (Anonymous Transnational Activist 2005; Dillon 2008).

IFIwatchnet is an excellent example of the growing transnational networking and research capacity of NGOs and CSOs. In 2001 the Bretton Woods Project commissioned a report to examine how civil society groups monitoring the IFIs communicated with each other and strategized for the future. In response, in early 2003 the IFIwatchnet project was established to build civil society networks and enhance communications on the IFIs. For its first two years it was funded by the Ford Foundation under its Strengthening Civil Society Programme and coordinated by the Bretton Woods Project. In early 2005 the coordination of IFIwatchnet was transferred to Instituto del Tercer Mundo in Uruguay (IFIwatchnet 2006).

At FONDAD the Global Financial Governance Initiative Working Group conducted research on crisis prevention and development finance. The Center for Global Development at the Washington Institute for International Economics (IIE) produced research on the international financial architecture from a critical perspective (Rodrik 1997; Kenen 2001). Jubilee Research continued to release new research as part of the NEF and started the "Real World Economic Outlook", a bi-annual publication designed to provide a forum for economists and activists. Finally, EURODAD launched the "Economic Policy Empowerment Program" in order to coordinate the economic policy initiatives of its members (EURODAD 2006).

A norm cascade (Sikkink 1998: 2) started to develop as government representatives and members of the business community increasingly expressed concerns similar to those expressed by debt cancellation campaigners. In November 2001 the RBWC and the Conference Board of Canada organized a luncheon in Ottawa. Then Finance Minister Paul Martin gave an address in which he expressed his view that the "crushing burden of debt" should be lifted from the "shoulders of the poorest of the poor" (Finance Canada 2005b). In his years as finance minister

Martin became increasingly interested in international finance, and his involvement made a huge difference with respect to NGO and CSO access to decision makers. Members of the NGOs and CSOs campaigning for debt cancellation and reform of international finance were increasingly included in high level discussions (Anonymous International Public Servant 2008; Rayfuse 2008; Culpeper 2008; Tomlinson 2008). When the events of September 11, 2001 made mass public demonstrations more difficult CSOs and NGOs continued to target the G8, sometimes with the help of state officials. In the lead up to the 2003 G8 summit in Evian, France, French diplomats arranged meetings between representatives of American and French civil society groups to build transnational coalitions on the environment, trade, reforming of IFIs and debt (New Rules 2006).

The two-year period after Seattle was marked by large-scale protests and public confrontation, but the attacks of September 11, 2001 changed all this. After the shocking events of that day large-scale demonstrations were less impressive. Furthermore, escalating security concerns made public protest more difficult (Dillon 2008). Even after Genoa, institutional donors had found their faith in the alter globalization movement shaken by the escalating violence (Smithey 2008). As demands for security increased, remote, easily policed sites were sought out for major international meetings. Protests and demonstrations did continue but they were more constrained and other means of campaigning became more important (Jubilee South 2006; Kairos 2006).

At the 2002 WSF the International People's Tribunal on Debt produced the verdict that "the external debt of the countries of the South…is illegitimate, unjust and ethically, legally and politically unsustainable" (Jubilee South 2006). Later that year the G8 meeting was held at Kananaskis in the Canadian Rockies, a site deliberately selected for its remoteness. But as it became more difficult to mount large demonstrations and counter conferences at the site of the G8 meeting, media coverage of civil society campaigns improved (TOES 2005). Parallel civil society events in other locations provided effective counterpoints (CADTM 2003). Furthermore, at Kananaskis alternative views were presented within the G8 meeting itself, as the host, Canadian Prime Minister Jean Chrétien, placed the particular challenges faced by Africa squarely on the table (Fried 2008).

At the 2003 WSF Jubilee South organized a conference "New perspectives and insights on globalization and debt" and concentrated on exchanging ideas, experiences and lessons useful in the struggle against debt (Jubilee South 2003). The WSF continued to provide an opportunity to publicize the goals of the campaign for debt cancellation as well as to network and explore potential working relationships. Debt cancellation campaigners strove to make their arguments meaningful to grassroots participants. They worked to demystify the technical aspects of finance at the same time as reframing the issues and emphasizing the moral and normative aspects of debt. Furthermore, as Denise Comanne of CADTM advised, they remained alert to opportunities to exert pressure on governments (Jubilee South 2003a; CADTM 2006). While public protests were much reduced, behind the scenes lobbying was an important factor. National and transnational NGOs and CSOs campaigning for debt cancellation continued their efforts to develop support at popular and elite levels simultaneously.

The fourth WSF took place in Mumbai, India. Seventy-five thousand were expected to attend but thousands more came. Stiglitz spoke. By 2004 a sort of "forum circuit" had developed with activists, politicians, officials and businessmen attending both the WSF and the WEF which usually took place within a few days of each other. Jubilee South continued to be an important participant at the WSF. Their slogan was "Don't owe! Won't Pay!" Jubilee South and several other debt cancellation NGOs continued to organize major events around debt and debt cancellation at the WSF (Jubilee South 2004). In June 2004 the G8 was held at another remote site, Sea Island, Georgia. Once again public protests were made difficult by the remote location; however, although the proceedings were dominated by the ongoing war in Iraq, development and debt remained stubbornly on the agenda.

In the fall of 2004 a new kind of grass roots civil society organization started to take shape. In response to the limited opportunities for staging mass demonstrations at important international meetings, these groups created a kind of virtual space for demonstration and networking on the increasingly accessible internet. Through these new organizations a wide range of individuals could become involved in campaigns for economic justice. They could express their support through the website, as well as become involved in more conventional organizations and activities in their own communities. On October 15, 2004 the Micah Challenge was launched in conjunction with the UN ceremony for the International Day for the Eradication of Poverty 2004. In January 2005 the Global Call to Action against Poverty (GCAP) was launched at the fifth WSF in Porto Alegre.

The GCAP and its White Band campaign captured the public's imagination. In less than 12 months the GCAP grew into the world's largest anti-poverty coalition with organizations from over 100 countries representing more than 150 million globally (Whiteband 2006). The Micah Challenge, launched in 2004, is a complementary organization to the GCAP aimed at the global Christian community. It is a joint project of the World Evangelical Alliance (WEA) and the Micah Network, a network of 270 Christian organizations providing relief, development and justice ministries throughout the world (Micah 2006a). It challenged world leaders to achieve the MDGs by 2015 (Micah 2006b). The Micah Challenge aims to connect North and South as well as faith based civil society organizations with secular civil society campaigns in a pragmatic political partnership.

In 2005 the G8 summit was held at Gleneagles, Scotland. For the first time since Genoa a variety of large scale demonstrations, civil society events and other innovative means of applying pressure on the G8 leaders to "do the right thing" were organized to coincide with the summit. As early as September 2004 Dissent! Network was set up to facilitate and co-ordinate support for the "convergence" in Perthshire, Scotland (Dissent 2006). On July 2 "Live 8", a series of "Live Aid" inspired rock concerts, took place around the world to stimulate and demonstrate popular support for debt cancellation prior to the G8 summit. Bob Geldof and Bono were key organizers. By this time NGOs and CSOs recognized the usefulness of the G8 in shaping IMF and WB policy or, as one campaigner put it, they recognized the G8 was the place to give the IMF and WB their "marching orders." To this end, they lobbied actively in the lead up meetings, especially the meetings of the G7 finance ministers, and made every effort to ensure their views were well represented to the G8 participants (Fried 2008; Culpeper 2008; Rayfuse 2008).[10]

HIV/AIDS

In order to understand the impact of the campaign for the cancellation of third world debt two other factors need to be discussed. The first is how growing concern with the HIV/AIDS epidemic is connected to the campaign for debt cancellation. By 2000 there was a growing sense that the official response to the HIV/AIDS epidemic in Africa had failed and that this had resulted in needless human suffering. In June 2001 the WDM published an article making an explicit link between AIDS and third world debt (WDM 2001), and the UN General Assembly held a special session on HIV/AIDS in which it was argued that debt relief was necessary to help finance the response to the AIDS epidemic in hard hit debtor states (NGLS 2001a). In 2002, at the 14th International AIDS

Conference in Barcelona, the human toll of the epidemic was communicated by AIDS activists and development NGOs and in response, the desire among policy makers and state officials to "do the right thing" increased (PBS 2006). In 2002 a new organization DATA, Debt AIDS Trade Africa, was founded by Bono, Bobby Schriver and activists from Jubilee 2000 Drop the Debt campaign to "raise awareness about and spark response to the crises swamping Africa: unpayable debts, uncontrolled spread of AIDS, and unfair trade rules" (DATA 2006). By 2004 G8 leaders supported a call for more resources for HIV vaccine research, and the Bill and Melinda Gates Foundation provided much of the funding (PBS 2006). In 2005 Kairos wrote about the connection between debt and HIV/AIDS (Kairos 2006b) and Stephen Lewis, UN Special Envoy for HIV/AIDS in Africa, implicated the IMF and SAPs in the failure to combat the AIDS epidemic earlier (Lewis 2005: 5–6, 14–16).

The HIV/AIDS epidemic ravaging Africa produced some unusual political alliances. Even among those who continued to adhere to the neoliberal approach, the question became how much "short term pain" could possibly be justified? US Senator Jesse Helms apologized for his prior opposition to AIDS spending, said "I am ashamed to have done so little" and promised he would "do better" (PBS 2006). Lobbying by Bono and other norm entrepreneurs played an important part in convincing Senator Helms and other American decision makers to support debt relief (Busby 2007: 248–269). The human toll of the AIDS epidemic in Africa undermined the moral case for market discipline put forward by supporters of the Washington Consensus and strengthened the campaign for the cancellation of third world debt. As Sikkink suggests when debt became linked with bodily harm and the death of innocent victims this linkage increased the cross cultural and transnational impact of the campaign for the cancellation of third world debt (Sikkink 1998: 4).

The United Nations

A second important overarching factor in this campaign is the role of the United Nations. In 1948 the United Nations proclaimed the Universal Declaration of Human Rights, a document which played an important part in legitimating the human rights claims of the campaign, but the UN also played an important role in facilitating civil society networking and co-operation between the various NGOs and CSOs involved in the campaign for debt cancellation. Large international meetings, such as the 1992 Earth Summit in Rio and the 1995 Social Summit in Copenhagen, allowed activists to meet and work together, both in the summits themselves as well as in the preparatory meetings which led up to the summits (Tomlinson 2008). This participation granted civil society activists a degree of legitimacy in the broader international community as well as giving them experience in, and an appreciation for the potential uses of high level policy discussions as a means of achieving their goals. This foreshadowed the use of boomerang politics.

Furthermore, although largely ignored, the United Nations Conference on Trade and Development (UNCTAD) had been expressing its concern about the inherently destabilizing effects of the globalization of finance since 1990. Not surprisingly, after the Asian financial crisis it experienced a renewed relevance. In November 1998 UNCTAD organized a Partners for Development Summit in which NGOs took an important part in discussions about international taxation and human rights oriented approaches in investment (NGLS 1999a: 1–3). In 2000, two months after the collapse of the WTO meetings in Seattle, the UNCTAD X meeting was held in Bangkok. A particular effort was made to ensure the meaningful participation of civil society, and the conference was preceded by five days of civil society meetings.[11] The conference was followed by an NGO Forum "Alternatives to Neo-Liberalism: Building in the Spirit of Seattle" (NGLS 2000: 1). UNCTAD X was intended to provide a venue where conflicting views could be freely expressed. Finance and debt were important topics of discussion, but there was no breakthrough on debt cancellation and fundamental differences of opinion remained obvious. For example, in his farewell speech, Michel Camdessus, the outgoing director of the IMF, described poverty as the "ultimate systemic threat facing humanity", admitted that markets can have major failures, but called for the increased liberalization of international capital movements as the remedy. When challenged from the floor, Camdessus completely rejected the view that the IMF's structural adjustment policies had played any part in causing the crises in poverty and development in the third world (NGLS 2000: 12).

Second, in addition to facilitating transnational civil society networking, the UN provided an important source of legitimacy. The UN UDHR (1948) was only the first of an ongoing series of United Nations declarations that were important in reinforcing claims related to economic rights as well as human rights. The 1995 United Nations Social Summit produced the Copenhagen Declaration which called for "people to be put at the centre" of development (UN 1995). At the Millennium Summit, in September 2000, the world leaders unanimously adopted the Millennium Declaration pledging, "we will spare no effort to free our fellow men, women and children from the abject and dehumanizing conditions of extreme poverty, to which more than one billion of them are currently subjected." The Millennium Declaration led to the articulation of eight specific Millennium Development Goals (MDGs) (Millennium Project 2006).[12] The MDGs, especially Goal Eight, "creating a global partnership for development" subsequently became an extremely important source of legitimacy for the NGOs and CSOs campaigning for debt cancellation. Since civil society activists are not selected through a conventional political process, their claims to speak for anyone other than themselves is rightly subject to some skepticism. Therefore CSOs and NGOs face an inherent problem with legitimacy but, by invoking the 1948 Universal Declaration of Human Rights, they found a way around this particular democratic deficit. The MDGs provided an even more specific set of goals similarly backed by the international authority of the United Nations.

The UN's International Conference on Financing for Development (ICFfD) took place in Monterrey in March 2002. The preparation for the ICFfD involved extensive consultation with civil society representatives (NGLS 2000b). Prior to the conference several thousand representatives from NGOs and CSOs gathered for a three-day "Global Forum: Financing the Right to Sustainable Development." The ICFfD adopted the Monterrey Consensus, which was heralded by many in attendance as a break with the Washington Consensus and a promising means to meet the standards laid out by the MDGs and achieve a "fully inclusive and equitable global economic system" (UN 2003: 5). However, civil society representatives and some developing country delegates were disappointed (NGLS 2002: 1–2). They rejected the Monterrey Consensus and proposed an alternative economic model, but despite this they expressed their desire to continue to be included in the financing for development process (NGLS 2002: 6).

In the same year the Millennium Project, an independent advisory body headed by Jeffrey Sachs, was commissioned by the UN Secretary General to develop a concrete action plan for the world to reverse the "grinding" poverty, hunger and disease affecting billions of people (Millennium Project 2006). It was linked to the Millennium Promise, a non-profit organization which provided links to grassroots groups fighting poverty and malaria as well as providing online networking opportunities (Millennium Promise 2007). The Millennium Campaign, another UN initiative, was launched in 2002 to support citizens' efforts to hold governments to account for the MDGs (Millennium Campaign 2007a). In 2005 the campaign worked closely with the GCAP (Millennium Campaign 2007b). By 2005, the UN itself was coaching NGOs on how to best frame their campaigns in the context of the MDGs (Herfkens 2005). This was an innovative variation on boomerang politics.

Therefore the UN played an important role facilitating transnational civil society networking and legitimizing the involvement of civil society campaigners in international politics. Furthermore, the United Nations provided CSOs and NGOs with an important means of legitimizing their demands. From the UDHR to the MDGs, the UN provided a means to underscore the links between negative economic outcomes and broadly defined human rights violations. It helped create a space in the debate for normative ideas and moral values and, through its authority as an international institution, legitimized and established the relevance of these concerns.

Change

It is difficult to measure how successful transnational advocacy networks were in achieving their goals with respect to challenging the "proper" role of international finance and reframing the issue of debt cancellation. The gap between rhetoric and action coupled with ongoing innovation in lending and borrowing complicates the question of measurement and comparison. In this case study the two most important changes that came out of the civil society based campaign for the cancellation of third world debt are, first, the way moral values and normative ideas relating to human dignity and economic justice moved from the periphery to the mainstream debate and second, the adoption of innovative political strategies by NGOs and CSOs working outside the formal channels of political authority.

The issue of debt cancellation provided a way into a renewed debate in which the tensions between broadly defined human rights and the outcomes of a liberalized international finance order were recognized. In 1984 the WCC (1985: 79) made their position clear – a given economic system should be evaluated on the basis of economic justice and its effect on the most vulnerable in society. In 1985 at the Havana Conference on Debt Luis Ignacio Silva or "Lula", a Brazilian labour leader and later President of Brazil, urged participants to recognize the power of finance:

> Without being radical or overly bold, I will tell you that the Third World War has already started – a silent war, not for that reason any the less sinister. This war is tearing down Brazil, Latin America and practically all the Third World. Instead of soldiers dying there are

> children, instead of millions of wounded there are millions of unemployed; instead of destruction of bridges there is the tearing down of factories, schools, and hospitals, and entire economies...It is a war by the United States against the Latin American continent and the Third World. It is a war over foreign debt, one which has as its main weapon interest, a weapon more deadly that the atom bomb (George, S. 1988: 238).

As market discipline and economic restructuring were embraced as the way out of chronic debt, new lending and debt restructuring became conditional on structural adjustment. The IMF adopted the role of coordinator and enforcer of the Washington Consensus. In the debtor countries themselves, however the effects of the SAPS were met with increasing civil society based opposition. Concerns were communicated from the South to the North through established faith group networks as well as grassroots development organizations. In the campaign for the cancellation of third world debt transnational civil society campaigners were able to put a "human face" on the impact of debt rescheduling and economic restructuring in the third world.

The campaign challenged the claim that market discipline and financial liberalization provided the best approach to maximizing welfare. They reframed the issues, brought the human impacts to the forefront of the debate and eventually generated a norm cascade. Slowly, the focus of the debate shifted from the moral necessity of repaying one's debts to the immorality of demanding repayment at any price. This was a fundamental change. The campaign raised awareness of the socially intolerable impact of the debt crisis, and, in Polanyian terms, contributed to a transnational countermovement. The cultural and emotional resonance of the third world debt crisis provided an effective challenge to the hegemony of the Washington Consensus. The campaign shifted the global agenda.

Of course, one could argue that human rights were always on the agenda in the sense that many who adhered to liberal and neoliberal theory sincerely believed that strict market discipline would improve economic efficiency and eventually increase global welfare. However, the campaign for debt cancellation was able to challenge this view and force concepts such as justice, conscience and morality onto the agenda. Human rights became part of the debate in a way that they had not been before. The economistic, empirically oriented methodologies of those forging the policies of the Washington Consensus had little room for the messy, anecdotal objections raised by early debt cancellation campaigners. And yet the movement took hold. Based on human rights claims, driven by public outrage at perceived human rights violations and fuelled by carefully orchestrated communication and research networks over the course of 20 years, civil society campaigners were able to make a connection between financial structures and their impact on individual welfare. They were able to undermine the argument that short-term suffering was a justifiable and necessary cost of long-term gain. They brought into question the capacity of the Washington Consensus to achieve the goals of third world development. By basing their critiques on human rights values they were able to shift the focus of the discourse from technocratic analyses of abstract economic relations to a focus on the immediate human costs. The discussion shifted from efficiency to welfare and finally to questions of right and wrong. Eventually, even within the mainstream institutions, doubts took hold.

In addition, the campaign served to remind the IFIs of their original raison d'etre and the idealistic hope for a better world that had led to their creation in 1944. Furthermore, it made the links between financial rules and practices, debt cancellation and human rights outcomes clear and accessible to interested publics in the developing, as well as the developed, world. Campaigners not only challenged the rules but also highlighted the political nature of the process which generated these rules. By emphasizing that the rules governing international finance were political constructions, the campaigns opened the door to renegotiating these rules.

The debt cancellation campaigners made their demands explicit and immediate. If the Washington Consensus approach could not deliver results, and the campaigning organizations assembled evidence to show that it had not and, indeed, probably could not achieve its goals, then changes would have to be made. It was both the "right" and "necessary" thing to do. They reframed the question of debt and successfully shifted the terms of the debate to redefine the measure of success. This was an enviable strategic position. Campaigners demanded "another world" but did not propose exactly how this should be achieved. They strategically left the technical details and the ultimate responsibility for success or failure with the international financial institutions.

There has been substantial debt rescheduling and cancellation over the years, but it is important to recognize that, originally, this had little to do with normative considerations. In the early 1970s and 1980s debt was rescheduled as necessary to preserve the larger financial system. As early 1988 the Paris Club first cancelled 33% of the bilateral debt of the poorest debtor states (Paris Club 2006).[13] But it was not until 1999, when HIPC 2 was adopted at the Cologne G8, that normative concerns started to have an effect. After the Cologne summit there was a growing concern with the human costs of the debt crisis and the social impact of structural adjustment policies within official circles and even in the IMF itself (2006).

The shift in the language around debt cancellation is important. Early campaigns called for debt "forgiveness" and made an appeal to charity while later campaigns called for debt "cancellation", and some even demanded reparations for the costs of colonialism and the debt crisis. By 2005, the term "cancellation" had largely replaced "forgiveness" indicating that this was not an act of charity but rather an act of economic justice. The use of the terms "odious" and "illegitimate" debt as a means to justify demands for debt cancellation indicated a further implicit criticism of the international financial system. These terms refer to debt that should never have been made and therefore should not be collected. From this it follows that if the international financial markets generated substantial amounts of odious debt, they might not be as automatic and welfare maximizing as some would like to believe and they may instead be in serious need of regulation and reform.

A second major change associated with the campaign for the cancellation of third world debt is tactical. In this campaign CSOs and NGOs became part of international and eventually transnational networks campaigning for economic justice and debt cancellation. They worked simultaneously at the grassroots level and the elite level using a variety of tactics from public education to street protests to high level lobbying to move their concerns forward. At the same time as building a resilient popular base, campaigning CSOs and NGOs developed an equally impressive number of research centers, think tanks and umbrella organizations to provide research and policy analysis, coordination, networking opportunities and funding.

NGOs and CSOs campaigning for debt cancellation employed a number innovative tactics including several variations of "boomerang politics" which complemented conventional political mechanisms. In classic boomerang politics, when civil society actors in state A find their access to their own state blocked or ineffective, they enlist civil society actors in state B who exert pressure on state B and that state, in turn, exerts influence on state A (Keck and Sikkink 1998: 12–13). This relationship, diagrammed in Figure 2.1 is reproduced as Figure 3.1.

Debt cancellation campaigners employed a number of variations on this. In one variation state B in turn targets a responsive international organization that in turn exerts pressure on the unresponsive state A. (See Figure 3.2.)

Figure 3.1 Classic boomerang politics

Domestic civil society actors work through external civil society, state and international organization actors to target unresponsive state policy i.e. debt cancellation and human "dignity" discourse.

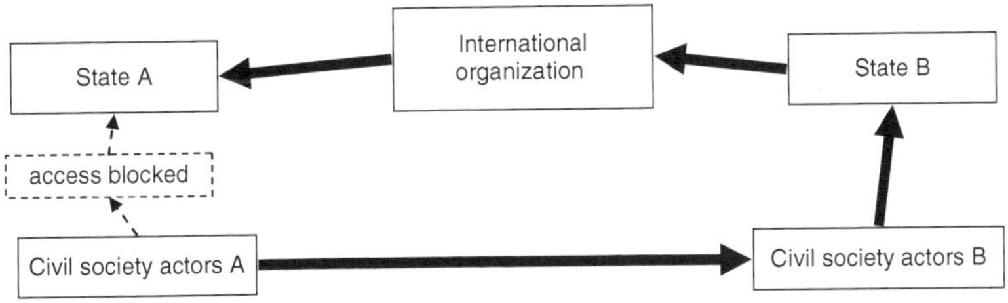

Figure 3.2 Boomerang politics, variation 1

In another variation of this civil society actors working in transnational advocacy networks target a number of key states (state B, state C) simultaneously in order to get a responsive international organization to exert pressure on state A (see Figure 3.3). An example of this is the high level lobbying efforts that took place at the G8 meetings in 2002 and 2005.

Finally, in a case where both civil society actors and state actors seek the same policy outcome but find their way blocked by an unresponsive international organization, they may join together and work to influence another influential international organization and in this way achieve their goals. An example of this is the way high level lobbying within the G8 was able to exert pressure on the IFIs (see Figure 3.4).

In the course of the campaign NGOs and CSOs came to recognize the potential of the G8 as a key moment to exert pressure on the IMF and the WB and they brought considerable expertise and analytic strength to bear in lobbying key actors in G8 states. By 1998 many NGOs campaigning for debt cancellation had learnt how to communicate in the

Transnational advocacy networks work through states and international organizations to target unresponsive state i.e. high level lobbying at G7/G8.

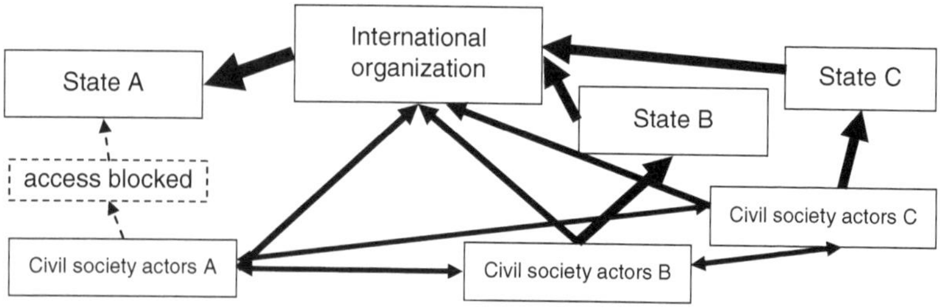

Figure 3.3 Boomerang politics, variation 2

Transnational advocacy networks and states target an inaccessible international organization through another international organization i.e., civil society actors and state actors seek the same policy and seek to circumvent an unresponsive international organization.

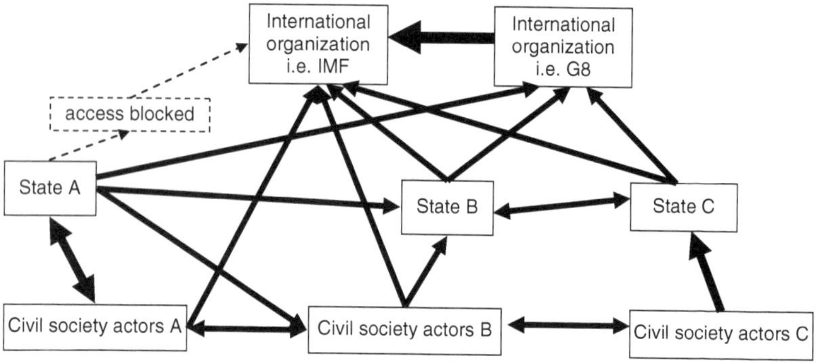

Figure 3.4 Boomerang politics, variation 3

language of policy elites and had become respected participants in the process. This generated a norm cascade around putting human factors, not just economic indicators at the center of development. The debt cancellation campaign contributed to and benefited from this cascade (UNDP 2009; UN 2003; Millennium Project 2006).

Whether there was more rhetoric than real change is difficult to say. But whether or not the rhetoric was merely lip service, the agenda had been shifted and social and economic justice had become an indispensable part of the debate. In June 2003 private sector banks adopted the

Equator Principles as a benchmark for the financial industry to provide guidelines for dealing with social and environmental issues in project financing (Equator Principles 2009). By 2005, at the annual meeting of the Institute of International Finance (IIF), a global association of financial institutions, the agenda included a panel on "fair debt restructuring" and the keynote speaker was the Nigerian minister of finance (IIF 2006).

Debt cancellation was linked with fighting global poverty and the G8 became an important site of change. At the Okinawa G8 in 2000 leaders from the indebted poor countries were included in informal discussions about debt relief for the first time (BBC 2000). In 2002 the G8 African Action plan was adopted at Kananaskis. British Prime Minister Tony Blair and Gordon Brown, the Chancellor of the Exchequer, were extremely receptive to NGO and CSO arguments regarding poverty alleviation and debt cancellation (Fried 2008). By the spring of 2005 debt cancellation was the new consensus. At the 2005 Gleneagles G8 summit, leaders announced the Multilateral Debt Relief Initiative (MDRI). Although this was the first time that the G8 had agreed to full cancellation of multilateral debt for highly indebted countries, other external debts remained. In addition, only one-third of the 60 countries most burdened by poverty were included in the plan and, under the MDRI, debt relief remained subject to conditions (Reilly-King 2006; Hallinan 2006; Monbiot 2005). Even so the Jubilee Debt Campaign stated, "The decision to cancel all World Bank and IMF debts for some countries – up to a certain date – is a hugely important step forward, and represents a fundamental shift in official approaches to debt cancellation" (Jubilee Debt Campaign 2006).

Although 2005 was undoubtedly a step forward for the debt cancellation campaign, it was not a total success. Indeed the growing conflation of debt relief with poverty reduction detracted from the original strength of debt cancellation as a critique of international finance. The debt crisis provided a means of making the power of the rules and practices governing international finance visible. This insight however, was largely overshadowed by the goal of poverty alleviation. In 2005 the Gleneagles G8 summit seemed like a breakthrough but one year later the criticisms abounded. While the debt cancellation portion of the 2005 agreement was promptly fulfilled in the following year, there were concerns that overall levels of aid were not being increased and, as a sense of "mission accomplished" took hold there were growing concerns that poverty, as well as debt, might fall off the agenda (Hallinan 2006; Beattie 2006).

Ending global poverty is a compelling goal. It is a worthy cause for popular mobilization, but the danger is that it is so compelling that it draws attention away from the baffling details of international finance. Finance has often been considered too technical to provide a basis for popular action but the success of the debt cancellation campaign seemed to disprove this. Yet in 2005 the question remained, could public pressure be maintained or would support diminish as the public came to believe that debt cancellation, the most intuitively appealing part of financial reform, was accomplished? Furthermore, even if debt cancellation made meaningful progress and reforming international finance remained a top priority, could the rules and practices governing international finance and the system which produced the debt crisis in the first place, be addressed? Even today in the light of the ongoing economic difficulties and new series of debt crises, this time centred in the developed world, the public remains confused and overwhelmed by conflicting claims which it has little capacity to evaluate.

Conclusion

This chapter started by asking how non-state actors mobilized to challenge the rules and practices governing international finance in the campaign for the cancellation of third world debt. This case study found evidence in support of the four related hypotheses. First, in the emerging context of transnational civil society based politics, moral values and normative ideas; in other words ideas about how the world *should* be, are a powerful force in shaping change, even with respect to the rules and practices governing international finance. Second, the campaign for the cancellation of third world debt is part of a Polanyian double movement taking place at the transnational level in which the effects of market discipline and economic restructuring administered by the IMF produced a societal backlash. Third, in this campaign civil society actors redefined the global agenda with respect to debt cancellation and produced a crisis in one elite discursive framework, the Washington Consensus and a (partial) shift to a more inclusive discursive framework which incorporated the demands of non-elite actors. Finally, by means of activism and innovative political strategies the campaign for the cancellation of third world debt changed the process of decision making to include actors and points of view that were previously excluded.

The concept of norm emergence and norm cascade is useful in analyzing the campaign for the cancellation of third world debt. In this campaign, norm entrepreneurs participated in transnational networks of NGOs and CSOs to create a change in discourse with the goal of reforming the rules and practices governing third world debt cancellation. Sikkink (1998: 2–3) argues that norm entrepreneurs work to reframe issues according to their strongly held principled ideas. While some CSOs and NGOs, most obviously debt cancellation activists in debtor countries, can be loosely understood as acting in pursuit of their own material interests, others are more puzzling. Many of the organizations and activists involved in campaign for debt cancellation were motivated by their values and a desire to "do the right thing." For them the effects of the debt crisis became intolerable due to its impact on what they held to be fundamental human rights.

Furthermore, debt cancellation campaigners found their normative reframing of debt particularly resonant due to the longstanding ambivalence or even disapproval of finance which is a characteristic of many cultures (see de Goede 2005: 45–87, 108; Chernow 1990: 375–377). Campaigners deliberately tailored their demands for debt cancellation to powerful societal norms in specific societies. For example, Jubilee USA, the American member of the Jubilee 2000 network, adopted the slogan "Break the chains of debt" and referred to the condition of the debtor nations of the third world as "debt slavery." The linkage between debt and slavery was a particularly powerful image for the American public.

In Polanyian terms, the transnational campaign for the cancellation of third world debt can be understood as a countermovement challenging the Washington Consensus on the basis of moral values and normative ideas.[14] Previously, the Washington Consensus, or at least the neo-liberal revolution which inspired it, had challenged the hegemony of embedded Keynesian liberalism and the regulated financial order of the Bretton Woods system in the name of economic efficiency. This ongoing process of challenge and change is an important part of the adaptive capacity of capitalist systems. As long as major, catastrophic disruptions in the form of security crises or environmental disasters do not occur, this process has the capacity to allow the capitalist economic system to adapt indefinitely. This is not to say it is a pleasant process, nor to minimize the suffering of those caught in the quiet violence of famine or epidemic. It is, however, a process well worth understanding and one which shapes the economic, political and social rules of the world in which we all live.

By 2005 the campaign for the cancellation of third world debt had successfully redefined the agenda with respect to debt cancellation and produced a crisis in one elite discursive framework, the Washington Consensus, and a partial shift to another, more inclusive framework which rejected the economistic logic which underpinned the Washington Consensus. Through the impact of the third world debt crisis and the effects of SAPs the campaign was able to connect the abstract world of international finance with what they framed as intolerable human rights abuses resulting from excessive market discipline. A multitude of CSOs and NGOs took it upon themselves to defend the most vulnerable citizens in debtor states and campaign for reform. After the Asian financial crisis, the international financial institutions themselves became somewhat skeptical of neoliberal policy prescriptions of the Washington Consensus, and when several important opinion makers, within these institutions expressed their doubts this gave additional momentum to the civil society campaign. While the civil society campaigners had never lacked for financial expertise, being well grounded in a number of research institutes and think tanks, the apparent conversion of prominent economists like Stiglitz and Sachs added a new level of credibility and authority.

Thanks to advances in communications and travel civil society actors were able to create networks of activist organizations and networks of networks. Access to up-to-date information was only as far away as the nearest internet connection or telephone. Modern travel facilitated networking opportunities as well as popular mass demonstrations. Modern media and the use of celebrity in supporting these causes made activism fashionable as celebrity spokespeople reinforced the message. Documentaries and interviews with those negatively affected by the debt crisis aroused feelings of empathy and anger. Research and analysis provided by the campaigning organizations provided an alternative means of understanding the origins and implications of the crises. In short, as Keck and Sikkink (1999: 5) predict, the campaigning CSOs and NGOs were instrumental in communicating the problem, making the public care about the problem, and facilitating and directing popular demands for change. They were also effective when meeting with politicians and officials and lobbying for their point of view. A measure of their success is that by 2005 the idea of linking human rights violations and the negative effects of neoliberal economic restructuring seemed obvious. In contrast, 30 years earlier this claim would have seemed quite foolish because market discipline was seen by definition, to be, automatic, apolitical, welfare maximizing and, if not above ugly political contests, at least outside of them.

Innovative political strategies on the part of NGOs and CSOs were important in changing the process of decision making to include alternative perspectives and actors. In this case study norm entrepreneurs founded and participated in advocacy networks at domestic, international and transnational levels; they participated in a myriad of tactics to persuade actors at all levels to adopt a new cognitive frame for their view on debt cancellation in particular, and international finance in general. Sympathetic norm entrepreneurs in government, international organizations and civil society collaborated to influence the agenda. These networks cultivated the support of powerful state actors in the international system as they sought to achieve a change in the policies of the G8 and the IMF with respect to debt cancellation. When these CSO and NGO networks found their path to conventional lines of influence blocked, for example as in the case of a powerless state or an unresponsive organization, they pursued various strategic variations on boomerang politics to exert pressure on relevant actors and organizations (Keck and Sikkink 1999: 4).

In conclusion this chapter demonstrates how the concept of transnational advocacy networks can help in understanding the importance of moral values and normative ideas in new forms of transnational contentious politics. It highlights the innovative political tactics of the NGOs and CSOs involved in the campaign for the cancellation of third world debt and outlines a number of variations on the original concept of boomerang politics. The next chapter considers the case of the World Economic Forum (WEF) as a transnational advocacy network and a site of innovative political contestation and civil society activism.

4
The World Economic Forum as a Site of Contestation

The World Economic Forum, whose high-powered membership gathers each winter at Davos, Switzerland, appears to be an elite club devoted to organizing the world in the interests of big business and free market economics, yet as the years have passed the WEF has embraced an increasingly public role and normative agenda. Today the motto of the WEF is "Committed to improving the state of the world." This chapter examines the role of the WEF as a transnational advocacy network and analyses the WEF annual meeting as a site of innovative political contestation in the campaign by non-state actors to change the rules and practices governing international finance in general and debt cancellation in particular.

As argued previously, the resilience and adaptive capacity of capitalist systems is not only the result of their impressive capacity to mobilize technical and material resources through market relations, but also is due to their relation to social and normative structures which have historically, supported, as well as generated, societal limits on market processes (Ruggie 1982; Polanyi 1944/1957; and Gramsci 1971). This case study examines how non-state actors at the WEF have mobilized to challenge the rules and practices governing debt cancellation. Although the WEF can be understood as simply another CSO in the multitude of civil society based organizations campaigning for the cancellation of third world debt that were addressed in Chapter 3, it is worth examining as a separate case study. The WEF is a CSO like no other. From its inception in 1971 to 2005, the end point of this study, the WEF became increasingly connected to the broader campaigns of civil society, but there has been little research focusing on its power and influence in transnational and international politics. Each year a kind of "conventional wisdom" comes out of Davos. Over the years the content of this has changed, and substantial shifts in the discourse at the WEF have both reframed the global agenda and contributed to the success of innovative political strategies such as "boomerang politics" (Keck and Sikkink 1998: 12–13) with respect to attitudes to economic globalization in general and the cancellation of third world debt in particular.

This chapter starts by outlining some of the main lines of continuity in the Davos meetings and then focuses on contestation and change. It tests four hypotheses. First, that moral values and normative ideas, in other words beliefs about how the world *should* be, were important in shaping the way the WEF defined its role in the world and in changing its approach to debt cancellation. Second, that this is part of a Polanyian countermovement emerging at the transnational level. Third, that contestation over moral values and normative ideas at the WEF redefined the agenda with respect to debt cancellation and produced a crisis in one elite discursive framework, the Washington Consensus, and a (partial) shift to another discursive framework which incorporated the demands of non-elite actors. And finally, that the innovative political strategies used by CSO and NGO actors, both within the Davos meeting as well as those targeting the WEF from outside the meeting, changed the process of decision making to include actors and points of view that had previously been excluded.

Background to the World Economic Forum

The WEF has developed from its rather modest origins as the European Management Forum (EMF) into an almost mythical institution, imbued with both glamour and mystery. At first the Forum met only once a year in Davos but, over the years, the WEF expanded its activities in scope and scale to include regional meetings as well as an impressive number of specialized programs and initiatives. This chapter, however, will focus on the WEF Annual Meeting usually held in Davos in January or February of each year. Klaus Schwab, at the time a professor of business at the Centre d'Etudes Industrielles, took charge of organizing the first meeting, which took place in January, 1971 (Graz 2003: 329). At first the Forum was conceived as an opportunity for European firms to learn about American management practices (Wadler 2002); however, in 1973 the EMF expanded its focus from management to include economic and social issues, and, in January 1974, political leaders were invited for the first time (WEF 2008a).

At Davos the week-long meeting was set up to provide a sense of easy access and intimacy among a select group of highly accomplished individuals. Entourages were deliberately limited. Simply being a participant facilitated introductions and chance meetings led to fruitful dialogue. For business leaders, Davos was a place to discuss economic issues and formulate business strategies. During the late 1970s and the 1980s the organization became increasingly global in outlook, and in 1987 the EMF changed its name to the WEF. At the same time the WEF leadership started to realize the political uses of this informal elite venue, not just in facilitating business and economic cooperation, but also in enhancing cooperation between political leaders, and the WEF annual meeting became the site of a number of important diplomatic initiatives (WEF 2008a). While business members pay a substantial membership fee, others attend as guests of the Forum. As the WEF sought to define itself as a uniquely informative experience it invited interesting non-members to Davos in ever increasing numbers. These non-paying, invited guests, ranging from Nobel Laureates to heads of state, were carefully selected to add intellectual stimulation and often a little glamour to the event.

Over the years the size of the meeting grew and the proportion of paying, business participants shrank. In 1988 there were 700 businessmen and only 200 non-business participants; by 2004, 1,255 of the 2,280 participants were non-paying (Dullforce 1988; WEF 2004j). However, this decline in the proportion of business participants is not evidence of a lack of interest. On the contrary, much of the shift is due to the WEF's deliberate policy of limiting the number of business members at the annual meeting in order to maintain the sense of equality and easy access that was such an important part of the early meetings at Davos (Pigman 2007: 24). Today a typical WEF member company is a global enterprise with more than $5 billion US in turnover (WEF 2008e). A company that falls behind is not invited back and each year new prospective members apply.

The annual meeting follows a formal program. Each year a new theme is selected (see Table 4.1). The opening plenary sets the tone of the meeting and the closing plenary summarizes and emphasizes the WEF's perspective on the events. Sometimes carefully placed opinion pieces in international newspapers or articles in the Davos edition of *World Link* magazine or *Global Agenda* magazine reinforce the theme. A schedule of events is required to negotiate the impressive array of panels, plenary sessions, dinner discussions and breakfast meetings available to participants.

The panels cover a wide variety of topics including, not surprisingly, business, finance and economics. More unexpectedly there are also a

Table 4.1 European Management Forum/World Economic Forum themes, 1984–2005

1984	European Management Forum Warming up for Economic Recovery
1985	European Management Forum
1986	European Management Forum The Courage for Globalization
1987	Name changed to World Economic Forum (WEF)
1988	The New State of the World Economy
1989	Key Developments in the 90s: Implications for Global Business
1990	Competitive Cooperation in a Decade of Turbulence
1991	The New Direction for Global Leadership
1992	Global Cooperation and Megacompetition
1993	Rallying all the Forces for Global Recovery
1994	Redefining the Basic Assumptions of the World Economy
1995	Leadership for Challenges Beyond Growth
1996	Sustaining Globalization
1997	Building the Network Society
1998	Managing Volatility and Priorities for the 21st Century
1999	Responsible Globality: Managing the Impact of Globalization
2000	New Beginnings: Making a difference
2001	Sustaining Growth and Bridging Global Divides: A Framework for our Global Future
2002	Leadership in Fragile Times
2003	Building Trust
2004	Partnering for Security and Prosperity
2005	Taking Responsibility for Tough Choices

number of panels that have little to do with business. These have been a feature at the annual meeting for years and are a popular part of the program. Over the years the panels on offer have shifted with the preoccupations of the times. In the early days the forum was primarily concerned with business and management issues, and general interest panels tended to focus on individual health or scientific interest. After 1995 however, panels on globalization, security, corporate social responsibility, economic justice and individual responsibility came to occupy a substantial place on the program.

At Davos, personal networking connects investors with opportunities from around the world. The potential for informal meetings at Davos is legendary. As the organizers intended, everyone one encounters at Davos, or at least everyone with an all access white badge, is likely to be worth at least a few minutes of conversation. There are also a number of private meetings and invitation only events formally scheduled within the larger Davos program. For example, the Informal Gathering of World Economic Leaders has become an annual tradition at Davos. It is restricted to senior ministers, presidents and prime ministers without their entourages. During the annual meeting this group meets to discuss finance, trade and public policy. Similarly, the Davos Governors' Meetings, initiated in 1983, are industry-specific gatherings which provide a private venue to discuss issues affecting specific industries (Steinberg 2003a).

In addition to the annual meeting the WEF is involved in a long list of regional forums, publications and initiatives. The WEF has become well known for its competitiveness reports which each year provide analysis and data on the relative competitive positions of an ever increasing number of states. The WEF first published the "Report on the Competitiveness of European Industry 1979" for use at the annual meeting in 1980 (Pigman 2007:101). By 1990 the name of this publication had been changed to the "World Competitiveness Report" (WCR) although it profiled only countries from the developed world and the Asian "tiger" economies (WEF and IMD, 1990). Even in 1996, when the name was changed to "Global Competitiveness Report" (GCR), the definition of "global" employed by the WEF was still remarkably limited (WEF 1996a).

In January 1988 the WEF launched its own magazine called *World Link*. This attractive, bi-monthly publication was part of an ongoing effort to promote the WEF and build an elite community around the organization (Schwab 1990). As was the case in the GCR, the "truly global view" in the early editions of *World Link* magazine is remarkably narrow; for example, in the July 1989 issue there are no less than three articles on Antarctica but one is hard pressed to find any mention of Africa (WEF 1989). *World Link* magazine was given to attendees at Davos and made available to others by subscription (Pigman 2007:101). It was used to set the tone at the annual meeting, call attention to issues the organizers wished to highlight, and to provide a space for those interested in promoting specific states and regions. In 2003 the name of this publication was changed to *Global Agenda* (GA) but the use of the magazine as a companion publication to Davos, as well as a way to reinforce and explain the theme chosen each year by the WEF leadership, continued.

World Link was originally conceived of as a publication which would help the WEF community to keep in contact but developments in communications technology soon provided new and better ways to accomplish this. The WEF had many high tech companies as members, and it was well positioned to pioneer the possibilities of communications technology. In January 1991 the WEF launched "WELCOM", an electronic communications system intended to enhance the formidable networking potential of the forum (WEF 1991a: 29). After a slightly difficult start WELCOM took off and subsequently the forum continued to embrace new technological possibilities (*Financial Times* 2001; Pigman 2007:16). The WEF set up its first website in 1999 and shortly after made coverage of several events available online (WEF 1999h). Today the online presence of the WEF is substantial.

It is important, however, to remember that the WEF is a private membership organization and is not subject to the transparency requirements of public institutions. Its public image is carefully constructed and controlled, yet unlike other elite forums, the WEF appears to court the media. It invites selected journalists to participate in its activities and, to a limited extent, facilitates public coverage of these events; however, the WEF leadership makes and enforces rules with respect to which elements of the meeting can be reported (Freeman 1998; WEF 2004i). They strive to provide a respectful venue for constructive discussion. Reports on panels do not always exist and, when they are available, they tend to be brief summaries of the discussion which cast all of the participants in a positive light. No comment may be attributed to a specific speaker without their consent. This is very much in the spirit of Davos. The organizers strive to create, not only a useful and informative experience for their 1,000 business members, but also a pleasant and interesting experience.

At Davos there are two classes of journalists, each distinguished by badge color. The media leaders are invited guests, able to participate in the forum as equals with other participants and as such have white badges. The reporting press, assigned to cover the meeting, are issued orange badges. They have more restricted access and are not usually invited to the private receptions and dinners which complement the formal program of the meeting. Both media leaders and ordinary journalists publish reports and articles, but they usually comply with the rules of disclosure set down by the WEF. This is not really surprising. Such is the mystique of Davos that it seems almost everyone who has ever attended would like to be invited back, and preferably invited back wearing a white badge (Russell 2002).

Although the WEF has a much higher public profile than other elite clubs such as the Trilateral Commission or the Bilderberg Group, it continues to be not quite public and yet not quite private. It is an organization that remains very difficult to classify. On one level it is nothing more than a private club but the power and wealth of its members make it a private club like few others. While the WEF is not an easy organization to track, what is clear is that today the public image of the WEF is very different from that of its early years. Over the years it has transformed itself in a way that reflects the changed preoccupations and intellectual fashions of the times. The prominently featured motto, "Committed to Improving the state of the World", adopted in 1999 indicates that the WEF is an organization which works hard to make the world a "better" place (Freeman 1999). Arguably, this is the intention of the WEF. The real question, however, is exactly what constitutes "improving" and how this might be achieved. As will be seen in the following sections, in its own way the WEF has always been committed to making the world a better place but it has not always succeeded.

Continuity at the Annual Meeting

While Davos has undergone many changes in the years leading up to 2005 this section outlines three important areas of continuity at the annual meeting: leadership, networking and providing a meaningful experience for business members.

Perhaps the most obvious source of continuity is the leadership role of Klaus Schwab, the founder of the WEF. The WEF is a private membership organization, and at its annual meeting in Davos Klaus Schwab is the host. The activities of the WEF are shaped by his vision and guidance. In building the WEF, Klaus Schwab and his team were careful to create a mystique around the annual meeting. Not only did they create an ideal atmosphere for business networking, they also created a heady and exclusive atmosphere which drew a loyal following of business members back each year. In a kind of virtuous circle, an ever more impressive guest list enhanced the cachet of the WEF while the growing cachet of the WEF added to world wide interest in participating.

The Forum was founded as a business forum and, even though business members now constitute only half of the participants at the annual meeting, the WEF remains an organization which depends on their interest and support. Politics and geopolitics are, of course, of vital interest to business but more recently, the leadership of the WEF shifted its emphasis to address the effects of economic globalization. This fits well with the economic emphasis of the forum, but it also shows the continuing efforts of the WEF to address the important issues of the day. The WEF is politically sensitive. It is characterized by a fluid response to the mood of the times combined with a well-developed sense of what is politically possible within its membership community. From its origins as the EMF to the prestigious, globally oriented transnational organization that it is today, the WEF has always kept a careful eye on both the world situation as well as on the interests and enthusiasms of its membership.

The strong leadership has resulted in a clear hierarchy in the organization of the WEF. Despite its high public profile the WEF remains a private organization and ultimately is answerable only to itself. No one has the right to demand membership in the WEF. Yet it is ironic that an organization which itself has such a clear hierarchy has become so willing to exert political pressure outside the traditional state-centric hierarchy of international diplomatic relations. The leadership of the WEF has carefully cultivated its transnational networks for decades and, as a result, has a multiplicity of ways and means to apply political pressure. Paradoxically, the hierarchical discipline at the WEF, which successfully insists on the polite glossing over of fundamental differences within the Davos meeting itself, has contributed to the creation of an environment at Davos in which dissenting and unfamiliar views can be heard, or at least presented, in formal as well as casual encounters. In general participants are pleased to be included in the elite circles which attend the Davos meeting and, with very few exceptions, the WEF has succeeded in keeping the tone of discussion civil.

A second continuity in the WEF annual meeting is the ongoing importance of networking. Since its start, the Davos meeting has, in effect, served as a private introduction service and provided its attendees with excellent opportunities for networking. Famously much of the business at Davos is accomplished outside the formal sessions and workshops in private meetings and in informal encounters, in the hallways, restaurants, and on the ski slopes. The success of the WEF in facilitating informal meetings and helping to improve communication in international conflicts demonstrates its value as a site for diplomacy. The Davos meeting presents equally impressive opportunities for business networking. The intention of Davos has been to provide a forum for discussion where issues can be discussed, ideas communicated and insights developed in a way that is not possible where outcomes must be negotiated and interests are at stake. At Davos privacy is possible and discretion is valued. With only a few exceptions the atmosphere at Davos is ruthlessly polite. Opponents routinely appear on the same stage and only rarely do they refuse. As a result, at Davos unlikely alliances have been forged and future lines of communication opened.

Finally, the WEF depends on the support of its business members for its continued existence. As such it must maintain this support and one of the ways it can ensure ongoing interest is by providing a meaningful experience for its business members. Although the definition of "meaningful" has evolved over the years, the sense that Davos provides an extraordinary experience, uniquely in tune with the times, has remained constant. The WEF frequently refers to the "spirit of Davos." It envisions Davos, during the time of the annual meeting, as a special place which provides unique benefits to those in attendance. The WEF strives to create an enjoyable and stimulating environment at Davos. It works at being a good host, seeing to accommodations, planning professional and social events, considering the comfort and security of its guests, and facilitating the interaction of those in attendance.

There are strong pragmatic reasons for attending Davos. The meeting provides an extremely useful venue for businesses, states and others seeking investment as well as those seeking new investment opportunities. Davos provides an excellent opportunity to get a sense of global events and developing trends and to develop a sense of the economic environment business will have to work within during the coming year. As early as 1980 the *Economist* (1980a) wrote "After some shaky moments, the symposium got and has kept a firm hold on its high-level, high paying participants by giving them what the OPEC years required: not advice on how to run their businesses, so much as on the disrupted environment they have to run them in." Davos became a place where business could take a reading of the world (Carr 1984b; Warner 1998; Uchitelle 1998; Pfanner 2004).

Over the years the fame, status and wealth of those attending the annual meeting has grown and for many members there is undoubtedly a certain satisfaction in being included in this exclusive group. At the same time some business members have become celebrities in their own right. For example, Bill Gates was transformed from the CEO of a technology company to a global venture philanthropist, Jeffrey Sachs from an economist to a campaigner to end global poverty and George Soros from a financial wizard to a promoter of democracy. At Davos there has been a shift to a more overt concern with the "state of the world" and whether it is Sharon Stone shaming participants into funding bed nets to prevent malaria, or Bono and Bobby Schriver, in the company of Bill Gates (2008), inventing the RED initiative, Davos now provides opportunities to network and coordinate philanthropic, as well as business, initiatives. The satisfaction of being involved in these initiatives, no matter how peripherally, adds to the meaning of the Davos experience for many business participants.

Contestation

This section examines how the WEF transformed from a meeting focused on European business to a forum which drew participants from around the world and in which the business agenda, while still important, shared space with a substantial social and ethical focus. The discussion is divided into four periods which mark different stages in the development of the WEF.

From European Management Forum to World Economic Forum: 1989 and before

In this period the Davos meetings were focused primarily on the needs and interests of the business community in the developed world. Intensive work sessions and seminars filled the program, and in 1984 "brainstorming sessions", where world political and economic leaders moved from one group of businessmen to another, were introduced. The opportunity for access and interaction at Davos was extremely useful to business and non-business participants alike and over time Davos came to be the site of informal high level diplomatic and policy discussions. In 1987 a high level group of international officials and politicians met at Davos in preparation for the G7 finance ministers meeting that was scheduled for the following week (Wyles 1987; JiJi 1987).

The environment, the third world debt crisis, business ethics and AIDS were also on the agenda but, although these issues were not that different from those which preoccupied the WEF in later years, the approach was. In this period issues were viewed through the prism of what they might mean in terms of narrowly defined business interests. The conference was "unashamedly capitalist" (*The Economist* 1987), and there was little sense that business activity could possibly be responsible for any negative social effects (Ferguson 1988). Even the emerging HIV/AIDS epidemic was viewed primarily in terms of its effect on business in the developed world (*Herald* 1988). It was not that business leaders at Davos were indifferent to human suffering but, at the time, the conventional wisdom held that the way business might best contribute to global welfare was by working through existing economic structures in the most efficient manner possible. The goal was to work with the rules, not change them.

Each year however, the organizers made an effort to include a few dissenting voices. In 1983 Arthur Scargill, the British miners' leader, and Petra Kelly of the West German Green party shared a stage at Davos. Unfortunately, the event turned out to be a demonstration of prejudice and gender bias as a number of German businessmen, who objected to Kelly being invited, "reacted by splattering her with insults and expressions of male chauvinism" (*Financial Times* 1983). This most un-Davos-like moment underlines the gendered nature of the Davos meeting. Before 1989 the business participants at Davos were primarily men, and, although the WEF has made efforts to address the gender imbalance the disparity between male and female participants continues even today. In 1987 the WEF invited Andrew Young, a US civil rights leader and Daniel Cohn-Bendit, previously well known as "Danny the Red", a 1968 student leader who had become an activist in the West German Green party. Against the background of ongoing antinuclear protests in West Germany, the two men discussed the uses and abuses of activism and reminded the Davos participants that not only activists, but also business had a "responsibility to bring about a reduction of violence in the world" (Stevens 1987). In the same year Maurice Strong, a Canadian businessman who was closely involved with the WEF, called for an ambitious plan of action to address environmental crises, the AIDS epidemic, reform the international economic system and "launch a world campaign against the poverty of the Third World" (Crane 1988). In this period, the WEF invited celebrated individuals to participate, not only to enhance the international prestige of Davos, but also to help communicate a message that might be considered somewhat beyond the scope of a business forum. But while business participants listened, there is little evidence that it spurred them to action. Instead these sessions were rather like the general interest sessions on health or science those were so popular at the time. Business participants became aware of new cutting edge research on a variety of fascinating topics, but they felt little personal responsibility to act on this information.

Contestation and challenge, 1989 and before

By the mid-1980s the third world debt crisis had become impossible to ignore. At Davos, however, debt was seen as technical problem and the impact in human terms of the "debt trap" that became so prominent in later discourse, was noticeably absent. In 1984, when A. W. Clausen, President of the World Bank, spoke out against "negative transfers"; he was careful to stress the rights of capital and his strongest criticism was that it was *premature* that the developing economies be net exporters of capital to the developed economies. There was no discussion that it might be unfair that the poorest countries of the world should be exporting capital to the richest or what this might mean in human terms for the citizens of debtor countries. Instead Clausen argued that the debt crisis must be addressed, not because of its impact on the developing world, but because it would have a negative impact on economic growth in industrialized countries (Carr 1984a).

In 1986 the debt crisis continued to be seen primarily in technical terms (Carr 1986) but in 1987 Daniel Cohn-Bendit, one of the dissenting voices invited by the WEF leadership made the first clear link between the debt crisis and the moral responsibility of the developed world:

> The indebtedness of developing countries to the governments and businesses of the developed world poses a major moral question... If developed nations insist on repayment third world countries will be unable to afford the schools, hospitals and other essential services that their people need and violence will become unavoidable.

He concluded, however, by connecting the moral argument with a pragmatic one stating, "If we don't solve the problem, there will be more violence and violence is bad for business" (Stevens 1987). This is an early example of the kind of "two track" – moral and pragmatic – argument that in later years typified the discussion around debt cancellation at Davos. In 1987, however, the moral argument fell on deaf ears.

By 1989 debt was a growing problem. At Davos Michel Camdessus, Managing Director of the IMF, urged support for debt relief but he was careful to stress that such relief would involve "appropriate amounts, in appropriate forms and on appropriate terms" (Rowan 1989). That year at Davos the Americans as well as the EU and the Japanese indicated that they were working on new ways to deal with the third world debt crisis (Crane 1989a). Carlos Pérez, the president elect of Venezuela, called for a new international agency to be created to assist in debt relief but the Americans firmly rejected this proposal (Hogg 1989). Instead there was a sense that the debt service burden would be eased if Mexico, Brazil and Venezuela – often with US-trained economists at the helm – exercised firmer discipline in introducing economic reforms and reducing public sectors.

Speaking at Davos in 1989 Senator Bill Bradley echoed Clausen by arguing that since debtor countries were devoting an estimated 30% to 50% of their foreign exchange earnings to repaying debt, they had no money to buy American exports and this was hurting American manufacturers (Hoagland 1989). There was still no discussion of the impact this might have on the welfare of the citizens of debtor countries struggling to service their debts. Rather there was a conviction that the people who had created the "mountains of debt" in the 1970s were the bankers and their third world clients and, since they had created the problem, they were now responsible for solving it. There was little criticism of the financial system that had at first rewarded the exuberant lending which led to the debt crisis. In contrast to later years, the rules were not brought into question. Instead, it was assumed that the moral imperative determined that debtors must somehow repay their debts and it was argued that debt relief "based on pity or the idea of good works rightly rubs Americans the wrong way" (Hoagland 1989). By 1989 plans for a debtors' cartel in Latin America had come to nothing, the Baker Plan had done little to remedy the situation and debt remained a persistent and distorting problem for the world economy. At Davos, representatives of Mexico, Brazil and Germany suggested that growth might provide the way out of the debt crisis (Crane 1989b; Crane 1989c).

The idea that economic growth could provide a remedy to the intractable problem of the third world debt crisis resonated with another theme which had started to take off at Davos earlier in this period: "the "magic of the market." In 1985 the US economy was booming and at Davos the emphasis shifted to the "Reagan miracle" (Carr 1985). America had once again become the place European businessmen turned to for inspiration as one American speaker after another spelled out the need to promote growth, liberalize capital markets and reduce structural "rigidities" in industry. While some CEOs such as John Akers of IBM scorned "this revival of economic Darwinism", 1985 marked the start of a turn toward neoliberalism at Davos (*The Economist* 1985).

Claude Smadja (1989), editor-in-chief of *World Link* published an editorial aimed at conveying to the WEF membership the complexity of the debt crisis in terms of its impact on the citizens of debtor states, but by 1989 adherence to the IMF's dictates on structural adjustment had become a condition of debt relief around the world (Selowsky 1989). Neoliberal ideology was being internalized within the leadership of the debtor states themselves. According to Tim McNamar (1989), former Deputy Secretary of the US Treasury,

> the countries themselves are adopting liberal economic reforms. The Prebisch Model is being rejected – even in Argentina. I am, therefore optimistic. Look at the successful reforms taking place in Mexico and Venezuela today…A combination of liberal domestic policies, realistic bank actions, and an attractive interest rate environment should provide the basis for the end of the international debt problem.

By 1989 the debt crisis was firmly on the WEF's agenda but, at Davos debt was viewed primarily as a technical, but not a political or social problem. The belief that adherence to neoliberal policy prescriptions of privatization, deregulation and economic restructuring would eventually provide a lasting way for debtor states to grow out of the debt crisis had taken hold. At the time debt forgiveness was employed as a part of the toolkit for managing the global economy but it was not associated with any normative project. Rather it was seen as a form of default, an emotionally neutral, unfortunate, but necessary side effect of the incorrect assessment of financial risk.

After the Fall: the World Economic Forum, 1990–1997

The Berlin wall came down in the autumn of 1989. This stunning event and all that it implied reinforced the ideological shift toward neoliberalism. At Davos the enthusiastic participation of new converts from the emerging economies of Russia and Eastern Europe added to the sense that free market capitalism had won the day and by 1990, the move from Keynes to Hayek seemed complete. At the WEF a multitude of panels emphasized the benefits of unfettered markets, the "distortion" associated with bureaucratic state "interference" in these markets and the connection between free markets, democracy and individual freedom. A new vision of a united Europe appeared possible as the forces of Soviet oppression had been vanquished, not by military might, but rather by economic forces. The road to progress seemed clear.

While the concerns of Western business continued to dominate, the diversity of the Davos meeting increased steadily from 1990 to 1997. In 1993 the WEF started the Global Leaders for Tomorrow (GLT) program which proved to be useful in recruiting members from up-and-coming sectors of the economy as well as a means of enhancing the geographic diversity of participants (WEF 1993b: 48; WEF 1995a: 122–123). The WEF also sought to increase the gender diversity of its membership through the recruitment of qualified women but, year after year, it noted its failure with regret (WEF 1993b: 48; WEF 1994a: 100; WEF 1995a: 122; WEF 1997a: 114).[1]

Davos continued to boast an ever more impressive guest list, and it was in this period that the WEF first started to articulate its intellectual quest. In his opening address in 1993 Klaus Schwab (1993: 100) stated,

> We have to confront the world as it is – complex and uneasy, with an overloaded agenda, with more questions than answers and certainly

> no simple choices. What we really want to do is re-establish a longer term global vision.

At this time it became increasingly apparent Schwab was seeking to set, not only the Davos agenda, but also influence the global agenda. This ambition is particularly clear in the revised purpose statement of the WEF (1992c: 14; my emphasis):

> The World Economic Forum is an independent foundation whose mission is to integrate the leaders from business, government and the sciences into a creative global partnership for economic and social progress. Since its creation in 1971, the World Economic Forum has become the world's foremost international organization for global, high-level, personalized interaction among *those who really shape the future*.

Throughout this period the Davos meeting continued to be an excellent place for business to take a reading of the world and those attending Davos and especially the WEF leadership, became increasingly aware of the potential of the meeting to, not only assess this environment, but also to shape it. Arguably, the turn toward neoliberalism at Davos in the early 1990s was the result of external events and shifts in economic fashions. However, the turn away from neoliberalism at Davos was largely the result of the intellectual leadership of the WEF. Through the power of communication and invitation Klaus Schwab could, and literally did, set the agenda at Davos.

By 1990 John Williamson had coined the term "Washington Consensus", and for a time it seemed as if the turn to neoliberalism was complete (Williamson 2004). At Davos, the appeal of this approach was tremendous (WEF 1990d; Strong 1990; Kaufman 1990). In 1992 the neoliberal consensus continued to dominate (Hutton 1992). Eastern European participants remained ideologically committed to free market principles and participants from Latin America and the developing world voiced their agreement:

> One by one the leaders of nations that are euphemistically termed to be "in economic transition" mounted the podium at the World Economic Forum...to extol the merits of their country as a place where markets are freer, tax incentives greater and the business climate warmer. The audience, more than 1,000 chief executives from global companies, applauded them and buttonholed their aides to find out more about the conversion to no-holds – barred capitalism.

> IMF managing director Michel Camdessus has said that, while his predecessor on the job spent all his time cajoling governments to reform, he spends his time listening to Third World governments telling him how much they want to change of their own volition (Cook 1992).

By 1993, however, cracks started to appear in the neoliberal consensus:

> Over the last few years there has been near euphoria in Davos over the triumph of markets but this year there is a long-overdue willingness to reassess some basic claims. Markets have led Japan to too much industrial capacity, the US to too little, the world to have too much financial instability, and have proved a poor guide to the transformation of Eastern Europe and the former Soviet Union. Even where they are supposed to work, at firm and industry level, there is growing scepticism (Hutton 1993).

In 1993 Klaus Schwab stepped into the role of visionary when in his opening address he proposed an ambitious role for the WEF in shaping the global agenda (Schwab 1993a: 100). The next year, in his opening address, he developed this theme arguing that "what we need now is to extend entrepreneurship to politics, economics and social interaction. Entrepreneurship does not mean just adapting to change, it means provoking change in a positive direction ... for the benefit of mankind" (Schwab 1994: 112). At Davos the debate intensified. European businessmen were looking for American-style growth but with European social cohesion (Hutton 1994). American panelists were critical of the welfare state, while German trade union representatives defended it (Cherian 1994a). The Russians in attendance were split between pragmatic reformers and younger, more ideologically pure, supporters of free markets (Hoagland 1994; Safire 1994). India's then Prime Minister P. V. Narasimha Rao stated "India will not be swept away by free market winds ... we want change but we want a certain amount of humaneness" (Cherian 1994b).

On January 26, 1995 Klaus Schwab and Malcolm MacLaren published an opinion piece in the *International Herald Tribune*. These pieces, which for several years appeared just before the start of the Davos meeting, were calculated to highlight certain issues and set the tone of meeting. In this piece their growing concern with the impact of economic liberalization is apparent and in his opening address in the same year Schwab reiterated many of these points for the benefit of those who had not read the editorial (Schwab and MacLaren 1995; WEF 1995b: 125–126).

The title of the meeting was "Leadership for challenges beyond growth" and the need for international frameworks for international cooperation was a dominant theme.

At Davos in 1995 the belief that one institution, the market, might have the capacity to meet the needs of global governance was increasingly challenged (Norman 1995a; Thorsell 1995). George Soros made his scepticism clear, "I am very much aware of the shortcomings of the market economy and I am not an unmitigated capitalist." Furthermore he expressed specific concern with liberalized financial markets:

> Since the explosive growth in derivatives means that financial disturbance can now be rapidly transmitted from one area of the world's financial system to another, regulators have good cause for worry. In recent years a dangerous cocktail of aggressive traders, speculative investors and complex financial instruments has emerged. The potential for a global liquidity crisis which could lead to a market crash is certainly not far-fetched. But in dealing with the daunting scale of the regulatory challenge, central bankers should not look for easy scapegoats like hedge funds. While they may be part of the problem, they are also a reflection of a liberalised financial system in which the concept of *laissez-faire* has been taken to dangerous limits. The stakes are too high to count on the self-regulating mechanism of the market (Cohen 1995).

The next year Schwab and Smadja (1996) wrote an opinion piece called "Start taking the backlash against globalization seriously." In this they emphasized that the benefits of markets must be considered in conjunction with their social impact:

> Economic globalization has entered a critical phase. A mounting backlash against its effects, especially in the industrial democracies is threatening a very disruptive impact on economic activity and social stability in many countries ... the globalized economy must not become synonymous with "free market on the rampage," a brakeless train wreaking havoc. The social responsibilities of corporations (and governments) remain as important as ever. What is on the agenda is the need to redefine and recalibrate them.

Although largely pro-market in tone this article opened the door to a more values-based discussion of social issues at Davos (Thorsell 1996).

By 1996, the Washington Consensus was no longer the consensus at Davos (Thorsell 1996; Elliot 1996a). At one event when European businessmen expressed interest in liberalizing their labour markets, several American participants cautioned that American labour markets had already become too flexible and had created "a demoralized underclass" (*The Economist* 1996). Yet at the same time as neoliberal policies were being criticized in one panel, in other parts of the forum, the success of neoliberal policies in New Zealand, the new "South Pacific Tiger" was being lauded (Metcalfe 1996). This diversity of opinion is also apparent in the 1996 "Davos Special Issue" of *World Link* magazine (Greenberg 1996). The 1996 GCR, however, took a decidedly pro-market tone (WEF 1996a).

The following year the WEF leadership continued to bring social issues and the human impact of economic relations to the forefront of the discussion at Davos. Schwab and Smadja published two opinion pieces in the *International Herald Tribune* which placed the social responsibilities of business and government squarely on the agenda (Schwab and Smadja 1997a; Schwab and Smadja 1997b). In the same year George Soros (1997) published a revolutionary article also timed to coincide with the Davos meeting. Writing with all the authority that he had earned through his brilliant career in international finance he stated,

> Although I have made a fortune in the financial markets, I now fear that the untrammelled intensification of Laissez-faire capitalism and the spread of market values into all areas of life is endangering our open and democratic society. The main enemy of the open society, I believe, is no longer the communist but the capitalist threat.

These concerns, which Soros repeated at Davos, presented a profound challenge to the neoliberal view of the proper market/society relationship. The mood at the annual meeting had shifted substantially. In his address at the opening of the WEF Arnold Koller, the Swiss President, stated, "It would be disastrous if the historic triumphal process of freedom ushered in by the fall of the Berlin Wall were to give way to a new kind of servitude, through inhuman application of the so-called market forces" (Crane 1997a). There was a growing sense that business and government had a responsibility to ease the social stress caused by rapid global economic change (Rubin 1997; Elliot 1997). Around the world,

> the inevitable backlash to market-worship is well underway. But to really hear the excesses of capitalism denounced listen to some of the

> world's confirmed capitalists... Evidence of this rethinking is everywhere. The latest meeting of the WEF in Davos, Switzerland – which views itself as the world-class assemblage of the free market elite – was devoted to ways of ameliorating the worst consequences of economic competitiveness (Sanger 1997).

Furthermore, representatives of the developing world were arguing that if market capitalism cannot promote both prosperity and justice, it would not succeed (Annan 1997: 17). At Davos royalty, politicians, CEOs, Nobel laureates and the Secretary General of the UN all encouraged business to consider its responsibilities in broader terms (WEF 1997b: 20–31; Crane 1997b; Polanyi 1997). In 1997 although most essays in the GCR continued to stress the benefits of economic liberalization, one essay stands out as reflecting a more critical view. In this essay Macha Levinson, a Director of the WEF, predicts that "soft issues" like the environment and human rights will have an increasing effect on competitiveness rankings in the future and concludes that "concern with the environment and human rights is now beginning to preoccupy the more public-minded chief executives around the world" (Levinson 1997).

The evolution of the conventional wisdom with respect to AIDS is a particularly striking illustration of the changes in attitude which took place within the WEF during this period. In the early 1990s AIDS was not really on the agenda at Davos. In 1992, however, *World Link* published an article on AIDS which is remarkable because it focuses on the impact the AIDS epidemic is expected to have on the profits of companies operating in AIDS-affected countries (Jebb 1992). The article includes a diagram of the "death of the family farm" in Uganda which traces how disease reduced a prosperous family of nine, working their own farm, to only two surviving children earning their living as farm day laborers. The human toll of this ordeal is ignored. Furthermore, the article recommends responding to the growing costs associated with the AIDS epidemic by rationing fixed healthcare budgets. No consideration is given to expanding healthcare budgets either for prevention or treatment.

This attitude started to change in 1997 when Nelson Mandela (1997: 19–20), a highly respected, long time Davos participant, gave a speech on the global threat of AIDS. At the same meeting Luc Montagnier, the discoverer of the AIDS virus, addressed the forum and spoke of the human toll of the disease as well as the economic impact of AIDS. He linked the fight against AIDS to the anti-apartheid battle. Slowly, AIDS started to be reframed from a purely economic consideration to a moral question and, in the coming years, concern over the AIDS epidemic came to play an important role in mobilizing support for debt cancellation at Davos.

Finally, with respect to debt and finance the neoliberal consensus continued to dominate Davos in the period from 1990 to 1997. Although it became increasingly clear that innovative and largely unregulated international financial markets increased the instability of the international financial system they also presented economic opportunities. A number of participants, from central bankers to successful financiers, warned of potential dangers but these warnings were largely ignored.[2] The ongoing third world debt crisis continued to be seen primarily as a technical problem. In the 1980s the debt crisis had brought the financial system to the brink of disaster, but by 1990 the way out of the crisis, through the rigorous application of market discipline and economic restructuring in debtor countries, seemed promising and the third world debt crisis was almost completely dropped from the agenda. In part this was due to the astonishing events in Eastern Europe and the Soviet Union but this was also due to the belief, shared by many participants from the developed as well as the developing world, that the debt crisis was well on its way to being solved through the "magic of the markets" (Kaufman 1990). Some participants, however, continued to emphasize that high levels of external debt were an ongoing obstacle to economic progress in developing countries (Crane 1990). But many others, from the developed as well as the developing world, believed that a solution had been found and at Davos, Carlos Salinas, the Mexican president, threw a fiesta to celebrate Mexico's debt rescheduling agreement with the commercial banks (Dullforce 1990).

By 1991, however a new debt crisis, this time in Eastern Europe, dominated the agenda. At Davos Jan Krzysztof Bielecki, President of Poland, called on Western creditors to forgive 80% of Poland's $46 billion foreign debt arguing that Poland deserved special treatment because it was a pioneer in moving toward a market economy. His speech was described as "an ode to entrepreneurship" (Greenhouse 1991). Later that year the WEF published an article "Debt Forgiveness: Dangerous Trend or Absolute Necessity?" in which two opposing viewpoints were presented (Aggarwal and Schulman 1991). In this article, Horst Schulman, Managing Director of the International Institute of Finance, argued that debt forgiveness was not a solution and predicted that there was a serious risk that once allowed, debt forgiveness would come to be considered a right. On the other hand, Vinod Aggarwal argued in favor of debt forgiveness as a solution, but all of his arguments were based on the negative impacts of the ongoing debt crisis for those in the developed world. In contrast to later debates, neither side invoked normative arguments or the impact of structural adjustment programs on the most vulnerable citizens of the debtor countries.

By 1992 the financial crisis had spread to Russia, and Davos was "simply overwhelmed" as representatives of Eastern European, Russia and the Soviet successor states sought to convince anyone who would listen that, because they were now ideologically committed to free market principles, they were worthy of aid and investment (Crane 1992; Rodger 1992). In 1993 at Davos the trend continued as representatives of debtor nations appeared unanimous in their support of neoliberal economic policies. The Russian Prime Minister Victor Chernomyrdin asked for a restructuring of foreign debt and pledged Russia's commitment to ongoing reform (*Globe and Mail* 1993). Latin America embraced the neoliberal solution (WEF 1993c). In 1994 Larry Summers, at the time US Treasury Undersecretary for international affairs, called for an international economics with a "human face" and expressed the hope that there would be more progress toward reducing debt over the next two years. This however, did not necessarily mean debt cancellation (Kiely 1994: 50). Rather it reflected the enduring belief that economic restructuring along neoliberal lines would solve the debt crisis through long-term economic growth and thus ensure that the problem did not recur.

By 1995 however, a renewed financial crisis in Mexico cast a long shadow over Davos (Hutton 1995). As concerns for the stability of the economic and financial system grew, Soros' critical assessment of the liberalized financial system and the "so-called self regulating mechanism of the market" added to the deepening gloom (Cohen 1995a; Norman et al. 1995; Brittan 1995a; Drohan 1995). The atmosphere was made even darker by the fact that none of the multitude of experts in attendance at Davos the previous year had seen the latest Mexican crisis coming (*Globe and Mail* 1995). Latin America was facing renewed problems while Russia continued to need loans (Drohan 1995).

Yet in 1996 optimism returned. The Mexican crisis seemed to have turned the corner, and at Davos this was credited to successful structural reform policies and firm neoliberal discipline (Elliot 1996b; Drohan 1996). Participants from the developed as well as the developing world continued to emphasize their enthusiastic adherence to neoliberal policy prescriptions and Stanley Fischer, the Assisting Managing Director of the IMF, argued that the way ahead for Africa and eastern

Europe in a political as well as an economic sense, lay with the adoption of structural reform policies (Crane 1996; Drohan 1996; Harris 1996). Similarly, in 1997 bringing debtor states more fully into the world economy by enforcing market discipline continued to be accepted as the best response. Although this view was increasingly challenged outside of the meeting, inside Davos only a few had started to openly question the conventional wisdom with respect to debt cancellation. In some parts of Davos there was a growing appreciation for the role of international institutions and government coupled with a concern that, in the global context, unfettered market processes might produce a social backlash. But while there was dialogue at Davos there continued to be a tendency to accept that with respect to finance and debt the prescriptions of the Washington Consensus provided the most promising means of moving forward. As will be seen in the next section, the Asian financial crisis dealt a severe blow to this belief.

Asia and after: 1998 and 1999

The Asian financial crisis, which emerged in the spring of 1997, blindsided the Davos community (WEF 1997b: 31). As its effects spread around the world, a number of important opinion leaders such as Sachs, Soros and Stiglitz became increasingly critical of the Washington Consensus and the policy prescriptions of the IMF. The Asian financial crisis brought the international financial system to the top of the Davos agenda.

Over the years the WEF had prided itself on providing timely information to its business members; therefore, in an effort to provide up-to-date insights into the fast moving Asian financial crisis the WEF added six new sessions in the three weeks prior to the 1998 annual meeting (Smadja 1998). In this period the WEF continued its efforts to expand its geographic scope (WEF 1998e; WEF 1999e) and, while participants from the developed world continued to dominate the Davos meeting, in 1998 African participants started to attract more attention as the WEF leadership continued to use its power of invitation to expand the diversity of voices taking part (WEF 1998f).

Business networking continued to be a major draw at Davos but, increasingly a normative intellectual project started to take hold. At the same time there was less emphasis on international diplomacy than in the past. In 1998, for the first time in many years, neither Palestinian Authority Chairman Yasser Arafat nor Israeli Prime Minister Binyamin Netanyahu (*Jerusalem Post* 1997) was invited to attend Davos. That year the meeting's planners decided that Davos would not focus on the politics of the Middle East but would instead focus on the international economy and especially the international financial system. After the 1997 crisis Schwab and Smadja's opinion pieces started to seem prescient, and at Davos in 1998 there was a growing scepticism of the "magic of the market" as speakers outlined the inadequacy of the neoliberal model and the difficulties of governing economic globalization. This started with scepticism of the IMF response to the Asian crisis, but it spilled over into a broader critique of neoliberal policy prescriptions in general (WEF 1991i). Financial instability and international debt became linked with concerns about the unequal benefits of economic globalization.

At the annual meeting there was a growing emphasis on social responsibility, and a number of sessions at Davos addressed the social consequences of business decisions. For years the Davos agenda had featured general interest sessions which focused on issues related to individual wellbeing, whether medical or spiritual. Originally, these were designed to appeal to exhausted CEOs seeking to "recharge their batteries." In 1998 these interest sessions took a turn to a search for deeper meaning and a number of sessions emphasized social responsibility and values (Cooperstone 1998).[3] In contrast to earlier meetings, there was a growing emphasis on the important role of society and government in the economy. In her 1998 keynote address, Hillary Clinton spoke of the economy, government and civil society as three legs of a stool and stressed that each must be strong if the stool is to stand (WEF 1998c: 11). In the same year the Informal Group of World Economic Leaders agreed that "there must be more effective partnerships between governments and the private sector in addressing the growing inequalities that could lead to social instability and human tragedy" (WEF 1998g). This shift can also be seen in the WEF motto. Although the WEF continued to use "Entrepreneurship in the global public interest", in 1999 it adopted the considerably more ambitious motto "Committed to improving the state of the world."

In 1998 Klaus and Hilde Schwab created a new foundation designed to foster and reward entrepreneurs working in the public interest: the Schwab Foundation for Social Entrepreneurs. Although separate from the WEF it was designed to complement the activities of the WEF because it had become "evident that social progress cannot depend only on high level cooperation among global decision makers, but also requires community driven social entrepreneurship on a broad scale" (Schwab Foundation 2007). In this period there was an element of "consciousness raising" about the WEF (WEF 1998b: 27). In their 1998 opinion piece Schwab and Smadja called for "new rules for a new game" and stressed the need for an international debate on how to "govern globalization" (Schwab and Smadja 1998). In their 1999 opinion piece "Globalization needs a Human Face" they argued,

> At a time when the emphasis is on empowering people... globalization has established the supremacy of the market in an unprecedented way... The forces of financial markets seem to be running amok, humbling governments, reducing the power of unions and other groups of civil society, creating a sense of extreme vulnerability ... If we do not invent ways to make globalization more inclusive, we have to face the prospect of a resurgence of the acute social confrontations of the past magnified at the international level (Schwab and Smadja 1999a).

In a 1998 interview with Lewis Lapham, Klaus Schwab said that the "more thoughtful of the world's landlords" were discovering that the global economy was "more complicated than anyone had thought," and that it was important that the corporate elite enhance their understanding of broader issues. Lapham concluded that Schwab believed that the "masters of the corporate universe had to learn to think like statesmen" (Lapham 1998: 40–41). At Davos the agenda was increasingly designed to enhance the participants' understanding of the complexity of the global environment, as well as develop a sense of the responsibilities and obligations of business to the broader global community. The project of turning CEOs into statesmen was high on the agenda at Davos.

Contestation and challenge, 1998 and 1999

After the 1997 Asian financial crisis the Washington Consensus came under greater scrutiny in Davos. Indeed, in the minds of many opinion leaders, events following the financial crisis in Asia effectively discredited the underpinnings of the Washington Consensus and brought into question the competence of the IMF. At the end of the 1999 meeting John Sweeney announced that the "Washington consensus was no longer a consensus, even in Washington" (Laurance 1999). At Davos scepticism of the Washington Consensus had been slowly growing for years but the neoliberal approach still had many adherents who believed that there was little cause for concern. However, as will be seen below, their complacency was substantially undermined in this period.

Early criticisms of economic globalization put forward by the WEF leadership warned of a potential backlash to neoliberal capitalism and expressed concern this backlash could make the system too difficult to manage. After 1998, however, the concerns started to take on a more normative tone (Schwab and Smadja 1998; Sachs 1998; Davies 1999; Schwab and Smadja 1999b). The assertion that there was a causal connection between free markets and democracy had been one of the cornerstones of the popularity of neoliberalism, but, in 1998 Soros turned this argument on its head. He argued contra Hayek, that under certain conditions unfettered free markets can actually generate antidemocratic conditions and likened the pendulum of market forces to the swing of a wrecking ball (Lapham 1998: 45). Soros had reread Polanyi while writing *The Crisis of Global Capitalism*, and insights related to the double movement featured prominently in his arguments (Soros 1998: v). In both 1998 and 1999, ethics, values and social responsibility appeared in discussions at Davos with increasing frequency while civil society and government were increasingly presented as having a positive contribution to make in moderating the impact of economic globalization.

At Davos the leadership of the WEF set about creating the conditions to turn businessmen into statesmen. This was in keeping with the original mandate of the WEF which was to give European business the insights and intellectual tools to adapt to changing conditions of competitiveness, and yet, at this time, the WEF seems to have expanded its mandate to not only help business compete efficiently but also to shape this competition in the most socially responsible way possible. This was linked to the "two track argument" which held that first, minimizing social dislocation is simply good business because it is necessary if capitalist economic relations are to survive and, second that minimizing negative social outcomes associated with economic globalization is the "right" thing to do. At Davos speakers as diverse as Hillary Clinton, Al Gore, Kofi Annan, Princess Anne, Nadine Gordimer and John Sweeney all stressed the human impact of the unequal distribution of the benefits of economic globalization and the potential role of values, society and government in addressing this. Kofi Annan (1998) framed the argument in terms of universal values:

> Freedom, justice and the peaceful resolution of disputes; social progress and better standards of living; equality, tolerance and dignity; these are the universal values set out in the [UN] Charter. They define the true human interest. They are also a pillar of the global economy. That is because markets are also a reflection of values. Markets do not function in a vacuum. Rather they arise from a framework of rules and laws, and they respond to signals set by governments and

> other institutions...Let us choose to unite the power of markets with the authority of universal ideals. Let us choose to reconcile the creative forces of private entrepreneurship with the needs of the disadvantaged and the requirements of future generations. Let us ensure that prosperity reaches the poor. Let us choose an enlightened way forward towards our ultimate, shared goal: a global marketplace that is open to all and benefits all.

In this period, George Soros, Jeffrey Sachs and Joseph Stiglitz, highly respected long time participants at Davos, expressed views highly critical of the policy prescriptions of the Washington Consensus. This was an important turning point. As noted earlier, Soros had expressed his concerns at the 1997 meeting, and after the Asian financial crisis his concerns grew. In 1998, speaking on a panel in Davos, he labeled the Washington Consensus "market fundamentalism" (Lapham 1998: 45). The term "market fundamentalism" proved to be a profoundly effective criticism of the Washington Consensus because it undermined neoliberal pretensions to having the monopoly on a coolly rational approach to economic policy. Previously, criticisms of the negative human impacts or social effects of neoliberal policy prescriptions had been easily dismissed as overly idealistic or for not taking the policy constraints of the "real" world into account. But, in this one phrase "market fundamentalism", Soros was able to emphasize the normative and dogmatic aspects of neoliberal ideology. This phrase when taken up by others inside and especially outside of Davos provided an important step in reframing the issues and creating the space to bring more openly normative approaches to the economy back into the discussion.

At the same time there was a growing emphasis on philanthropy among business participants at Davos. Ted Turner, Vice Chairman of Time Warner, who announced in 1997 that he would give over $1 billion to establish a United Nations foundation, had been openly critical of wealthy executives, including Bill Gates, who had not given generously to philanthropic causes. In 1999 Turner and Gates met at Davos and, shortly after this, Gates announced that he would donate over $3 billion to philanthropic causes (Saporta 1999). This marked the beginning of Gates' work as a philanthropist and activist. Up to this point Gates had been a Global Leader for Tomorrow and an important participant at Davos but his contribution had been primarily in terms of his business and technology expertise (Sennett 1998). After the 1999 meeting Gates became more politicized and involved in the major philanthropic initiatives at the global level for which he is famous today.[4]

At Davos personal interaction and "consciousness raising" played an important role in facilitating the social pressure and networking opportunities that generate change.

Much of Davos was designed to appeal to the better instincts of the corporate participants in attendance. Arguably those who came to Davos were already self selected for their desire to face intellectual challenges and many of them were also characterized by their "good intentions" (Lapham 1998: 36; Elliot 1998a). Although the "core" of Davos was what it saw as "hard economics", in 1998 observers noted "some businessmen can surprise you by their liberalism and social concern. They are developing a new value system around their capitalist beliefs" (Hutton 1998). In 1999, after Kofi Annan called on "the world's leading businessmen to initiate a global compact of shared values and principles which will give a human face to the global market", it was the corporate participants at the WEF who approached Annan to express their interest in developing an organization to promote corporate social responsibility (WEF 1999f; Fréchette 2008).[5] Furthermore the greater geographic diversity of the invited participants contributed to a more nuanced understanding of the issues facing the developing world (Kohli 1999; *South China Morning Post* 1999a). A sense that the Washington Consensus might not in fact provide an adequate basis for achieving development started to grow among the corporate participants at Davos (*Newsweek*, 1999a).

In this period the "two track" argument became increasingly common. According to this argument "globalization with a human face" or "responsible globality" was not only the right thing to do from a moral perspective, but it was also the correct approach from a business perspective. Schwab and Smadja (1999b) expressed strong criticism of what they believed to be the widespread but unwarranted faith in the capacity of the "invisible hand" of the free market to manage economic globalization. By 1999, according to one observer, it was clear that events had started to undermine the neoliberal consensus at Davos:

> There is something even bigger here, a feeling of fin de siècle...The people who go to Davos are at the top of the pile. Some display the arrogance that you might expect from people who take themselves very seriously. But many others seem uncomfortable about the future. Maybe it was the nagging concern that the world economy as a whole cannot prosper if large parts of it remain in recession. Maybe it is the perception that going global does not itself deliver an acceptable degree of social equality. Maybe it is simply that the past two years have brought shocks that would have seemed almost

> inconceivable: the experts have been wrong. None of this means that there is necessarily a great catastrophe looming but the more thoughtful people seem uneasy (McRae 1999).

In 1998 and 1999 AIDS was not high on the Davos agenda. But, although there was little discussion there were two important developments at Davos that were to have far reaching effects in reframing the debate and furthering the campaign for the cancellation of third world debt. First, Bill Gates became involved in supporting global health initiatives which targeted the developing world and second, in his keynote address Al Gore, then the Vice President of the United States, explicitly linked the pain and suffering associated with the AIDS epidemic to a need for debt relief in the developing world. In the following years this linkage was to become the basis of a compelling argument in favour of debt cancellation (WEF 1999c: 17).

In this period debt and finance dominated the agenda. As the Asian financial crisis developed into the Russian financial meltdown, the global financial system preoccupied Davos. In 1998 the Asian crisis was a point of reference for almost every economics and business discussion (WEF 1998c: 10). Previously, supporters of the neoliberal approach had held up the Asian economic "miracle" as a model for the rest of the world to follow, and when it collapsed like a pack of cards, this shook the Davos worldview (Elliot 1998b; Hutton 1998). As noted earlier, Jeffrey Sachs, Joseph Stiglitz and George Soros, three important opinion leaders at the WEF, were vocal in their criticism. They described liberalized financial markets as inherently unstable and criticized the IMF for its high-handed approach as well as the incompetence of its policies (Soros 1998; Sachs 1998, Elliot 1998a, Uchitelle 1998b; *South Morning Post* 1999a). But this view was far from unanimous. While some argued that the crisis was the result of financial liberalization, others argued that it was the result of political interference in markets (Elliot 1998b) or due to delays in implementing financial liberalization within the affected Asian countries (*The Economist* 1998; Mehta 1998).

Lewis Lapham's (1998: 43–46) description of a plenary session in the Congress Hall is worth quoting at length. In 1998, when John Sweeney, the president of the AFL-CIO, attempted to connect financial liberalization with negative economic and social justice outcomes, his comments,

> evoked murmurs of disagreement and an impatient rustling of programs and briefing books. A Dutch banker rose to suggest that

> perhaps Mr Sweeney hadn't been paying close attention in the conference rooms, perhaps had missed the news about the restorative tonic of privatisation sure to cure the illness of the Asian and European economies by making them more fiercely competitive.
>
> ... [Sweeney's] remarks would have been dismissed without further notice if he hadn't been followed to the podium by George Soros, the financier as famous for his political philanthropy as he was venerated for his vast fortune...
>
> Only imbeciles believed in the conscience of markets, Soros said, imbeciles and tenured professors of economics. Markets were as dumb as posts and as blind as bats, inherently unstable because dependent upon what people wish for, not what they have in hand... Imagine a pendulum," Soros said, "a pendulum that has become a wrecking ball, swinging out of control and with increasing speed, knocking over one economy after another"...
>
> The murmuring in the Congress Hall turned suddenly apprehensive... What had happened to the blessings of privatization? To the infinite wisdom of the good old invisible hand? "Market fundamentalism doesn't work,' Soros said. "Without the intervention in Asia of the IMF and the World Bank, the whole system would have fallen apart." The questions persisted until the time expired... and when the plenary session ended in what was still a clamour of anxious voices, [Soros] abandoned the company to its investigations and bid them a fond farewell.

Soros' remarks planted doubts but others continued to defend financial liberalization. The following year Howard Davies, Chairman of the UK Financial Services Authority and rapporteur of the annual meeting, wrote that at Davos "few voices were raised against market opening, trade liberalisation, and free flows of capital. Those who argued the case for capital controls typically saw them as a temporary expedient: more a case of "*reculer pour mieux sauter*' rather than a plea to "stop the world I want to get off." Davies continued, "It would be wrong, however to mistake this broad intellectual consensus for complacency or to interpret it as an endorsement of the status quo. There was a palpable sense of unease about the international community's ability to respond effectively to financial crises, though – it would be fair to acknowledge – far less certainty about the changes that need to be made" (Davies 1999: 14).

In 1999 a number of panels featured participants who were critical of liberalized financial markets alongside those who supported them.[6]

Stanley Fischer of the IMF expressed his indignation when other panelists characterized the IMF as lacking a social conscience (Cowell 1999). Although many of the panels on finance were predominantly concerned with the technical aspects of maintaining the stability of the financial system, in the more policy oriented panels there was discussion of the need for a new financial architecture (Crane 1999b). Canadian Finance Minister Paul Martin and UK Chancellor of the Exchequer Gordon Brown championed the need for an early warning system to head off future financial crises (Crane 1999a). Furthermore, by 1999 a number of participants had become concerned that an increasingly deregulated international financial system had a disproportionately negative impact on the developing world. In his address at the opening session of the WEF US Vice President Al Gore called for "decisive progress to debt relief and reform of the international financial system" (WEF 1999d; WEF 1999c: 17). Others argued that the Asian crisis proved that the neoliberal model of development had failed (WEF 1999c: 20; Vallelly 1999; Sachs 1998). Finally, in a break with previous meetings, representatives from developing countries no longer expressed support for deregulation and privatization but instead expressed their own concerns with the impact of the deregulated international financial system (Kohli 1999; *South China Post* 1999a).

By 1999 many at Davos had become concerned with the way the developing world had been "decimated" by the flight of capital (Hutton 1999). Although some influential participants continued to argue that the fault lay not in the economic system but rather with the governments of the developing world (Friedman 1999), a sense that the free market "playing field" was not in fact quite as level as previously believed started to take hold at Davos. The week after Al Gore put the issue of debt relief on the agenda at Davos, the G7 finance ministers meeting in Bonn considered three new proposals for more generous help to developing countries. In June of that year the Cologne Debt Initiative, also known as HIPC 2, was launched at the G8. As discussed in the previous chapter this process was spurred on by organizations such as Jubilee 2000 and Oxfam (Elliot 1999). For years CSOs and NGOs had lobbied government leaders in the G7 countries and in 1999 the support of Gerhardt Schroeder, Chancellor of Germany and the head of the G8 host government, in combination with the support of like-minded representatives from the US, UK and Canada, many of whom were in attendance in Davos in 1999, was crucial to the success of this initiative.

In 1998 and 1999 civil society organizations located outside the WEF started to target Davos and the pattern of popular protest which characterized the following years began to take shape. This was a very important development because it marked an innovation in boomerang politics as campaigning NGOs and CSOs targeted a forum attended by business elites, heads of state, finance ministers and those in leadership roles at the IFIs. In 1998, Peoples' Global Action (PGA) denounced "informal" business groups including the WEF (PGA 1998). In 1999 two counter conferences took place: The Other Davos in Zurich and The Alternative Davos in Davos (The Other Davos 2007; Brittain 1999b). During the WEF annual meeting a protest demonstration took place in the streets of Davos. These events, organized by networks of NGOs and CSOs, were designed to garner attention from both WEF participants and the press (McRae 1999). They were intended to challenge the neoliberal economic order, reframe the debate on the rules governing global economic relations, and generate support for reform of the rules and practices governing international finance in the pursuit of economic justice (Brittain, 1999a).

By 1999 events had started to undermine neoliberal certainties at Davos, and there was a growing sense that unfettered market processes might need to be constrained by governments and international institutions after all. In this period financial markets in particular had demonstrated their weaknesses and the negative social backlash predicted by Schwab and Smadja in 1996 became a reality. At Davos the social occupied an increasingly important place on the agenda. By 1999 most of the major forces and actors that were to play an important part in debt cancellation over the next five years were already in place but just how this would play out remained unclear. What was clear however was that Davos had become an important site in the contest to shape the global agenda and, in this way, define the limits of the possible.

After Seattle: Davos, 2000–2005

The demonstrations which took place in Seattle in the fall of 1999 had a profound effect on the WEF. At the subsequent annual meeting the WEF leadership chose "New Beginnings: Making a difference" as the theme, and they invited representatives from an unprecedented number of CSOs and NGOs, many of whom had participated on the streets of Seattle, to attend Davos. After 2000 critics of neoliberal globalization were located increasingly inside, as well as on the streets outside the meeting. At Davos there was a growing sense of the responsibilities of the business community in a rapidly changing world. Although formal and informal networking remained important, the Davos agenda reflected the increasingly diverse membership of the WEF, and there was an increased emphasis on the developing world (Schmemann 2002; WEF 2000d; WEF 2000k). The WEF continued to invite global leaders. In 2000 Tony Blair attended for the first time and Bill Clinton gave an important address. The WEF broadened its invitations to labour leaders (Freeman 2000a; Warner 2000a; Keegan 2000) and representatives from 49 NGOs including Greenpeace International, Friends of the Earth (FOE), Amnesty International, Human Rights Watch, Oxfam International, the New Economics Foundation and Focus on the Global South attended Davos in 2000 (WEF 2000i). This brought issues of social responsibility, especially those related to the environment and finance, to greater prominence (Juniper 2000; WEF 2000k; Atkinson 2000).

In 2000 the leadership of the WEF continued its efforts to place the human impacts of economic globalization high on the Davos agenda. In his opening address Schwab stated that "The most important challenge for the 21st century is to bridge the paradox between the harsh business reality and human and social values" (Schwab 2000a). Schwab and Smadja published an opinion piece which argued the need for multilateral structures to help "steer" globalization (Schwab and Smadja 2000a). In another article Schwab expressed his belief that the UN was "in a unique position to serve as a catalyst for the processes that will make for a more equitable form of globalization" and to help "avoid globalization running amok" and presciently suggested that the UN Millennium Summit, to be held the following September, might provide an opportunity for world leaders to strengthen the mandate of the UN to help achieve this end (Schwab 2000c: 15).

The WEF leadership continued to extend invitations to participants from developing countries (Jonquieres 2000; Kahn 2000a). It scheduled sessions on corporate responsibility, debt, African economic recovery, human rights, the digital divide, corporate philanthropy and global health. In 2000, the panels featured an unprecedented mix of participants and were designed to expand discussion beyond the previous limits (Murdoch 2000). Furthermore, at this time the leadership at the WEF started to provide strategic support to international actors they judged helpful in moving their agenda forward and developed initiatives whereby their business members could become involved in "making a difference" under the auspices of the WEF. The Annual Meeting Report concluded,

> The process of integrating wealthy and poor countries, political, civil society and business voices, is of course at the heart of Davos. The Annual Meeting 2000 marked an important step in examining

> many of the issues surrounding globalization – part of the "New Beginnings" referred to in the theme. The next step, "Making a difference", will require attention and action for far more that the six days in Davos (Knobel 2000:12).

In 2001 the WEF leadership continued in its efforts to locate the WEF on the moral high ground. In their opinion piece in the International Herald Tribune they wrote,

> Over the course of six days, participants will be asked to help find new ways to combat the spread of AIDS in sub-Saharan Africa, new approaches to bridging the divisions between haves and have-nots, and new ways to safeguard the environment in the developed and the developing world. They will also assess the strengths and weaknesses of the international economy and discuss ways to bring peace to nations in conflict…The work we do at the World Economic Forum may not have the romantic allure of a street demonstration, but it does, in concrete ways, make the world a better place in which to live. So, yes, there will be a moral high ground in Davos this week, but it won't be in the streets (Schwab and Smadja 2001).

The desire to "advance human well being" and "deepen thinking about the challenge confronting global society" is prominent in WEF publications of the time (Schwab 2001b; WEF 2000j; WEF 2001c). In 2001 the WEF launched the Global Health Initiative and the Digital Divide Initiative and encouraged its members to participate in the UN Global Compact (WEF 2001b: 4–5). The inside/outside dynamic is captured in this quote:

> The earnest breast-beating in Davos about the failings of globalisation took on the air of a collective confessional…Stung into action not just by the threat of anti-capitalist demonstrations but by many of its own members from poorer countries, the World Economic Forum turned into an unprecedented public expression of guilty conscience from the planet's most exclusive gathering of political and business leaders (Carnegy 2001).

In 2002, in the wake of the September 11 terrorist attacks, the WEF annual meeting was moved to New York. Many member companies had been directly affected by the attacks and, not surprisingly, these events brought the question of security to prominence on the WEF agenda but, rather than security concerns eclipsing the questions of social responsibility or human rights, as might easily have happened, security concerns were seen as *bolstering* the importance of these questions by the WEF leadership. The WEF continued to reinvent itself moving from what it saw as "its traditional role as a convener of events to a wider new role as a catalyst for progress on important items on the global agenda" (Schwab 2001b). It remained committed to the belief that the communication and collaboration made possible through the WEF could contribute to addressing these challenges:

> Global society faces an increasing number of common challenges, whether in the form of poverty, infectious disease, environmental degradation, intolerance or instability. During the economic exuberance of the 1990s, few paid sufficient attention to problems emerging in the wake of rapid global economic integration. And the events of 11 September sharply illustrated that globalization generates not only new economic and social opportunities but also new forms of vulnerability. Emerging freedoms have to be matched with social, cultural and environmental responsibility on a global scale. Participation in the economic benefits of globalization must be broadened across and within regions (Schwab 2002a).

In 2003, when the WEF returned to Davos, the meeting took place against a background of renewed concern over the impending invasion of Iraq. This, however, did little to distract the WEF from its increasingly activist stance. The *Global Agenda* magazine replaced *World Link* but the practice of using this publication to set the tone of the Davos meeting continued. In 200 glossy pages it laid out an agenda for change including articles on "What antiglobalization protesters want", "Why capital needs character" and corporate social responsibility. Information on how interested companies might become involved was included beside many articles (WEF 2003c). In the same year the WEF launched the Global Governance Initiative, designed to monitor progress toward achieving the MDGs, held the first Open Forum an alternative conference co-sponsored by the WEF and a group of Swiss NGOs (WEF 2003b: 17) and formally invited Social Entrepreneurs to attend Davos (Getz 2003).

In 2004, the theme of corporate social responsibility continued to be very important at Davos:

> We at the World Economic Forum see it as our duty to make the leaders of globally active companies in particular aware of the consequences of their actions. Their decisions have implications for millions of people (Schwab 2004b).

Global Agenda contained articles on poverty, inequality, "Living up to our responsibilities", "The human face of globalization", ethical banking, global health initiatives, Africa and fair trade (WEF 2004c). Elkington wrote that at Davos people "were adjusting their mindsets" and "many once forceful pro-globalisers are now off-balance. Some even take part in sessions on corporate social responsibility and sustainable development. The agenda is a lot more nuanced than it was just a few years ago" (Elkington 2004). In 2004 the WEF restructured its organization to facilitate its activism:

> Our new structure reflects and underlines the Forum's unique dual offerings: providing value to both business and wider society. This is particularly reflected in the twin pillars of the new organization: the Centre for Strategic Insight and the Global Institute for Partnership and Governance. The Centre devises dynamic, incisive and relevant content for our summits, including scenario building, based on an expert understanding of global business and emerging risks. The Global Institute promotes public-private partnerships to help address major international challenges, from greenhouse gas emissions to IT literacy. In doing so the Institute puts the non-business community at the very heart of the Forum (WEF 2004b: 2).

The leadership of the WEF wished to ensure that the conclusions drawn from the meetings would not "melt into nothingness" when the meeting was over and were increasingly interested in networking outside of the confines of the business community to achieve this (Pfanner 2004; Schwab 2004a). At the same time Schwab (2004b: 2) was careful to emphasize that no decisions were made at Davos:

> Let me make one thing clear from the outset: no decisions are taken at Davos. We simply bring decision-makers from relevant areas together, facilitate dialogue, offer analyses and help point the way to developing solutions. Decision-making is the task of governments and international organizations.

In 2005 the WEF took its efforts to a new level. Schwab (2005: 3; my emphasis) wrote,

> Our summits have always sought to anticipate the needs of member organizations and to reflect key issues and, in doing so, to drive the global agenda. In 2004/2005, we took this commitment even

further. **In a new move, the agendas of the Annual Meeting and the Africa Economic Summit were structured to give targeted support to the UK** as it chaired the G-8 group of industrialized nations and took over the presidency of the EU in the second half of 2005. **The programme outline was drawn up in close collaboration with senior UK ministers**, with Prime Minister Tony Blair and Chancellor Gordon Brown participating in the Annual Meeting.

The theme chosen for 2005 was "Taking Responsibility for tough choices", and Davos provided an opportunity to make the case for debt cancellation at the highest level. *Global Agenda* set the tone and featured articles on the Global Compact, MDGs, poverty, debt relief, Africa and global warming (WEF 2005c). On the first day of Davos a "Global Town Hall" was held during which 700 participants discussed, and eventually voted on, the six "top challenges" facing the world. Poverty and equitable globalization topped the list (WEF 2005d). Jacques Chirac (2005), the President of France, addressed the assembly and argued for the implementation of a number of innovative "levies" including a levy on international financial transactions to be used to help fund the fight against AIDS and global poverty. Lord Browne of Maddingley, the chief executive of BP, mused openly about the limitations of markets in delivering public sector services (Caulkin 2005). Tony Blair, the Prime Minister of the UK, publicly cited his conscience as an important motivator behind his involvement in the Report on Africa (Dugger 2005). At Davos it was now possible, not only to argue that poverty was "ethically unacceptable", but also that it was properly the concern of business to work with civil society and government to "eradicate poverty". This is not to say that the new agenda was without its critics (*The Business* 2005; Nordlinger 2005, Elliot 2005b). In 2005 the Davos meeting had a split personality. Networking continued to be important but many also came because the event was uniquely informative and intellectually challenging (O'Brien 2005).

In the period from 2000 to 2005, the development of the WEF's normative project is apparent in its Annual Report. Before 2002 the Report contained no mission statement but the 2002 report contains both a "mission and strategic vision statement" and a "statement of values and principles." In this the WEF states its ambition to be a "credible, independent broker, characterized by intellectual integrity, commitment and strong principles" (WEF 2002b: 31). This shift coincided with Schwab's statement that the WEF was seeking to change its role from a convener of events to a catalyst for change. Over the course of the next three years a "Mission and Values" statement was included in the Annual Report, and each year the social development component of the mission became more explicit (WEF 2003b:36; WEF 2005b: 36).

From 2000 to 2005 the leadership of the WEF expanded the Davos agenda and despite the renewed focus on security which took hold in much of the rest of the world, at Davos the normative and social responsibility aspects of economic globalization became more important each year. Davos shifted from a forum designed to help business understand the global business environment to an organization playing a part in shaping the global agenda. By influencing the world view of its members, by "consciousness raising", Davos had an impact. By 2005 the WEF had become, for better or worse, what one commentator called a "facipulator" and the annual Meeting at Davos was a key site in this campaign:

> WEF is the quintessential '**facipulator**', straddling the role of facilitator and manipulator.... again, this is not bad in itself, it is what anyone with a change agenda is every time they get up in the morning... but this is the complication in the model.... The agenda embraces corporate citizenship but forgets about the topic of corporate taxes, it talks about the need to increase official development assistance (ODA) but makes the mind numbing numbers and effects of the arms industry invisible.... These are deeply rooted gaps and fractures that do WEF no credit, but explain why they are still in business today, such gaps are not the inventions of evil men, but of a pragmatic and deeply political organisation working out the viable limits of what can and cannot be on the table if they want the world's most powerful people to turn up for the meal. (Zadek 2005a; emphasis in original)

Contestation and Challenge 2000–2005

In this five-year period the intellectual hegemony of the Washington Consensus was increasingly challenged at Davos. Through its power of invitation and the ability to set the Davos agenda, the WEF leadership was able to guarantee a hearing for points of view that profoundly challenged the fundamental assumptions underpinning the Washington Consensus. At Davos the challenge was based on two main factors. First, many participants were increasingly critical of the limitations of the market model as a means of understanding the complex processes associated with globalization. Second, many argued that, far from moving the world along a path to increased prosperity and welfare, the prescriptions of the Washington Consensus had resulted in outcomes which were intolerable to any socially responsible entity whether individual or corporate.

In 2000, critics of the Washington Consensus cited the dangers of over reliance on market logic, while supporters insisted that the free market mechanism presented the best way to ensure social justice.[7] In 2001 some argued that the problem was not too much "globalization" but rather too little (Bhagwati 2001; *The Economist* 2001). However, when Benjamin Mkapa, the President of Tanzania, expressed his scepticism by suggesting that globalization was as likely to "deliver" as Tanzania was to win the World Cup, his remarks were met by cheers from the audience (Elliot 2001a). By 2001 it was difficult to deny that, 10 years after the collapse of communism, old problems were unsolved and new problems had emerged. As Claude Smadja put it "globalisation has thus far failed to deliver the goods" (Kaur 2001). But the question remained why had it failed? Was this a flaw of the policy prescriptions of the Washington Consensus or the fault of their incomplete application?

At the 2002 meeting many continued to insist that increased economic liberalization would provide the answers. IMF Director Horst Koehler presented trade liberalization as a means of reducing poverty (Reuters 2002) and, although Dani Rodrik disputed it, the economic success of China, India, Taiwan and Vietnam was cited as evidence of the benefits of financial liberalization (Uchitelle 2000). On the other hand, enthusiasm for deregulation was somewhat undermined by the Enron scandal which had shocked many of the European executives in attendance at the WEF and highlighted the possible pitfalls of too little regulation (Jonquieres and Yeager 2002; Cernetig 2002; Carnegy 2002; Plate 2002).

By 2003 however, it was clear the Washington Consensus was losing support at Davos. Observers noted, "an emerging humility among some of the world's leading economists.... experts seemed less sure than in past years that the existing inventory of economic policies and ideas are sufficient to deal with the challenges at hand" (Naim 2003). At Davos participants from NGOs fuelled these doubts (Stocking 2003: 31). Arthur DeFehr, president of Palliser Furniture Ltd., who had attended the forum for years, commented, "If you go back three years there was a triumphalism that the market economy will solve the problems of the world. The self assurance of three years ago is gone" (Freeman 2003a; see also Jonquieres 2004). While there was a growing consensus on the potential benefits of liberalizing agricultural trade as a means of helping the developing world (Vanguard 2004a; Elliot 2004a; Staunton 2004) there was less consensus on financial liberalization.

By 2005 there was widespread questioning of the benefits of financial liberalization (Miller with Overdorf 2005) and a growing concern that unfettered financial markets may in fact produce destructive outcomes. The 2005 GCR included an article by John Williamson (2006), the originator of the term Washington Consensus, defending capital controls and the role of government in regulating financial markets:

> liberalization involves a tradeoff between an increased danger of crisis, versus an increased growth potential if crisis is averted. The obvious policy implication is that much greater emphasis should be placed on improving supervision and other measures to reduce the probability of a crisis. I do feel somewhat guilty that in early statements of the Washington Consensus I did not emphasize this need…. My reason for scepticism about capital account liberalization is that it increases the danger of crisis, in return for minimal – perhaps zero – benefits in terms of faster growth.

At Davos there was a renewed appreciation of the value of government in moderating financial market outcomes.

The WEF's changing attitude to the role of government can also be seen in a change it made to its macroeconomic environment index in the 2003–2004 GCR. This index had been accepted as an important measure of national competitiveness but up to 2004, in the calculation of this index, *any* government spending was seen as a negative factor, which would by definition damage the national competitive environment. When the WEF replaced this component with a measure designed to capture government *waste*, this "was done expressly to acknowledge that government expenditure can be productive and make positive contributions to competitiveness" (Pigman 2007: 105). It is remarkable that for years the WEF produced a document in which the overall Growth Competitiveness Index was based on the assumption that *all* government spending was *by definition wasteful*. This is both an illustration of the dominance of the Washington Consensus as well as evidence that, by 2004, these assumptions were being re-examined.

At Davos, however, the most effective challenge to the Washington Consensus was located on the terrain of social responsibility. In the previous decade the Washington Consensus had claimed to provide a set of rules that would improve both economic efficiency and global welfare. By 2000, however, there was a sense that the Washington Consensus had not "delivered the goods" and that the most important category of goods which it had failed to deliver was that of the social.

As Schwab and Smadja had argued as early as 1996, this was of concern to business participants at Davos because it threatened the future stability, and therefore profitability, of the economic system. In addition, many at Davos emphasized a second reason why social responsibility was properly of concern to the business community. They argued that the social effects of growing economic inequality globally were not, or should not be, tolerable in a personal, "human" sense to anyone, and certainly not to the kind of privileged individual who attended Davos. This version of the familiar "two track" argument played on economic interest as well as a kind of "noblesse oblige." In 2000 meeting the presence of CSO and NGO representatives on many panels had the effect of subtly shifting the debate as CEOs were urged to take a stronger stand on human rights and accept more broadly defined responsibilities, not just to shareholders, but to society as well (Kahn 2000; Uchitelle 2000). This normative agenda was internalized by many of the participants (WEF, 2000l). Both political and economic leaders reinforced the message of the rights, but also the responsibilities of business. President Clinton (2000), the first US president to attend Davos, drove home the costs of debt and poverty in human terms and framed debt cancellation as an important and legitimate tool in the creation of a more equitable form of globalization.

In 2001 the WEF continued to invite NGOs but not all accepted. Walden Bello of Focus on the Global South deemed Davos "not worth a second visit" and chose instead to attend the first World Social Forum (WSF) in Porto Alegre, Brazil (Bello 2001). The WSF styled itself as the "anti-Davos" (Jonquieres and Lloyd 2001). On Sunday, January 28, 2001 eleven representatives from the WSF debated four from Davos by means of a video link. Reportedly the WSF speakers demonstrated a "strong sense of their own moral worth" while the Davos speakers George Soros, Michael Moore (head of the WTO), John Ruggie and Pascal Lamy (European Commissioner for Trade) "bent over backwards" to appear open to dialogue but, eventually, the debate deteriorated into a "shouting match" (Lloyd 2001a, 2001b; MacKinnon 2001). The willingness of the WEF to engage in a televised debate with the WSF is indicative of its desire to be seen as part of the solution, not the problem.

Inside Davos many appeared to be in sympathy with the broader aims of the alterglobalization movement (Carnegy 2001; Carnegy and Barber, 2001; Cohen 2001; Geller 2001; Cookson 2001). As George Soros remarked, "It's not the digital divide, it's the capitalist divide [and I care] just as a human being. It's not for business, not everything is for business" (Soros 2001). At Davos social consciousness was "in." By 2001 the Global Compact was endorsed by BP, Daimler Chrysler, Unilever, Deutsche Bank, Novartis, Nike and Ericsson (Pike 2001). At Davos Kofi Annan was actively recruiting more corporate members to meet his goal of 1,000 by 2002. Representatives of NGOs such as Greenpeace, Amnesty, Civicus, Public Citizen and the New Economics Foundation were veterans of Davos. Issues alterglobalization protestors had first brought to the streets were now being debated inside the forum (Rubin 2001; Ash 2001; Crane 2001).

The trend continued in 2002. Even the tragic events of September 11, 2001 did little to change the growing emphasis on social responsibility and values at the WEF. Indeed the shock of the event may have contributed to an increased willingness among participants to re-examine some of their fundamental assumptions (Nunn 2002; Manuel 2002). There were repeated appeals to the better instincts of the participants. In his special message to the assembly Kofi Annan (2002) urged business to accept its social responsibility:

> Do not underestimate the attraction of the rival gathering, timed to coincide with yours, that has just finished in Porto Alegre, Brazil. Its title, "World Social Forum" is intended as a criticism of yours, implying that you are interested only in economics, or in profit, and that you do not care about the social effects of your economic activities. And that criticism resonates around the world. I believe that perception is wrong and that globalisation, so far from being the cause of poverty and other social ills, offers the best hope of overcoming them. But it is up to you to prove it wrong, with actions that translate into concrete results for the downtrodden, exploited and excluded.

At the opening plenary titled "For Hope", several members of the panel agreed that those protesting outside were right to be concerned about the world's injustices and the lack of action to address them (WEF 2002e).[8] Shortly after Bill Gates stated, "It's a healthy thing there are demonstrators in the streets. We need a discussion about whether the rich world is giving back what it should in the developing world. I think there is a legitimate question whether we are" (WEF 2002a: 31). At the session "Attacking Hunger and Poverty: The Other Global Campaign" Bono and Sachs called for a Marshall Plan for Africa (WEF 2002g). Debates at the WEF were gradually incorporating the views of campaigning NGOs and the alterglobalization groups (Strom with Uchitelle 2002a; Barrett 2002a). In 2002, even the closed summit of government leaders was dominated by two themes: growth and equity (Crane 2002b). While some saw this as evidence of a fundamental shift, others were less optimistic (Warner 2002; Juniper 2002; Jim 2002; Public Citizen 2002).

In 2003 the WEF continued to emphasize the responsibilities of business. Connecting social responsibility with enhanced competitiveness, the original goal of the WEF, Schwab (2003) wrote,

> To be truly competitive, today's corporations need to understand not only the fundamental economic, industrial and technological trajectories of change, but also the geopolitical, social and cultural forces shaping our future. To regain and maintain public trust, corporations must establish effective corporate governance and, furthermore, to live up to the demands of business's new global role, they must engage proactively in corporate citizenship.

Increasingly, the idea of responsibility to others challenged those who insisted that in the long term market discipline provided the best means of maximizing global welfare. Lula, the President of Brazil, came directly from the WSF to the WEF "to plead for the poor" (Smith 2003; Downic 2003; Colitt and Crooks 2003). Jacques Chirac (2003), the President of France, vowed to "bring fairness to globalization." President Mkapa of Tanzania called for the world to ensure "globalization with a human face" (BBC Worldwide Monitoring 2003). Implicit in all these statements was the belief that markets were not adequately addressing these goals. In 2004 Schwab continued to call for business, government and civil society to work together in the common interest (Schwab 2004c). Social Entrepreneurs became influential participants (Puttnam 2004; Clinton 2004) and at Davos participants from James Wolfensohn, President of the IMF, to Carley Fiorina, CEO of Hewlet Packard, talked about social justice and "doing good" (Nordlinger, 2004).

In 2005 the WEF's activism reached a new high. As noted earlier, the WEF deliberately shaped the meeting's agenda to support the UK goals with respect to debt cancellation and eliminating poverty, especially in Africa. A series of articles published in *Global Agenda* analyzed global challenges such as poverty, health, debt and climate change (Brown 2005; Held 2005; de Rato 2005). *Global Agenda* provided information on WEF initiatives and invited its readers to become actively involved in these programs (WEF 2005c). The 2005 Annual Meeting report was named "Strategic Insights the Agenda Review for Global Leaders." In this document the WEF listed a series of global challenges and then outlined "strategic insights", – step by step prescriptions for action to address them (WEF 2005a).

At Davos social responsibility was wrapped in a potent package of celebrity and authority in the persons of Bono, Jolie, Stone, Gates, Clinton, Blair, Brown and Soros to name but a few. Not many at Davos could resist the persistent arguments from so many quarters. By 2005, few participants were willing to be seen as uncaring or "uncool":

> this was the new caring sharing Davos in action – one where it is no longer cool simply to make money.... Ten years ago, in the days when trade union leaders were not allowed through the door, the agenda of Davos was how to thrive in the market place. The remedy to almost every problem was to embrace market forces. At a global town hall session this year the six priorities chosen by Davos participants were poverty, equitable globalisation, climate change, education, the Middle East, and global governance. Little wonder so many of those who used to be on the outside looking in were scratching their heads and trying to work out what it all meant. Some expressed the view that behind the warm glow of business rubbing shoulders with [celebrities] the more traditional Davos meetings were taking place in the private corporate sessions, where there was still strong resistance to trade unions and an emphasis on the need to take costs out of business. Overall, though, they were prepared to give the WEF the benefit of the doubt (Elliot 2005a).

In this period, at Davos and elsewhere, the AIDS epidemic came to epitomize much that was wrong with economic globalization (See Chapter 3). Just as the prospect of famine had been an important motivating factor in civil society activism during the mid-eighties so, in the early years of the twenty-first century, the prospect of the health crisis sweeping though Africa proved impossible to ignore. At Davos, the prominence of this issue grew every year and a number of prominent participants such as Annan, Clinton, Sachs and Piot became norm entrepreneurs and reframed the issue in a way that emphasized the social responsibility to act (WEF 2000g; WEF 2004a). The philanthropic work of the Gates Foundation drew attention to the cause (WEF, 2000m). It also drew attention to the limitations of markets. When Bill Gates described the failure to address the health crisis in the developing world as a "market failure", Davos was left with two disturbing prospects: first that market logic was an inadequate mechanism with which to address social issues and second that this was not a small defect but rather an enormous problem (Cookson 2001).

At the opening plenary in 2002 Bono made a connection between debt relief and the fight against AIDS (WEF 2002e). Many campaigning for debt relief argued that debt cancellation was a legitimate and necessary step to free up funding for fighting the epidemic. Some went further. They argued that the AIDS epidemic was the result of the cuts in government and health spending associated with IMF conditionality and therefore, responsibility for the AIDS epidemic lay, at least in part, with the IFIs that had implemented the policy prescriptions of the Washington Consensus (Lewis 2005; Stiglitz 2002: 20). By 2005 the fight against infectious disease was firmly linked to global philanthropy, debt cancellation and also to the fight against global poverty (Chirac 2005; Schwab and Taylor 2005; Duncan 2005).

At Davos from 2000 to 2005 panels on debt and international finance became ever more important but increasingly these two issues were addressed in separate panels. On the one hand, the 1997 financial crisis highlighted the technical challenges of maintaining a stable international financial system. On the other, a growing emphasis on social responsibility and economic justice highlighted calls for debt cancellation. In this period there was a growing tension between panels with a technical orientation and those panels with an activist orientation to finance. In essence the two approaches drew on different groups of participants, and, although some individuals could span both worlds, as time went on the separation grew. Ultimately, this would prove to be to the detriment of both.

In international finance maintaining stability without overly hampering financial innovation is a complicated and challenging task. At Davos in 2000–2005 there were a number of panels devoted to managing the technical challenges of finance and the difficult-to-balance relationship between regulation, trust and financial innovation. While there were some critical voices in these panels most of these sessions were devoted to helping participants assess the opportunities for profit presented by the burgeoning financial system.[9] The more fundamental criticisms of financial liberalization, such as those expressed by Soros, took place elsewhere and did not seem to penetrate the community of financial practitioners very deeply.

There were some initiatives however. The "Equator Principles", common environmental and social standards for lending activities, were adopted by the International Finance Corporation and some 20 leading banks (Lazarus 2004), but although the tension between the benefits of financial liberalization versus regulation continued to be a topic of discussion, at Davos there was little sense of urgency. While there was a sense that the financial markets might be a little "crazy", they seemed to be working fairly well as engines of prosperity, at least for those attending Davos (WEF 2004e). In some quarters, there was growing worry about the sustainability of growing global financial imbalances but others dismissed this concern (Warner 2004a; Keegan 2004; Warner 2004b; Beattie, 2004; Kaletsky 2004). Even in 2005, when the Davos agenda was focused on social responsibility and fighting poverty, a number of panels continued to look at financial issues in isolation. For example, panels on the hedge fund industry were concerned primarily with whether hedge funds could continue to be engines of wealth creation and whether they might require enhanced regulation to avoid collapse. Despite the high profile panels on global welfare which had taken place the previous day, in these panels there was no consideration of the potential negative impact a collapse of the hedge funds would mean for global welfare (WEF 2005k; WEF 2005b: 6–7).

In the period from 2000 to 2005, however, another kind of financial panel which linked the moral responsibilities of business, economic justice and debt cancellation began to take off at Davos. In these panels the human costs of economic globalization were invoked and normative arguments with respect to debt were placed firmly on the table (WEF 2000f; Clinton 2000; Sachs 2000; Martin 2000). In 2000 James Wolfensohn stated the protest movement was more than a nuisance; it was "getting its way" (*The Economist* 2000). In 2001 the question of debt cancellation continued to be reframed as a political question:

> as the debt campaign showed, it is possible to force change even against the most implacable of opponents, provided that economics plays second fiddle to politics.... The renaissance of politics has perhaps been the most important development of the past few years. It is now clear that the future of the planet cannot be entrusted to the divine workings of the market or left in the hands of corporations. There are choices to be made and they are political choices (Elliot 2001b).

Inside Davos representatives of NGOs pressed the point home. Justin Forsyth of Oxfam emphasized that some debtor countries were still spending more on debt service than on their entire health, education and development budgets combined (Hieber 2001). Representatives of IFIs were "contrite" (Carnegy 2001). In 2001 Bono, who had been an active Jubilee 2000 campaigner for years, was invited to participate on a panel called "Debt Relief: Is it just About Cancelling the Bill?" with Stanley Fischer First Deputy Managing Director of the IMF and Ed Mayo of the New Economics Foundation. The panel opened with a video prepared by Jubilee 2000 (WEF 2001h).[10]

By 2002 at Davos debt relief was increasingly framed as a necessary step in alleviating poverty and disease. In the opening plenary Bono made the link between AIDS and the urgent need for debt relief (WEF 2002e). In a later session Bono and Sachs reinforced this message (WEF 2002g). Kofi Annan spoke out in favour of debt cancellation (Annan 2002). Canadian Prime Minister Paul Martin announced Canada's plans to "lighten Africa's choking debt load" and announced that "helping Africa out of its worsening economic crisis will be the challenge of this year's G8 summit in Kananaskis, Alberta" (WEF 2002f). Many were eager to join the cause (Barrett, 2002a).

In 2003 the WEF continued to move debt cancellation forward. *Global Agenda* featured articles putting forward the benefits of debt cancellation (WEF 2003c). Speaking at the session "Globalization at a Crossroads" George Soros expressed his very critical view of the financial order, IMF policies and the impact of financial globalization. At "A World without the IMF" the technical discussion was overshadowed by comments from the two NGO representatives on the panel who stressed the link between debt repayment and reduced spending on health and education. In "Africa: seizing the moment" debt relief was framed as necessary to combat disease and poverty (WEF 2003d).

Momentum for debt cancellation continued to build in 2004, and the need to respond more effectively to the needs of developing countries was seen as increasingly urgent (Carter 2004; WEF 2004l; WEF 2004g). Because it had become part of this larger campaign it became almost impossible to be critical of debt cancellation but, at the same time there was a serious downside to this shift. As the antipoverty movement grew in popularity it eclipsed the focus on the rules and practices of international finance. Paradoxically, as the economic justice movement gained in strength it became less effective in addressing the root causes of the debt crisis, the causes which lay in the organization of the global financial system.

In 2005 the Davos meeting was structured to give targeted support to the agenda the UK had adopted as the chair of the G8 and debt cancellation was an important part of this agenda (Schwab 2004d). On the opening day a Global Town Hall was held in which 700 participants voted on the relative importance of six issues of concern. Poverty and equitable globalization topped the list. The next day the WEF scheduled two plenary sessions calculated to push Africa to the top of the agenda: in the morning, "Africa and the G8: Rhetoric or action?" and in the afternoon, "Getting the MDGs back on Track" (WEF 2005b: 6–9). In the first session Bono, UK Prime Minister Blair, former US President Clinton, Microsoft Chairman Bill Gates, South African President Thabo Mbeki and Nigerian President Olusegun Obasanjo, took their place on the stage to call for action. This session resulted in the iconic image of the six leaders, looking somewhat breathless and pleased with themselves, photographed against the background of an enormous WEF logo with Bono flashing a peace sign (WEF 2005b: 6–7). The mood was optimistic:

> It is easy to mock four rich middle-aged white men pledging to end Africa's grinding poverty from their comfortable perch in an exclusive Swiss ski resort.... And yet it seemed as if something is really on the move. You can almost taste the hunger of the billionaire, the rock star, the former President and the Prime Minister for one last achievement – bigger and more meaningful than the rest (Robinson 2005).

In the afternoon at the session "Getting the Millennium goals back on track" another star studded panel, including Angelina Jolie, Goodwill Ambassador for the United Nations, and Jeffrey Sachs expressed concern at the slow progress toward meeting the MDGs (WEF 2005f). The next day a session on "Funding the War on Poverty" was held to discuss the most efficient structural funding mechanisms through which to meet the MDGs. This panel included Gordon Brown, Jeffrey Sachs, Liuz Inacio Lula da Silva, Bill Gates and Benjamin Mkapa. At the end of this session Sharon Stone, an actress and AIDS activist, rose from the audience, offered to donate her own funds to buy anti-malarial mosquito nets, and asked whether others in the audience would like to join her. In response, "participant after participant took out business cards with figures scribbled on them and passed them along the aisle to the staff" (WEF 2005g). This anecdote illustrates both the desire to "do something to help" that characterized Davos in 2005 as well as the difficulties in determining just what the best way might be. As Ken Wiwa (2005) wrote,

> the impassioned speeches about Africa's poverty suggest, to my surprise, that the Davos crowd appears to have grown a social conscience.... It is easy to get blind sided by the glamour and glitter of Davos. But I would submit that the committed individuals, social

> entrepreneurs, enterprising business people, artists, academics and scientist I saw at the margins of the conference represent something more than a facelift of the WEF.

As noted above, in this period the WEF became increasingly focused on how it might produce concrete results. In 2005 this was evident in the way it structured the annual meeting and in the new format it adopted for its annual meeting report (WEF 2005a). The WEF was particularly well positioned to influence the G8 agenda with respect to financial policy. Not only did most of the G8 finance ministers, central bankers and representatives of the IFIs attend Davos but a G7 finance ministers meeting traditionally took place shortly afterwards. For years Davos had provided a convenient place to lay informal foundations for G8 initiatives. Therefore, through its power to set the agenda at Davos the leadership of the WEF was able to influence the atmosphere in which this informal foundation could be developed. This was the case in 2005 and, in its annual report, the WEF was pleased to conclude,

> The energy generated on day one of the Annual Meeting continues to reverberate across Africa and around the world. During the summer – as the Live 8 series of international concerts kept momentum strong – this energy ensured that Africa, debt relief, trade and global poverty held centre stage at the G-8 meeting in Gleneagles and beyond. (WEF 2005b: 6–7)

By the time the G8 met in Gleneagles in July 2005, it was almost impossible to adopt a public position critical of debt cancellation.

Support for debt cancellation gained momentum at Davos (Mulvey 2005), and a large part of the credit for this must go to the transnational debt cancellation campaigners who successfully reframed the debate. By 2005 the conventional wisdom had been transformed from the belief that a morally correct course of action required debts to be repaid to the conviction that, under certain circumstances, it was morally abhorrent to demand debt repayment. By 2005 at Davos debt cancellation was equated with the moral high ground. Just how far the pendulum had swung can be seen in the following blog posting:

> There is a lot of talk about debt relief, too, and may I say something terribly, terribly old-fashioned? Hopelessly 19th century? "Debt relief" often amounts to debt forgiveness or excusal. Is there not honor in paying off debt, both for an individual and a country?

> Does it not relate to character (personal and national)? Does not self esteem come into play? My gosh, you might just as well read Parson Weems[11], as talk like that (Nordlinger 2005).

Even Sir Digby Jones, who was outspoken in his criticism of NGOs "hijacking" the 2005 Davos meeting, was careful to clarify that he supported Blair and Brown's efforts to make progress on debt relief during Britain's G8 presidency (Elliot 2005b).

Unfortunately, from today's perspective the conflation between debt cancellation and ending global poverty ultimately served to obscure more than it illuminated. As Stephen King, Managing Director of the HSBC, wrote "If there was an overriding theme to this year's World Economic Forum, it was commitment to help the most vulnerable in the world. Gordon Brown should be a satisfied man." But as King continues, "All this suggests that the G7/G8 meeting in London this coming weekend will be busy focusing on poverty and debt relief, leaving discussions of currencies and the like on the sidelines" (King 2005). Over time this omission would prove to have serious consequences for the developed as well as the developing world. By allying itself with the global anti-poverty movement, the debt cancellation movement was able to more easily tap into popular support around the world but, at the same time, it weakened its capacity to focus on the dynamics of the international financial system that had contributed to the debt crisis in the first place. By allowing the technical panels on finance to proceed unchallenged, critics missed a key opportunity to drive home the potential downside of global financial markets (WEF 2005h).

Despite being a private membership organization the WEF has a relatively high public profile, and this made it a particularly useful site for innovative transnational politics in the period from 2000 to 2005. The WEF's simple but effective logo evokes the curvature of our beautiful and, apparently, endangered planet viewed from space while the motto "Committed to improving the state of the World" affirms the good intentions of the WEF. The WEF has been highly successful in creating its own brand but while this success added to its authority it also attracted attention of a more critical character.

After Seattle civil society protesters increasingly took to the streets in protest (Juniper and Wainwright 2001; Ash 2001). In 2002, the WEF annual meeting was held in New York, but even the altered security climate did not deter the public demonstrations as 7,000 people took part (Jonquieres and Yeager 2002; Associated Press 2002; Cernetig 2002; Jacobs 2002; Usborne 2002; Indypendent 2002). In 2003, the WEF returned to Davos and, as the possibility of a US invasion of Iraq grew, the protest marches took on a "No WEF No War" theme. About 1,000 people made it to Davos to protest while another estimated 1,000 people were turned back (New York Times 2003; BBC World wide Monitoring 2003b; Cowell 2003b). By 2004 however the street demonstrations at Davos were very much reduced (Getz 2004). Even though protests in Davos had been banned, about 50–70 people managed to reach Davos but the majority, approximately 500 protesters, were turned back (Bott 2004; Cowell 2004a, 2004c; Elliot 2004b; Fleck 2004a). This was not, however, evidence of the weakening of the alterglobalization movement. As Matthias Herfeldt of the Berne Declaration, the NGO organizing the Public Eye on Davos Conference, argued, by 2004 some felt that a different phase had been reached and that the most effective location for meaningful dissent had moved indoors (Fleck 2004b). In 2005 the importance of the protest march, as a key tactic in the NGO engagement with the WEF, was reduced even further (Neue Zurcher Zeitung 2005). When Swiss authorities proposed limiting anti-WEF demonstrations to a fenced off public square in Bern, demonstrators balked at the idea and instead vowed to use imaginative alternatives (Nordlinger 2005).

During this period the opportunities for meaningful dissent did indeed move indoors as counter conferences presented increasingly important opportunities for activists to network, debate, gain public attention and in this way influence the discourse of the WEF. In 2000 to 2004 the "Other Davos" was held in Zurich (The Other Davos 2007). The "Public Eye on Davos" took place from 2000 to 2005 (Public Eye on Davos 2000). In 2001 it featured a direct communication link to the WSF each afternoon as well as reports on new developments at the WEF from Public Eye on Davos participants who also attended the WEF (Public Eye on Davos 2001a; Public Eye on Davos 2001b). In 2002 Public Eye on Davos set up blocks away from the WEF in New York (ATTAC 2002; Crane 2002a). It returned to Davos in 2003 where it presented a four-day program in which participants gave "a critical analysis of corporate-driven globalization" and presented more equitable and sustainable alternatives (Public Eye on Davos 2003).

In 2003 the WEF co-sponsored the first "Open Forum" with a group of Swiss NGOs (WEF 2003e). The Open Forum was intended to provide "an open platform for frank discussion around challenging aspects of globalization" (WEF 2003b: 7), and the WEF seemed particularly interested in engaging with alternate points of view through the Open Forum (WEF 2004b: 11). In 2004 "The Public Eye on Davos", the "Other

Davos" and the "Open Forum" all took place. While concerns remained among some NGOs that the WEF was hiding behind a screen of philanthropy and secrecy (Lobe 2004a), interaction between the participants at the WEF and the counter conferences increased. For example, Mary Robinson, Director of the Ethical Globalisation Initiative, former UN High Commissioner for Human Rights and long-time WEF participant opened the 2004 Public Eye on Davos conference (Public Eye on Davos 2004).

However, the most influential counter conference of all in this period was undoubtedly the "World Social Forum" (WSF), first held in Port Alegre, Brazil in 2001. The WSF was conceived of as a sort of "anti-Davos" (Klein 2001). From the start the WSF was intended to provide "a space for building economic alternatives" and "an opportunity for developing concrete projects, to educate the public, and to mobilize civil society" (50 Years is Enough 2000). Its motto was "Another world is Possible." The first WSF produced an "appeal to mobilisation" which exhorted its followers to fight the "hegemony of finance" and demanded "the unconditional cancellation of the foreign debt of the nations of the developing South, along with reparations for 'the historic, social and ecological debts' of the wealthy countries" (Osavo 2001). As discussed above, the WEF linked to the first WSF for a video debate, and this recognition gave the WSF a certain measure of legitimacy, as well as a higher profile, among those attending Davos.

In 2002 50,000–60,000 participants attended hundreds of workshops and seminars at the WSF. At the opening an internet video hook-up broadcast live greetings from AFL–CIO President John Sweeney, a long-time participant at the Davos annual meeting, as he joined the protests against the WEF in the streets in New York (Cooper 2002). A number of high profile individuals including Lula, the President of Brazil, and Mary Robinson attended both the WEF and the WSF and, as discussed in the previous chapter, the International People's Tribunal on Debt held at the WSF in 2002 added momentum to the transnational campaign for debt cancellation (Jeremic 2002; Jubilee South 2002).

In 2003 the WSF continued its strategy of applying pressure to the WEF. While the mood at Davos in 2003 was reportedly gloomy the WSF was upbeat. Naomi Klein, a leading alterglobalization activist in attendance at the WSF said, "Over the course of only three years Davos has been transformed from a festival of shamelessness to an annual parade of public shaming." Walden Bello was similarly self congratulatory: "the world social forum ... has become the prime organisational expression of a surging movement against corporate driven globalisation...a voice for human rights, against violence and against imperialism" (Gumbel 2003). As Elkington wrote at the time, the WEF and the WSF were both crucial potential leverage points in shaping the future of the global system. He concluded that by 2003 a "bridgehead" had been established within the WEF, and this could be opened further (Elkington 2003). In 2004 Joseph Stiglitz and Irene Khan, the Secretary General of Amnesty International, attended both the WSF and the WEF. The WSF and the WEF were increasingly seen as complementing each other with each presenting "parts of the truth" (Arnold 2004; Schaeffer-Duffy 2004). The WEF wished to engage with the more "constructive" NGOs, while the WSF wished to "contaminate capitalism" (Ramesh 2004).

In 2005 the WSF continued to grow; however, ideological disagreements within the WSF became more serious at this time (Anthony and Silva 2005; Engler 2005c). Despite this, the WSF continued to play an important part in pushing the global agenda in general, and the agenda of the WEF in particular, toward a more critical view of the impact of economic globalization and the responsibilities of the developed world to the developing world (Engler 2005b). In 2005 the Global Call to Action Against Poverty (GCAP) was launched at the WSF. The GCAP or "white band campaign" was intended to coordinate "various forms of citizen mobilization in more than 50 countries around the world, with a particular focus on the G8 countries" (Naidoo 2005a). Like the WEF, in 2005 the GCAP aimed to further the agenda of debt cancellation and poverty reduction being promoted by the UK at the G8 meeting in Gleneagles.

When GCAP organizers took their message to the annual meeting at Davos they found a surprisingly receptive audience:

> Last week, several GCAP members also lobbied the World Economic Forum in Davos to put pressure on the political leaders attending the event. Surprisingly, the political and business establishment acknowledged that poverty and inequitable globalisation are the two key challenges facing the world (Naidoo 2005b).

By 2005 many panels at the WEF annual meeting "seemed like Ebenezer Scrooge after a Yoga retreat" (Loewenberg 2005). The leadership at the WEF had structured the conference to raise the visibility of debt cancellation and poverty reduction for their participants and the public at large. By 2005 the WEF was deliberately using its own celebrity in conjunction with celebrity participants to draw the attention of a broader public from around the world (WEF 2005b: 6–7; Cowell 2005; Duncan 2005):

> When Angelina Jolie or Sharon Stone stand up to help poverty, to fight AIDS or talk about climate change, what they say is often understood by people who would not get it the same way if the message was coming from their governments or other sources of information (Lemeur 2005).

From 2000 to 2005 the contestation which took place outside the Davos meeting itself was closely linked with the contestation which took place within the meeting. When the WEF leadership extended invitations to representatives of CSOs and NGOs this allowed their views to be heard in a new way by members of the business elite. The invitation bestowed a kind of legitimacy in the view of the participants at Davos. At the same time the WSF's assertion that "Another world is possible" meshed with the Davos mission to "Improve the state of the world." Just as Jubilee 2000 reframed the debt cancellation debate in terms of what *had* to be accomplished but did not prescribe exactly *how* this was to be achieved, the multitude of civil society organizations and social movements involved in this period inspired a vision of the possibility of a "better" world while leaving the exact terms of how this might be achieved somewhat open ended. This challenge proved irresistible to many at Davos and, for better or worse, inspired them to set about doing their bit to achieve this.

Change

So what changed? This section considers this question in two parts, first what changed at the WEF annual meeting at Davos and second, what changed in the world at large. At Davos the conventional wisdom with respect to the responsibilities of business and the way these responsibilities might best be fulfilled changed substantially. Over time the annual meeting became an important site of political contestation over the rules and practices governing economic globalization and this is particularly clear in the case of debt cancellation. At first the third world debt crisis was seen primarily through the lens of its impact on business interests in the developed world and in the early 1990s, the WEF embraced the Washington Consensus as a promising approach to resolving the ongoing third world debt crisis. After 1994 however, campaigning NGOs and CSOs started to reframe debt cancellation as a human rights and economic justice issue. It would have been difficult to speak of "economic justice" at Davos in 1990. At this time economic justice was equated with equality of opportunity to participate on the "level playing field" of the free market. By 2005, however, economic justice was viewed differently and many at Davos had come to recognize the market society relation as potentially problematic.

Civil society campaigners both inside and outside Davos were important in reshaping the conventional wisdom and employed a number of variations on boomerang politics in this campaign. One particularly effective tactic described in the previous chapter involved civil society groups from debtor countries getting their counterparts in creditor countries to lobby, educate, and exert pressure on officials and influential individuals in creditor countries with respect to debt cancellation. As a result, when these individuals attended the Davos meeting they brought with them new perspectives on the issues involved and many subsequently became influential advocates for debt cancellation at Davos.

Furthermore campaigning NGOs and international policy institutes like the Transnational Institute played an important part in challenging the Washington Consensus and laying the intellectual foundation for debt cancellation. An important measure of their success can be found in the fact that, while arguments in favour of free trade as a means of eliminating global poverty through the discipline of the market were popular at Davos in 2005, at the same time there was almost unanimous agreement that, in international finance, market discipline must be moderated by debt cancellation. This is evidence of the success of the lobbying efforts of Jubilee 2000 and other debt cancellation campaigners in reframing the issue. The conventional wisdom that market discipline must prevail and debts must be repaid was successfully challenged, partly for technical reasons, but also because it came to be seen as morally repugnant to insist on repayment from those who could least afford to pay. Figure 4.1 diagrams how the WEF became an important site of political pressure on the G8.

Davos was an important site of contestation and the WEF an important opinion leader. At the annual meeting the "two track" argument was made with increasing frequency. According to this line of reasoning, embracing social responsibility and initiatives such as debt cancellation was the "right" thing to do it but was also good business practice. At Davos debt cancellation and anti poverty campaigners created a growing sense of uneasiness with being wealthy and privileged in a world of

Transnational advocacy networks and states target an international organization i.e. the G8 through a transnational organization i.e. the World Economic Forum.

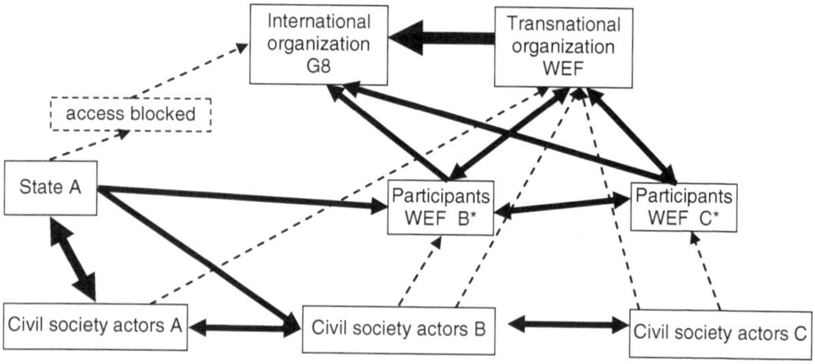

Figure 4.1 Boomerang politics, variation 4
*WEF Participants include state and non-state actors.

extreme poverty. They reframed the argument so that wealth was no longer seen as a reward for hard work or a sign of divine approval. For some this uneasiness was linked to traditional faith values and emphasized by the declarations of religious leaders. For others, with a more secular approach, human rights, economic justice and empathy provided a way into questioning the existing arrangements. These criticisms had a powerful cultural resonance. They were not easy to dismiss.

There was an especially sharp contrast between the extreme wealth of the business attendees at Davos and the plight of much of the rest of the world. At the 2000 meeting the unequal outcomes of economic globalization were reframed as "unacceptable" and a growing sense developed that "something must be done". Peer pressure and the dictates of fashion also played a role. By 2005 Schwab estimated that 50% of the corporate membership was "enthusiastically committed to the forum's goal of uniting politicians, business, and nonprofits to improve the world"; 30% while "loyal" were not actively involved; and finally 20% were primarily interested in networking opportunities (O'Brien 2005). The annual meeting provided a means for the leadership of the WEF to bring certain issues to prominence and push the Davos agenda beyond the narrowly defined interests of business. The WEF created initiatives through which corporate members could become involved in WEF approved good works. By 2005 the WEF had become a successful "facipulator" and was actively involved in a variety of forums, partnerships, and initiatives around the world.

Both the WSF and the WEF were "crucial leverage points" in the contest to shape the conventional wisdom on the global economy (Elkington 2003). For years Davos provided a convenient forum for state leaders and G8 finance ministers to meet informally in the weeks leading up to the G7 finance meeting, usually held shortly after the Davos meeting. Placing debt cancellation higher on the Davos agenda made it easier to include on the G8 agenda. In this way the agenda at Davos affected real material outcomes. When the moral arguments for debt cancellation were taken seriously enough to be extensively debated at Davos, this changed the agenda outside Davos. It expanded the limits of what was believed to be possible in the "real" world. As noted above, in 2005 the WEF deliberately constructed its agenda with the intention of providing support to the UK agenda of debt cancellation and poverty eradication, one of the key goals set for the G8 meeting in Gleneagles. In July 2005 the MDRI was adopted at Gleneagles and although it was not as inclusive as some of the campaigning organizations had wanted (Dillon 2005; Kairos et al., 2005), by 2006, there had been a remarkably high level of compliance with the new provisions for debt cancellation (Kirton et al. 2006).

The most important outcome of this process of contestation lies in the change in discourse or in other words, the change in the policy environment in which debt cancellation was considered. The WEF leadership provided a forum in which a number of previously marginalized voices could be heard by members of the world's business elite. Critics found a receptive audience at Davos and when many of those gathered there expressed their own criticisms of "market fundamentalism" and their belief in corporate, as well as individual, social responsibility, this was an important endorsement of the goals of the alterglobalization movement. Increased welfare had long been the goal of the Washington Consensus but the consensus on how best to achieve this goal changed. Blind faith in the benefits of unfettered free market processes was undermined and politics was brought back into the economic debate. Similarly, the tolerance for collateral damage, in the form of the negative human impacts of structural adjustment programs, was questioned. As previously marginalized voices became more difficult to ignore the very definition of success changed.

There is little doubt that the WEF expanded the worldview of many of its members beyond the economistic logic of competitiveness but, what is much more difficult to say is if there is any measurable positive change that one can point to as resulting from this process of contestation. Success can be difficult to measure. As Marie Dennis, head of the

Maryknoll Office for Global Concerns wrote, "the issues we are dealing with are so enormous that it's hard to see what success will look like and whether we will recognize it when it shows up" (Fraser and Jeffrey 2004). Furthermore, as Kumi Naidoo (2005a), the prominent activist and chair of GCAP as well as a long time participant at Davos, reminded his readers shortly after the Gleneagles G8 concluded "This struggle is not a sprint but a marathon". These quotes convey the ongoing nature of this contestation and underline the point that stamina and endurance are vital.

Arguably the biggest change resulting from the contestation at Davos is not any specific outcome but rather a shift in what is accepted as belonging on the agenda, what can be served for "dinner", not just at Davos, but at other high level meetings around the world. As the WEF (2004h) wrote,

> There are three good reasons to care about what happens at Davos. First, the annual meetings are a unique global barometer of elite attitudes and perceptions. Second, although the World Economic Forum produces no laws, no regulations, and no binding international treaties, its participants return home armed with what they have heard and discussed, frequently translating those thoughts into action. Third, and perhaps most important, the relationships that forum participants forge can be a remarkable catalyst for both understanding and initiative, bridging gaps that defy more quotidian efforts at social and professional intercourse.

Davos provided an innovative example of networking, consciousness raising and agenda setting. It highlights the importance of networking and discourse in governance. As Zadek (2005a) wrote,

> last week I came face to face with what looks to me like tomorrow's model of global governance ... the World Economic Forum itself. Here we have the convening space that brings together the most powerful people and institutions in the world today ... .the participants come and go, politicians and business leaders last a while ... but the WEF remains ... its networks are infinitely better than any one CEO or civil society leader could ever hope to develop during their moments of glory. ... My aim is not to exaggerate the significance of, demonise or celebrate the WEF ... it is merely to point out that it is an increasingly important part of today's global governance process ... and that is not just about what it does itself, but that the process it points us towards is likely to be a crucial model in the coming decades.

Conclusion

This chapter addressed the question of how non-state actors at the WEF mobilized to transform attitudes to economic globalization and in particular change the rules and practices governing debt cancellation. This case study provides evidence that supports the four related hypotheses put forward in this book. First, that moral values and normative ideas, beliefs about how the world *should* be, matter. The WEF started as an elite forum concerned primarily with business management but by 1991 it had become interested in pursuing a more ambitious agenda and contributing to "worldwide economic and social progress" through "effective global cooperation and entrepreneurial dynamism" (WEF and IMD 1991: 1). At first the WEF embraced neoliberalism as the best means to achieve this end but after 1994 this consensus weakened. As a series of crises in the global economy empowered critics and undermined the neoliberal consensus, at Davos concern with the negative social and political impacts of economic globalization grew. Moral values and normative ideas were important in shaping the way the WEF defined its "proper" role in the world and in its changing approach to the rules and practices governing debt cancellation.

Ideas have the power to shape not only understanding but also the very possibilities of action. As discussed in Chapter 2 Lukes' three-dimensional view of power clarifies the immense power of rules and practices and emphasizes that the privilege to set these is determined in a political contest, either overt or latent (Lukes 1974: 24). Polanyi's concept of movement and countermovement underlines the power of societal norms in changing, as well as maintaining, economic systems (Polanyi 1944/1957; Birchfield 1999). This case study provides evidence in support of the second hypothesis that ideas are influenced by developments in capitalism and that the campaign for the cancellation of third world debt can be understood as part of a Polanyian double movement taking place at the transnational level as the debt crisis and structural adjustment policies generated a societal backlash. This also supports the third hypothesis that moral values and normative ideas are important in defining agendas, in other words in defining what can and cannot be "on the table" (Zadek 2005). At Davos contestation over the impact of economic globalization and the negative social impact of neoliberal policy prescriptions redefined the agenda with respect to debt cancellation, and this produced a crisis in one elite discursive framework and a (partial) shift to another at Davos. Finally this case study supports the fourth hypothesis that by means of reframing and innovative political strategies civil society actors, both within the Davos meeting as well as those located outside the meeting changed the process of decision making to include actors and points of view that had previously been excluded.

As seen in the Chapter 3, transnational networks of debt cancellation campaigners worked to reframe the issue of debt cancellation. Previously a failure to repay debt was a seen as a moral failure on the part of the debtor but, by the time the Jubilee 2000 campaign had reached its peak, this point of view had been replaced by the belief that, in some circumstances, the greater fault lay with a creditor who demanded repayment from those who could not pay. In the winter of 2001 the WSF seemed to represent everything the WEF was not and the comparison was not flattering to the world business elite gathered at Davos. The WSF challenged the WEF to show that it was in fact "committed to improving the state of the world" in any meaningful sense. At the WSF and in the debt cancellation campaign at large, debt cancellation was reframed as a matter of social and economic justice. At first this argument was taken up by only a few opinion leaders at Davos but, by 2005, support for debt cancellation on the basis of economic justice had been embraced by the majority.

Innovative political strategies were important in broadening the debate and the effect of these strategies was felt inside Davos, as well as outside, as Davos participants brought their new perspectives to bear in other fora. As discussed previously, finance is a set of practices, beliefs and ideas and, in order to study finance, one must consider the discursive practices which bring finance into being (Geske 2000: 302; de Goede 2003: 79, 94). At Davos agents played an important part in putting the issues into context in new ways and in this way reshaping the discourse. Furthermore, as de Goede (2003: 96) writes, financial agents "may reformulate, rearticulate, transform and even fundamentally question financial orthodoxies." This "fundamental questioning" by influential agents located both inside and outside the WEF itself can be seen in this case study. Since the WEF was designed as an informal forum for the communication and the exchange of ideas (albeit the ideas of a limited elite) and not for the binding negotiation of international agreements, there were fewer constraints on the individuals attending Davos than existed in many other international or transnational meetings. Yet due to the power or the influence of the participants, pronouncements made at Davos carry weight in the forum as well as on the international scene. The WEF, therefore, provides an ideal site to challenge orthodoxies and reframe issues, a fact which was not lost on the WEF leadership nor on the NGOs and CSOs campaigning for reform.

At Davos many participants proved to be particularly open to normative arguments. Events such as the 1997 Asian financial crisis undermined faith in the practical benefits of financial liberalization and the subsequent criticism of the neoliberal approach and the policies of the IMF by influential participants such as Soros, Sachs and Stiglitz brought the theoretical worth of the Washington Consensus into question at the annual meeting. Outside Davos, CSOs and NGOs participated in counterconferences and public demonstrations to express opposition to the existing form of economic globalization and support for debt cancellation. In addition, for years a variety of civil society organizations and research centers had worked to generate alternative approaches to globalization, and by the late 1990s CSOs and NGOs had developed a substantial expertise in the area of finance. This was used to reframe the debate and influence the way economic issues were understood, both at the grassroots level as well as at the elite level. After 2000, when representatives from CSOs and NGOs were invited to Davos this allowed them to exert influence on other participants from inside the meeting itself.

A part of the puzzle remains, however. How does a shift in discourse at the WEF contribute to a change in the rules governing international financial relations which are, after all, determined by institutional or state actors formally answerable only to states and not accountable to the WEF in any conventional way? Clearly a shift in the consensus of the elite opinion within the Davos community can influence the views of those heads of state and the leaders of international financial institutions in attendance at the WEF annual meeting. However, in addition to this, through a number of variations on the tactic of "boomerang politics" (Keck and Sikkink 1998: 12–13), debt cancellation activists were able to generate additional effective political pressure on states through other channels. This supports the fourth hypothesis that at Davos innovative political strategies changed the decision-making process to include alternative points of view and actors.

A number of possible variations on this tactic were discussed in the previous case study. For example, as described in Chapter 3, debt cancellation campaigners in the South reached out to their counterparts in the developed world and, in turn, these groups mounted successful grass root campaigns for international debt cancellation within a number of G8 states. Over the years, popular democratic pressure at the grassroots level, in combination with more conventional lobbying efforts by national and transnational NGOs, affected the policy goals of a number of G8 states whose representatives then became leading advocates for debt cancellation within the multilateral institutions. At Davos a number of state leaders and finance ministers, who had been previously influenced by transnational advocacy networks, acting through their domestic constituencies, became important opinion leaders. In the case of the WEF, the potential impact of boomerang politics increased exponentially with the number of potentially effective pressure points available at the Davos meeting and the Forum's other activities. In this case "ricochet politics" might be a more apt term but, although the challenge of controlling and directing the path of a given intervention became correspondingly more difficult, the tactic remained appealing because its potential impact is high.

The discourse of the WEF annual meeting has undergone a number of transformations over the years, and this provides an interesting measure of economic fashions and the beliefs of international business elites as well as a window into the process by which these values and beliefs are constructed, reconstructed and reproduced. By 2005 a number of ideas and proposals, which previously would have been considered irrational and beyond the proper scope of consideration of the elite body, were brought forward for serious consideration and debate. At Davos opinion leaders became "norm entrepreneurs" and were instrumental in presenting these ideas to the WEF membership in the language they understood and respected. Due to the status and influence both of the WEF and the individuals involved alternative approaches to the rules governing the global economy achieved a level of legitimacy among many in attendance. This resulted in a norm cascade at Davos and in turn, this eased the progress of these approaches to being accepted as serious potential alternatives when presented in other international venues and, in this way, enhanced support for reforms to the rules governing debt cancellation.

As Keck and Sikkink (1998) argue, norms and identity can form a basis for political action independent of material interests (see also Sikkink 1998; Seidman 2001). While one may be skeptical of "non-material" explanations (Jacobsen 2003: 50, 60; de Goede 2003: 91), it is difficult to deny that moral values and normative ideas play a part and, indeed, sometimes seem to take on a life of their own in political causes. At the WEF agents, influenced by normative ideas contributed to the reshaping of the discourse. This ultimately had an impact on the rules governing debt cancellation. However, it must be clarified that this is not a case of what one might typically define as identity politics. In this case identity had less to do with ethnicity, race or sexual orientation than with a desire to publicly and perhaps privately define oneself as a "good" or ethical human being. At Davos the question of debt cancellation was linked to combating disease and eradicating global poverty. It was reframed in terms of morality and responsibility, something which had been virtually expunged from the discussion in the previous era, dominated as it was by neoliberal orthodoxy, the magic of the market and the long-term benefits of Adam Smith's invisible hand of the market.

This is not to say that material considerations did not play a part in this process nor is it to deny that an appearance of morality can and has been used in the pursuit of material advantage. It is to say, however, that there was something more at play here than the straightforward pursuit of material gain. As was seen in the previous case study, there are ways of framing demands that shift the foundations of the discussion in such a way that the immediate human costs of events or policies are brought to the foreground and overwhelm the previous conventional wisdom. In this situation, it is difficult for influential actors not to respond, or at least appear to respond, to the ethical dilemma. Arguably a similar process was at play in shifting the discussion and shaping the discourse of the WEF in this period.

At Davos many participants developed a more nuanced and sophisticated view of capitalism and a broader understanding of the challenges facing the capitalist system. For many at Davos success was based on material success but there was also an element of individual conscience included in this. Many WEF participants shared a desire to take pride, not just as the CEOs of profitable enterprises but also, in a broader sense, to take pride in themselves as responsible human beings making an important contribution to the global community. At Davos, it had always been important to be able to hold one's head up and be proud of one's actions. After 1997 a growing number of norm entrepreneurs in attendance at Davos made it difficult for many participants to ignore certain negative outcomes associated with the rigid application of market-based solutions. Outside the meeting CSOs and NGOs campaigned and lobbied to drive this point home. As the search for the "human face" of capitalism moved onto the Davos agenda, the force of arguments based on empathy and individual conscience became more obvious. Over time the importance of normative considerations as part of the definition of being "truly successful" grew at Davos. As long as participants subscribed to the view that, in the long run, free markets would by definition maximize global welfare it was easier to accept that the proper role for business was to operate within these constraints. In this case, while one might deeply regret the human impact of negative short-term outcomes, one could still believe that in the long term this pain would result in a positive contribution to global welfare. When this ideological certainty was brought into question at Davos, it became more difficult to feel one was occupying the moral high ground simply by fulfilling one's narrowly defined responsibilities in a business sense. This reframed the issues, started the debate around corporate social responsibility and eventually led to the shift in discourse which produced support for debt cancellation.

In 2005 there was a growing sense that "something had to be done" and that the current state of affairs was "unacceptable." At Davos the argument in favour of debt cancellation and other forms of action reflecting the social responsibility of business was made along "two tracks." Again and again it was argued that "something must be done" because it was the "right" thing to do but it was also frequently added that, not only was this the right thing to do in a moral sense, but it was also the right thing to do in a business sense. As Schwab and Smadja had argued in 1996, such adjustments were necessary, in a practical sense, to avoid a backlash as well as to assure the future security of the capitalist system. In other words it was possible to have one's cake and eat it too. In this way, normative considerations complemented material considerations in shaping the rules governing the global economy.

However, one must note that, when the debt cancellation campaign linked itself to the GCAP campaign to eradicate extreme poverty, it greatly enhanced its capacity to mobilize popular support but, at the same time, it weakened its capacity to address the fundamental issues of the organization of international finance. Arguments challenging the rules governing finance had been particularly difficult to make at the grassroots level, and it was a reflection of the particular genius of the earlier civil society activists that a movement which called for debt cancellation but also had a substantial capacity to educate its supporters on the fundamental principles governing the international financial order came into being. When the focus shifted to an anti-poverty agenda, the debate on reform of the rules governing the international financial system was eclipsed. Arguably this was a tactical error and one which continues to have a negative impact even today. At Davos the anti-poverty agenda came to overshadow the critique of the structure of the international financial system. By conflating debt relief, anti-poverty work and Africa, the capacity to fundamentally challenge the structure of the financial system and address the root causes of debt and economic dislocation was undermined. The potential to wage a popular campaign to reconstruct a financial system "with a human face" was reduced. And, perhaps even more importantly, at Davos the opportunity to draw the attention of elite members of the business community to other potential dangers brewing in international finance was missed. It was not the case that no one at Davos understood the potential dangers (King 2005). Rather these risks were not politicized in a coherent manner in the way that debt cancellation had been. As a result at Davos and elsewhere other potential negative impacts of the international financial system were not subject to the same kind of popular scrutiny. They remained the subject of dispassionate discussion largely by financial experts personally well insulated from the negative effects of potential financial reversals.

The popular campaigns criticizing the overall organization of international finance which had been so promising in the late 1990s lost momentum and focus as they were incorporated into a global anti-poverty movement. At Davos in 2005 Gordon Brown's agenda on poverty and debt relief appeared to have won the day but, at the same time, in other financial panels business went on as usual. While elsewhere the conference was enveloped in a pleasant haze of moral superiority, in this corner of Davos growing concerns were obscured by promising new opportunities to make money. Ironically, the focus on poverty and debt cancellation at the G8 drew attention away from other problems and risky practices taking place in international finance – practices which, when they started to unravel, would have an immensely negative effect on the welfare of both the developed and the developing world (King 2005). In the fall of 2008, as the international financial system came close to collapse, this came into sharp focus. At the time Klaus Schwab noted with regret that although the WEF began issuing warnings as early as 2003 "the financial community didn't listen." Instead they "treated him like a 'Cassandra' whenever he questioned the logic of their wisdom on asset-price bubbles in housing, stocks and other financial instruments" (Copetas 2008). By losing their focus on the structure of international finance the debt cancellation campaigners, as well other groups campaigning for the reconstruction of international finance, lost sight of their most important target, the immense power inherent in the rules and structures governing international finance.

This chapter explored the role of the WEF both as a transnational advocacy network and as a site of contestation in the campaign for the cancellation of third world debt. This contestation was part of an ongoing process that continues to be of relevance not only in the case of the third world debt crisis but also in understanding the current financial crisis. The key points to be drawn from this case study include the importance of transnational actors and innovative political strategies in shaping the rules and practices governing international financial relations as well as the role that moral values and normative ideas play in the creation, maintenance and transformation of the conventional wisdom – the invisible belief system that shapes our actions in such an all encompassing manner that we are barely aware of its influence. For better or worse this ongoing process, which adapts the rules governing the economy to the social context it must function within, is an important element in the adaptive capacity of capitalist economic relations.

5
Conclusion

In this book I have examined the civil society based campaign for the cancellation of third world debt in order to explore the question of how transnational non-state actors can mobilize to challenge the rules and practices governing international finance and what impact they have had. The two case studies on the campaign for the cancellation of third world debt provide a way to explore how new actors, transnational networks and innovative political strategies made possible by advances in transportation and communication are shaping global politics. At the moment this question is of particular interest because it bears on the question of how and with what degree of success civil society actors might mobilize in the future. The period from 1980 to 2005 examined in this research was characterized by increasing levels of engagement and activism by civil society actors from the local to the transnational. They embraced new political strategies and innovative tactics but, because they worked outside the conventionally defined lines of authority of the state system, these CSOs and NGOs had to develop alternative means of legitimizing their claims and enhancing their authority and influence.

Lukes' three-dimensional view of power provides a means of understanding the power of rules and practices in defining a particular agenda and, in this way, limiting the choice of possible alternatives. Lindblom highlights the power of the rules and practices governing economic relations and, in contrast to the view which associates the market mechanism with liberty and even democracy, Lindblom emphasizes the potential for market discipline to "imprison" behaviour. He describes the "automatic and punishing recoil" market forces can present to those who do not conform to the logic of the market or seek to act outside this logic. Finally, Polanyi's concept of the double movement emphasizes the power of societal norms and values and how they provide a foundation for the countermovement which reacts to "intolerable" market outcomes and seeks to set limits on the movement of unfettered market forces. Similarly, Gramsci points to the power of beliefs and ideas not only in hegemony but also in counter hegemony. These theoretical insights into the relationship between power, ideas and resistance all shed light on the civil society based contestation over the rules and practices governing international finance. They provide a means of understanding what is at stake, what is being challenged and suggest new possibilities for how change might be achieved.

The power of ideas to shape rules and practices is by no means limited to international finance, but international finance presents a particularly interesting case. While an active, stable and yet innovative financial system is vital to a modern economy, finance remains prone to instability and crisis. Finance itself is a construction, based on an abstraction, and maintained by a collective leap of faith. In terms of setting the limits of the possible on a broad range of issues, international finance is one of the most powerful structures in the world today and yet it is almost invisible. It is a complex system of rules and practices with real material outcomes. It is highly naturalized. It consists of formal and informal rules, practices, understandings, treaties and agreements in combination with a number of enormous and innovative markets dealing with an ever-changing array of financial products.

The assumptions underpinning market relations are so highly naturalized that they are difficult to challenge or expose. While recent work has gone a long way in revealing the contingent and constructed nature of the rules and practices governing international finance, even so, the idiosyncrasies of market relations remain hidden behind the myth of the mathematical "elegance" and efficiency of free market logic. Money permeates our culture and our decision-making processes. Through the mechanism of the market money can become a means of decision making, and this mechanism is tremendously appealing because it appears to de-politicize distributive decisions. If decisions are generated by market logic they appear to be fair and the outcomes just. Wealth and poverty appear to be based on merit but these outcomes can only be as just as the original conditions and assumptions on which the rules and practices governing market relations are constructed.[1]

Ideas are central to the reproduction of finance but they are even more important in contesting and reconstructing the rules and practices governing international financial relations. The power of ideas to challenge the existing financial order is particularly visible in the campaign for the cancellation of third world debt. Many of those who subscribed to the neoliberal policy prescriptions and the rhetoric of the Washington Consensus, as well as those who challenged the emphasis on liberalization and market discipline in international finance, shared the common goal of improving international economic welfare and finding a way out of chronic debt. But they differed sharply on exactly what this meant and how it might best be achieved.

During the 1980s market discipline and structural adjustment policies came to be accepted as presenting the best means to achieve a lasting resolution to the chronic problem of an ongoing series of debt crises in the third world. The apparent failure of Keynesian policy prescriptions cleared the way for a neoliberal approach as the assertion that each individual was responsible for their economic success or failure took hold. As the belief in the "magic of the markets" and the negative effects of government "interference" grew, a defence of the benefits of increased regulation for financial markets or state intervention in the economy became increasingly difficult. Economic beliefs were fundamentally reframed and, although the argument in favour of market discipline was not only economistic but also simplistic, it resonated widely. Soon, talk of "belt tightening" (preferably someone else's belt), the "magic of the market" and the need to "create a level playing field" dominated as the discourse shifted toward the Washington Consensus and market fundamentalism.

However the NGOs and CSOs campaigning for the cancellation of third world debt found a way to challenge the neoliberal discourse on third world debt. A complex argument against the excesses of a liberalized international financial system was implicit in their demands for debt cancellation. If free markets were by definition welfare maximizing and self regulating how then could they have generated so much unserviceable debt? Furthermore, the campaign for debt cancellation captured the public's attention, and its criticisms resonated with old prejudices against finance. It reinforced moral and normative concerns that the debt crisis, as well as the IMF response to it, were producing intolerable outcomes for the most vulnerable citizens in the most vulnerable debtor states. Campaigning NGOs and CSOs reframed the issues around debt so that SAPs and the economic restructuring required by the IMF as a condition of its assistance came to be equated with human suffering and economic injustice. The campaign reframed the ongoing debt crisis as an affront to human dignity and equated it with a modern form of slavery.

Criticism of the way the IFIs and the international financial system dealt with the third world debt crisis provided support for broader critiques of the claim that strict market discipline would, in the long run, generate a stable economic system, increased prosperity and just economic outcomes. When NGOs and CSOs successfully challenged the neoliberal remedy to the third world debt crisis this provided a way into a broader criticism of the Washington Consensus. The campaign undermined neoliberal certainties and planted seeds of doubt which had broader implications than debt cancellation, and this created a slight opening in the debate for those who held views opposing the neoliberal approach. Structural adjustment and economic restructuring came to epitomize the destructive side of international finance and, after the 1997 Asian financial crisis as the project of reconstructing the international financial architecture grew in importance, NGOs and CSOs found themselves well positioned to participate in the contestation.

Two case studies were selected: one on the civil society based transnational campaign for the cancellation of third world debt and the other on the WEF annual meeting at Davos as a site of contestation over the rules and practices governing debt cancellation. Although at first glance they may appear to be quite different, they are connected by the important role culturally resonant values and the reframing of economic issues play in both case studies. At these two different sites, one at the grassroots and one at the elite level, the rules and practices governing debt cancellation, were challenged in a remarkably similar manner. The case studies explore how, in the period from 1980 to 2005, civil society actors contested the rules and practices governing the organization of international finance. As civil society actors explored new ways to work transnationally and in networks of all kinds, these years saw new possibilities for challenge and change. Technological advances facilitated networking, coordination and the reframing of issues in a surge of innovation in popular communication whose equal has not been seen since the invention of moveable type. As CSOs and NGOs engaged with international actors and institutions they shifted the global agenda and redefined the limits of what was believed to be possible.

The case studies examined four hypotheses and in the following sections these will be discussed with respect to each case as well as with respect to the way the two sites of contestation complemented each other. The first hypothesis suggests that in the emerging context of transnational civil society based politics, normative ideas – ideas about how the world *should* be – are a powerful force in shaping change, even with respect to such an opaque, highly technical and apparently empirically based system of rules and practices as those which govern international finance. Under the Bretton Woods order the international finance was highly regulated but after the fixed exchange rate system broke down in the early 1970s, there was a shift away from the Keynesian approach to financial regulation. This eventually developed into a broad based ideological shift toward a neoliberal approach. As the international financial system grew in scale and scope, expert opinion seemed almost unanimous in support of financial liberalization at the same time as advances in technology facilitated innovation and exponential growth in financial markets.

The discourse of this period is dominated by accounts of the failure of Keynesian solutions, the need to "free" markets from the inefficient and destructive effects of government "interference" and the conviction that in the long run, not only will economic welfare be maximized but democracy will also be strengthened by ensuring unfettered market processes are allowed to work their magic. Despite this optimism, the 1980s were a time of upheaval with periodic financial crises taking place around the world, yet the neoliberal consensus only appeared to grow. As the Washington Consensus came to dominate international finance and the policy of IFIs toward debt rescheduling and economic restructuring the obvious question was where were the counter movements?

In both these case studies civil society actors presented the most important challenge to the Washington Consensus and they did this most effectively on the basis of moral values and normative ideas. Their challenge was based on a normative vision, either secular or faith based, of what it meant to be human and the rights, but also the responsibilities, this entailed. Although material interests clearly play a part in defining the market society relationship, the power of normative interests, visions of how the world should be and the power of normative ideas to produce change, are also very important. Changing material circumstances can change interests and, as discussed above, this provides an important part of the explanation of the evolution of international finance in the twentieth century. Undoubtedly material explanations are important but they are also incomplete. As has been shown in the case studies the power of moral values and normative ideas to shift the agenda and, in this way, redefine the limits of the possible, is substantial. Although quantifiable, empirically measurable interests are very important; they may, in some cases, conflict with goals based on normative ideas and, it is by no means certain that the materially oriented interest-maximizing goal will always dominate.

This is most obvious in the first case study. The Jubilee movement demonstrates the power of normative arguments to shift discourse. In the Jubilee movement there was a strong faith based religious element which was used to strengthen the human rights claims of the movement. Furthermore, the Jubilee movement likened the debt crisis to a new form of slavery. By linking debt service, economic restructuring and slavery, the Jubilee movement reframed the issues and brought added legitimacy to their demands for what was first referred to as a debt "forgiveness" and later called debt "cancellation." In this case study, the campaign for debt cancellation successfully shifted the discourse from the view that it was the moral obligation of debtors to repay their creditors to the view that, on the contrary, in some cases it was immoral for creditors to insist on being repaid. Jubilee argued that it was immoral to enforce economic policies which, in practice, amounted to enslaving debtors through the terms of debt rescheduling agreements. They chose to campaign on the terrain of moral values and normative ideas.

The faith based connection underlines the moral foundation on which the campaign to forgive third world debt was framed. The moral foundation helped emphasize that the campaign was not about economic efficiency or even inefficiency, but rather about economic and social justice. As discussed earlier this argument was very difficult for the IFIs to answer. Furthermore, the involvement of faith groups gave the debt cancellation movement access to ready made international and transnational networks ideally suited to mobilize public opinion and coordinate activism. Both faith based organizations as well as those who took their mandate from secular human rights values, provided committed activists who were comfortable campaigning at the intersection of idealism and pragmatism. Although some in the debt cancellation movement stood to have their material interests served by debt cancellation, there were many other committed campaigners whose material interests were not served by their involvement. Many campaigners, who can be described as "conscience adherents", were drawn to the campaign for debt cancellation by their values, whether faith based or secular, and the conviction that to do nothing would be a betrayal of themselves, their values and their beliefs.

The second case study demonstrates how, in the period from 1980 to 2005, the WEF annual meeting came to place greater emphasis on moral values and normative ideas. The desire to "improve the state of the world" had long been a goal of the WEF. At Davos the move to embrace the Washington Consensus had been part of seeking a practical strategy to remedy the chronic third world debt crisis and achieve this goal. However in this period just what was meant by "improving" the world and how this might best be achieved underwent a profound transformation. At Davos a "two track" argument is often made. According to this logic it is, first of all, good business to consider the potential social impacts of business outcomes in order to avoid a "backlash." This will keep the economy stable, society on an even keel and maintain a climate conducive to successful business activity. But there is a second part to this argument which was made with increasing frequency at Davos. It is that business should embrace its corporate social responsibility because it is the "right" thing to do. This kind of "noblesse oblige" or human rights based argument put forward a normative vision of how the world should be and asked how members of the WEF might best contribute to achieving this. It is striking how the WEF embraced a more activist agenda. By 2005 it had evolved from the strictly business oriented European Management Forum to what one commentator called a "facipulator", a combination of manipulator and facilitator that emphasized the social responsibility of its members (Zadek 2005).

In both case studies norm entrepreneurs were active in creating a norm cascade with respect to debt cancellation. In the first case transnational advocacy networks made up of a wide variety of CSOs and NGOs were vital in publicizing and reframing the issues, lobbying national and international decision makers, educating the public and recruiting support. In the second case the leadership of the WEF created a unique environment which became highly conducive to the presentation of alternative points of view and facilitated the recruitment of influential and motivated individuals to the cause. As Keck and Sikkink (Sikkink 1998: 520; Keck and Sikkink 1999: 8) suggest the normative argument with respect to debt cancellation became particularly compelling when it was connected to negative outcomes which included bodily harm to vulnerable and "innocent" victims.

For example the campaign to forgive "odious debt" asserted that many of the loans which contributed to the debt crisis did not benefit the most vulnerable citizens of the developing countries and, in some cases, contributed to their oppression by corrupt and illegitimate states. They argued that these loans should never have been made, that the citizens of these countries had no say in accepting or rejecting the terms of these loans and, therefore, they bore no responsibility for them. Furthermore, the economic rights enshrined in the Universal Declaration of Human Rights and later the MDGs provided support for the claim that not only the debt crisis but also the austerity measures implemented in response to the debt crisis violated the fundamental human rights of the most vulnerable individuals in debtor states. Finally, SAPs and cutbacks in health and education spending were linked to the AIDS/HIV epidemic in Africa, and this linkage emphasized the physical harm experienced by "innocent" individuals as a result of the debt crisis. The conviction grew that "something had to be done" to end the victimization. Therefore, due to the particular characteristics of debt and the relatively obvious connections between the debt crisis and negative human outcomes, the campaign for debt cancellation had the potential to provide the basis of a powerful critique of both the rules and practices governing international finance and the assumptions of neoliberal theory which formed the basis for the Washington Consensus.

It is interesting to note that in both cases transnational advocacy networks demanded change but were careful not to focus on the details or potential differences between their diverse members. They voiced their demands in general terms: "break the chains of debt", "another world is possible", "committed to improving the state of the world," They relied on the authority of faith leaders, human rights norms and even the reputation of the WEF to support their claims. This reflects a strategic appreciation of the wisdom of striving to provide a receptive environment for channeling the energies of a broad range of potential allies who share a common commitment to the moral values and normative ideas underpinning the campaign.

The second hypothesis posits that ideas are influenced by developments in capitalism and that the campaign for the cancellation of third world debt was part of a Polanyian double movement taking place at the transnational level in which the effects of international financial markets produced a societal backlash. In both case studies an effective tactic in furthering the case for debt cancellation was to emphasize the socially intolerable outcomes associated with the adoption of policies based on increased market discipline. Campaigning NGOs and CSOs emphasized the economic injustice and human toll of both the debt crisis and the SAPs and economic restructuring policies originally intended to provide a remedy. At Davos the need to put a "human face" on capitalism grew. Soros likened the effects of unregulated financial markets to a wrecking ball destroying economic and political stability. This sense that the third world debt crisis and the policies designed to remedy it were producing socially intolerable conditions in debtor states reinforced the civil society campaigners reframing of economic rights as fundamental human rights.

Polanyi's double movement describes an iterative process of movement and countermovement in which a movement toward unfettered market relations eventually produces socially intolerable outcomes. At this point society reacts against these conditions and a countermovement develops which subsequently seeks to set renewed limits on market processes. As Polanyi argued counter movements can be profoundly regressive; however this dynamic can also have a more positive aspect. It can provide a means of fine-tuning the market/society relationship and contribute to change and adaptation in capitalist systems over time. From the embedded liberalism of Ruggie to the Polanyian double movement and the Gramscian concept of hegemony and counter hegemony, social relations have a well-documented role in the processes by which the rules and norms which govern economic relations are reproduced and also how they are challenged and changed.

The third hypothesis posits that normative ideas are also important in defining more specific agendas. In the campaign for the cancellation of third world debt CSOs and NGOs redefined the global agenda and produced a crisis in one elite discursive framework, the Washington Consensus, and a (partial) shift to another discursive framework, which incorporated the demands of non-elite actors. Resistance to the Washington Consensus became particularly visible in the campaign for debt cancellation. In both case studies transnational civil society actors were influential in shifting the agenda and reframing the issues, and this created space to explore and eventually adopt a new discursive framework for debt cancellation. Normative ideas were important in redefining the definition of success in international finance. By highlighting examples of the negative impacts associated with economic restructuring in debtor states the campaign was able to bring into question the wisdom of unquestioning adherence to the Washington Consensus or as George Soros renamed it, "market fundamentalism."

In this period concern grew that the existing international financial system was unable to provide a stable, innovative and just means to foster economic progress for everyone including the most vulnerable individuals and states. In addition to debt cancellation campaigners many other CSOs and NGOs were working energetically to reform other aspects of the international financial order. Some advocated for a more ambitious agenda of reform of the international financial institutions. Supporters of the Tobin tax called for a tax on international flows of capital as a means of limiting excessive speculation. Others proposed innovative international taxes as a means to raise funds for international good works. Still others called for an end to financial tax havens, independent jurisdictions which allowed the wealthy to evade taxes. At the other end of the scale, the microcredit movement sought to work outside the conventional framework of international finance and provide small-scale lending to individuals in developing countries who would not otherwise be eligible to receive credit. While this proliferation of challenges provides further evidence of the discursive shift this book focuses on the civil society based campaign for the cancellation of third world debt.[2] The two most important outcomes of this campaign are first, its contribution to a shift in the climate of opinion or discursive framework with respect to debt and second, the change in the rules and practices governing debt cancellation.

The first case study traced the emergence of moral values and normative ideas in the CSO and NGO based challenge to the rules and practices governing debt cancellation. It found that the roots of the networks of NGOs and faith groups involved in this activism were very deep. For example, Oxfam was founded in 1942 to provide famine relief to Greece. In the following years Oxfam undertook development work, became involved in policy development and eventually it became an effective participant in the campaign for debt cancellation. In this campaign, networking took place from the third world to the developed world, through churches and faith related communities as well as secular NGOs. The campaign benefited from existing civil society based organizational frameworks which connected likeminded individuals in the developed and developing world. This provided a solid foundation for the international and transnational networking which became so important in furthering the demands of non-elite actors and in their challenge to the Washington Consensus.

The second case study focused on the World Economic Forum and the shift in the discourse which took place at its annual general meeting. The WEF is a private membership organization that was founded in 1971. Each year it holds an annual general meeting, which usually takes place at Davos, Switzerland. The Davos meeting has traditionally been a venue for business networking and a place for the business elite to take a reading of the global business environment, but in the period leading up to 2005 it became the site of substantial "consciousness raising" efforts. In this case study I followed the change in discourse at Davos, paying special attention to the attitudes to debt cancellation.

After 1989, at Davos as elsewhere, there was a marked turn to embrace the values and economic policies of the apparently newly triumphant neoliberalism. By the mid 1990s, however, a shift away from neoliberalism was slowly starting to take shape at Davos. It was based on normative as well as material considerations. It started in a general unease with the outcomes of unfettered capitalist market processes. As early as 1995 the leadership of the WEF expressed concern about a potential "backlash" against global capitalism and in 1998, in the wake of the Asian financial crisis, many at Davos openly expressed criticism of the Washington Consensus and the IMF response. In 1999 the idea of corporate social responsibility started to be a topic of intense interest and by 2005 the WEF leadership deliberately organized the Davos agenda to further the goals of the UK in promoting debt cancellation and ending global poverty. By 2005 the discourse had shifted to the point that debt cancellation had become the "right" thing to do and, at Davos, it had become almost impossible to speak out against debt cancellation.

The fourth and final hypothesis posits that CSO and NGO activism and innovative political strategies can change the process of decision making to include alternative perspectives and actors that were previously excluded. This is also supported in the two case studies. By reframing the issues or bringing new information to the debate a new conventional wisdom can be generated. Agents are important in challenging the existing discourse and shifting the agenda, and the process of contestation takes place not only between agents but also within agents. Clearly agents have a tendency to pursue their own perceived material interests but some agents also have a tendency to pursue more normative goals. They have a view of how things *should* be and are capable of convincing others to share their vision. By reframing an issue in a manner that resonates with existing widely held beliefs it is possible to motivate actors and mobilize the pressure of public opinion. A shift in the discourse can produce a shift in the agenda, and this can produce a shift in real outcomes. As was seen in both case studies, in the campaign for debt cancellation transnational advocacy networks and boomerang politics provided new ways in which political pressure could be applied to decision makers within the states and the institutions governing international finance.

In the first case study three major tactics proved to be successful: networking, research, and reframing. First, in this campaign institutions and organizations networked locally, nationally, internationally and transnationally. Networking was both formal and informal and this exchange of ideas, information and experiences shifted the discourse around debt cancellation. For many, the third world debt crisis and the impact of SAPs ceased to be a problem confined to distant others and became a problem of immediate concern shared by members of one's own community. Furthermore, as predicted by the concept of boomerang politics, these organizational links facilitated campaigning by transnational advocacy networks at the grassroots level within creditor states, and this ultimately generated political pressure on decision makers in the governments of G8 states. This created an atmosphere within the G8 that was more open to the demands of the debt cancellation campaigners.

Second, the campaigning NGOs learned to speak the language of the decision makers. They developed important research institutes which produced credible alternative analyses of the pressing issues around development, debt and finance. These groups lobbied key decision makers and eventually became respected sources of alternative expertise at the highest levels. At the same time they carried on a campaign which educated the public on why the third world debt crisis mattered. As popular education initiatives demystified the technical language of finance this challenged the authority of economic experts to monopolize discussion of debt cancellation. NGOs gave a coherent voice to an alternative approach at the same time as the quality of their research, presented in the language of the mainstream, but from a very different point of view, gave authority to these alternative voices.

Finally, NGO and CSO campaigners shifted the terrain on which the debate over debt cancellation took place. Despite an impressive command of the technical aspects of debt and finance, civil society campaigners did not propose detailed technical solutions. Instead they argued that the existing situation was not "right" and insisted that it must be fixed. However the civil society campaigners strategically chose to leave the details of just how this might best be accomplished up to the experts. In this way they placed both the responsibility and the expectations of the public on the financial experts and international leaders and challenged them to succeed. The campaigning groups linked their demands to powerful normative arguments which invoked basic faith based values, human rights values and the Universal Declaration of Human Rights as well as the Millennium Development Goals. In this campaign a multitude of actors in interconnected organizations and networks kept up the political pressure for years. Finally, not only civil society actors but also previously marginalized actors located within the IFIs themselves became more vocal in their criticisms of the neoliberal approach to the debt crisis.

In the second case study the WEF leadership, opinion leaders within the Davos meeting, and the pressure of civil society campaigners located both within and outside the meeting were important factors in achieving the inclusion of alternative perspectives and actors at the annual meeting. The WEF is a top-down organization and each year the leadership takes an active role in drafting the meeting agenda. They determine the composition of the panels, the topics under discussion and they set the tone for the meeting. Their power of invitation determines who attends the meeting. Over the years at Davos a number of influential and charismatic opinion leaders were important in shifting the discourse. For example, after the Asian financial crisis Soros, Sachs and Stiglitz all expressed opinions highly critical of both the Washington Consensus and the actions of the IMF. These criticisms, made by such well-respected individuals and expressed in the elite forum of Davos, were undoubtedly influential in planting seeds of doubt in the mind of the WEF business participants, doubts which eventually permitted the conventional wisdom with respect to debt cancellation to be successfully challenged at the annual meeting.

After Seattle the WEF leadership invited an unprecedented number of civil society representatives to the annual meeting, and this provided opportunities for their views to be heard in formal as well as informal meetings at Davos. These representatives included a number of prominent debt cancellation campaigners such as Ed Mayo of the New Economics Foundation and the charismatic Bono, who had been a Jubilee 2000 campaigner since 1999. Davos was originally designed to take the measure of the world environment that business would have to contend within the coming year; therefore it is not surprising that the WEF leadership was sensitive to the challenges to globalization being articulated by civil society campaigners. The WEF became a popular target of civil society efforts and, in addition to those NGOs and CSOs who were willing to accept invitations to participate in the Davos process, many others engaged in the debate from outside the meeting. Demonstrations, counter conferences and, of course, the World Social Forum provided important spaces in which to present alternative points of view or in some cases, even set up dialogue with participants at the Davos meeting.

In this period at Davos the issues were reframed to place greater emphasis on the broader responsibilities of business or as the new WEF motto stated the responsibilities of business in "improving the state of the world." By 2005 the Davos agenda was deliberately designed to support the goals of the UK at the G8 meeting scheduled to take place at Gleneagles, Scotland in July. In the process of including actors and points of view that were previously excluded the transnational, civil society campaign for debt cancellation and the elite WEF complemented each other. By 2005 the pressure from the grassroots and the elite, the developing and the developed world, creditor and debtor states, activists, academics, CEOs, spiritual leaders and celebrities had come together to create a feeling of unanimity in support of debt cancellation.

However, in this large and complex field of contestation it is difficult to precisely measure the impact of the campaign for debt cancellation in producing change in the rules and practices governing international finance. As discussed previously there is a danger of confusing public relations strategies with real change. It is therefore useful to assess the impact of the campaign on the basis of four factors: the consistency of the shift in discourse; the diversity of the voices expressing support for an alternative vision; the inclusiveness of the formal and informal fora at which these issues were debated and the change in policy outcomes with respect to debt cancellation and compliance with this change in policy.[3]

The two case studies provide evidence of a consistent shift in the discourse on debt cancellation that became more marked over time. The issue of the cancellation of third world debt was successfully reframed, and debt cancellation was transformed from a morally neutral technique for dealing with large scale defaults to a highly moral question which emphasized the experience of the most vulnerable citizens in debtor states. By 2005 the conviction that morality required debtors to repay their debts had been widely replaced by the view that, in certain cases, it was immoral of creditors to extract debt repayment. As responsibility shifted to the creditor, in the case of the HIPCs debt cancellation became more than a technical fix; it became the "right" thing to do. Furthermore the campaign for the cancellation of third world debt undermined faith in the benefits of financial liberalization and the belief in the efficiency and welfare-maximizing outcomes of strict market discipline. After the 1997 Asian financial crisis this critique was strengthened and new voices joined. At this time not only attitudes in favour of debt rescheduling and economic restructuring but also support for the fundamental assumptions of the Washington Consensus were undermined.

Second, as the case studies demonstrate, the diversity of voices participating in the campaign was enormous. They included NGOs, CSOs and individuals from the grassroots to the elite, from the developed and developing world, and state as well as non-state actors. They included faith based actors, human rights activists, politicians, academics, bureaucrats and business leaders. The diversity of the voices was matched by a diversity of tactics and innovative strategies. Through a number of variations of boomerang politics, political pressure was transmitted from one group to another in search of the most effective strategic opening to further the goals of the campaign.

Third, the formal and informal fora at which debt cancellation was debated became increasingly inclusive in the period under study. At first faith groups provided longstanding, ready made networks between civil society actors in debtor and creditor states. Starting in the 1980s and 1990s international meetings and summits, often associated with the UN, provided new opportunities for NGOs and CSOs to meet and network. Later the WSF provided a spectacular meeting place for an unprecedented variety and number of interested individuals and groups. The possibilities presented by new communications technology to facilitate discussion, networking and the organization of everything from counter summits to public protests, was equally impressive. Even high-level international meetings became an opportunity for CSOs and NGOs to campaign. If their views were not welcome inside the meeting itself, they were expressed in public demonstrations and counter summits planned to take place at the same time. Towards the end of this period high-level meetings became more inclusive, and representatives from NGOs and CSOs were formally invited to participate. In several influential G8 states debt cancellation campaigners became effective lobbyists and well-regarded sources of information and expertise for state actors.

Fourth, the most important change that came out of the campaign for the cancellation of third world debt was the change in discourse around debt cancellation. This brought with it a more critical view of the Washington Consensus and the value of policies based on the assumption that market discipline would provide an effective way out of chronic financial crises. This change in discourse changed the global agenda and opened up a process of contestation over the rules and practices governing international finance. Items such as economic justice or corporate social responsibility that had been struck from the international agenda by the turn toward neoliberalism in the 1980s were back on the agenda by 2005. The hope that market discipline could provide an efficient and fair means of addressing these issues without resorting to political contestation over international financial relations was disappointed.[4] Politics was back on the agenda and the political contestation that had always underpinned the rules and practices governing international finance became increasingly apparent. Nowhere was this more clearly visible than in the campaign for the cancellation of third world debt.

At the G8 summit in Gleneagles in 2005 the Multilateral Debt Relief Initiative (MDRI), a $50 billion debt cancellation and aid package was announced. While impressive this was not the end of the struggle but merely another stage in the campaign for debt cancellation and the broader campaign for financial reform and economic justice. Gleneagles was a turning point and, although it has been taken as the end point of this case study, the contestation remained ongoing (Jubilee Research 2005). Debt cancellation remains a moving target and as new sovereign debt defaults occur, this time in the developed world, it is clear that debt crises are an ongoing feature of the international political economy. This book does not argue that the campaign for the cancellation of third world debt solved the problem of chronic indebtedness nor does it suggest that the campaign achieved "economic justice." Rather it argues that there are lessons which can be drawn from these events. The response to the Latin American debt crises transferred the burden of repayment to taxpayers in the debtor states but subsequently, in the largely African case which culminated in the MDRI, taxpayers in creditor states joined the campaign and in effect exerted political pressure to be allowed to accept the burden of debt cancellation in the HIPCs (Lavelle 2011). I argue that the difference between these two responses was the result of the civil society based campaign for debt cancellation.

Arguably this somewhat counterintuitive dynamic is most important when the likely costs of a given action lie in what I think of a "middle range." That is to say that the cost of given action does not put into jeopardy in any significant way the survival of the actors themselves. Civil society is an important site where values are negotiated, and while normative ideas can help define what proper behaviour might be, this dynamic has its limitations. The kind of contestation examined in this book is of most importance in a fairly secure world where interested actors have the luxury of caring, not only about their own feelings but also about the welfare of others. In the case of a crisis where survival is at stake the positive normative aspects of this analysis are less relevant and, although power relations rooted within civil society may become even more important in shaping state actions, the civil society response is more likely to take a more regressive but perhaps equally normative form.

The one hundred percent compliance rate with the terms of the MDRI in the year following its adoption is evidence of the G8 states' commitment to debt cancellation (Kirton et al. 2006). In contrast the goal of increasing aid expenditures to 0.7 percent of GDP met with only mixed success. In the campaign for debt cancellation norm entrepreneurs succeeded in creating a norm cascade. Sikkink (1998: 3) argues that the path to power can be circuitous for both norm entrepreneurs and transnational advocacy networks and the lines between "insiders" and "outsiders" often blur. In this case there were actors both within international organizations and government who internalized the values and helped pursue the goals of the campaign for debt cancellation.

Furthermore, as Keck and Sikkink (1999: 8) suggest, a normative argument becomes particularly compelling when it is connected to negative outcomes such as bodily harm to vulnerable and "innocent" victims. The resonant connections between debt and negative human outcomes added to the capacity of the campaign for debt cancellation to challenge both the rules and practices governing debt cancellation and the assumptions which formed the basis for the Washington Consensus. However, this process of contestation is not without pitfalls. Just as civil society movements can be regressive as well as progressive they can also be easily distracted. In 2005 it seemed a natural progression to link the campaign for the cancellation of third world debt to the campaign to end global poverty and improve global health. At first it seemed as if this would strengthen the debt cancellation campaign; however, the emphasis on poverty eradication took the popular focus away from the much more difficult-to-understand critique of international finance that had originally been an important part of the debt cancellation campaign. Educational initiatives flagged. Furthermore, after the adoption of the MDRI in 2005 there was a widespread sense that debt cancellation had been "taken care of" and that the battle had been won. With only a few exceptions, international CSOs and NGOs shifted their emphasis to anti-poverty initiatives and once again left the organization of international finance largely to the experts.

The demands for debt cancellation had contained an implicit critique of the organization of international finance but, as the campaign for debt cancellation was transformed into an anti-poverty campaign, the popular political potential of the financial critique was undermined. The renewal of financial crisis in the summer of 2007, this time centered in the developed world, returned public attention to the profound impact and practical importance of the rules and practices governing international finance, but the civil society response was weak and confused. As the financial crisis peaked in the fall of 2008 fear and disbelief dominated, but early outrage did not transform into an effective civil society response either nationally or transnationally. At the G8/ G20 counter conference in Toronto in the spring of 2010 financial reform was only one of a multitude of diverse demands presented by CSOs and NGOs. By the American mid-term elections in the fall of 2010, the blame for the financial crisis and ongoing economic problems had been successfully shifted from a condemnation of "market failure" and the reckless greed of financial speculators to the much more familiar theme of a "failure of government regulation." At the same time the blind faith in self-regulating markets that had effectively tied the hands of financial regulators for decades was conveniently forgotten. Blind faith in markets coupled with the belief that government must not "interfere" completely misses the social constructedness of the rules and practices governing market relations and especially those rules and practices which underpin financial relations. Markets do not emerge solely out of a physical reality. They do not reflect unchanging laws of science, mathematics or even logic. They are instead embedded in a changing social and cultural environment which has the capacity to construct and reconstruct the very definition of rational behaviour.

The campaign for the cancellation of third world debt demonstrates how rules and practices can be challenged by shifting the terrain of contestation. By emphasizing the moral and normative aspects of the political economy the NGOs and CSOs campaigning for debt cancellation were able to shift the discourse and rewrite the global agenda in a way that gave more explicit attention to the negative effects of the rules and practices governing international financial relations with respect to the most vulnerable of debtors. The campaigners succeeded in linking financial processes to their impact on the ground and reminding at least some of those responsible for defining the rules and practices governing international finance of their responsibilities to other human beings, as well as the need to moderate the economic and social outcomes of international finance to make the system sustainable.

The campaign made the assumptions which underpinned the Washington Consensus visible and therefore subject to challenge. In Lukes' terms the campaign made the third dimension of the power of the Washington Consensus visible, and this was the first step in challenging its hegemonic control of the economic agenda. Reframing the issue of debt cancellation, shifting the discourse and redesigning the political agenda translated into effective political power which the civil society campaigners used in conventional political contests as well as in a variety of innovative variations of boomerang politics. The campaign for the cancellation of third world debt provides an important example of the political power inherent in economic beliefs and makes the contested and contingent political foundation of economic relations visible. It demonstrates the potential of civil society actors to challenge economic orthodoxy and transform marginalized points of view and interests into legitimate concerns. The case studies demonstrate the importance of three lessons for transnational civil society campaigns: first, the value of broadly defined goals and inclusive coalitions and networks; second, the power of culturally resonant issues in mobilizing broad based support; and finally, the value of innovative political tactics including reframing issues, shifting the agenda and pursuing indirect, as well as direct, paths to political influence.

It remains to be seen whether transnational civil society campaigners will be able to take a more politically effective role in the ongoing contestation in future. At present the linkage between economic justice and international finance remains on the agenda however tenuously. Although the public's memory appears to be short, in recent years, scandals, defaults and bankruptcies have further undermined public confidence in financial elites. At the worst point in the financial crisis in the fall of 2008 it was government action that was required to save a paralyzed international financial system from total collapse. At present there still is a chance to build on the lessons learned by the debt cancellation campaign to mobilize opinion around the world to rein in global finance. It remains a moment of possibility and a large part of the credit for this must go to the NGOs and CSOs who first campaigned for debt cancellation and who continue to campaign to bring moral values and normative ideas back into the rules and practices governing international finance.

Notes

1 Introduction

1. "Power" is a term which is used to describe many relationships, and the concept of power as it is used in this research will be discussed more fully in Chapter 2.
2. The events of the interwar and the ongoing Second World War were well within the living memory of the negotiators at Bretton Woods. Keynes had been an official representative of the British Treasury at the Paris Peace Conference but he objected to the economic provisions of the Treaty of Versailles and argued that they set the stage for further conflict. He resigned in June, 1919 and the next year published *The Economic Consequences of the Peace* (Keynes 1920/2004: vol. 6).
3. This discussion draws on Keck and Sikkink (1999).

2 Power and Resistance

1. Reitan draws on Johan Galtung's conception of the three forms of structural violence to help explain the power of framing. Galtung defines three categories of violence: direct, structural and cultural. Galtung's third category, cultural violence, is similar to Lukes' three-dimensional view of power as well as Galbraith's definition of conditioned power. Galtung argues that when one refers to cultural violence, one really should speak of cultural power or the ability to "shape actions by framing what is right and wrong." Reitan argues that the concept of cultural violence in Galtung is very close to the Gramscian concept of hegemony and illustrates how, through the power of framing, "common sense" can legitimate particular relations of power (Reitan 2007: 17).
2. For example in recent years financial market actors, who were unwilling to become involved with what they considered to overly risky or even recklessly irresponsible financial practices, faced a difficult choice. Due to the high, albeit short-term, returns associated with such investments, if they refused to be involved, they would produce reduced returns on investment in comparison to their competitors. Clients would move their capital to more lucrative opportunities and therefore the more cautious market actors would be left behind and perhaps even be forced out of business.
3. John Williamson (2008, 2004), who coined the term has since distanced himself from the more extreme version of the Washington Consensus. For example he rightly argues that his original 10 points did not call for the liberalization of capital markets but, as Rodrik (2008) argues, his "creation took on an independent life of its own" and came to both stand for and justify greater reliance on market discipline than Williamson had originally envisioned thereby, as Rodrik and Held (2004: 55–56) both argue, becoming a legitimate target for critics.

4. That Keynes understood the power of ideas, as well as the importance of lived experience in determining how a given idea will be received, can be seen in the following passage from the General Theory:

   > At the present moment people are unusually expectant of a more fundamental diagnosis; more particularly eager to receive it; eager to try it out, if it should be even plausible. But apart from this contemporary mood, the ideas of economist and political philosophers, both when they are right and when they are wrong, are more powerful than is commonly understood. Indeed the world is ruled by little else. Practical men, who believe themselves to be quite exempt from any intellectual influences, are usually the slaves of some defunct economist. Madmen in authority, who hear voices in the air, are distilling their frenzy from some academic scribbler of a few years back. I am sure the power of vested interests is vastly exaggerated compared with the gradual encroachment of ideas. Not indeed, immediately, but after a certain interval; for in the field of economic and political philosophy there are not many who are influenced by new theories after they are twenty-five or thirty years of age, so that the ideas which civil servants and politicians and even agitators apply to current events are not likely to be the newest. But soon or late, it is ideas, not vested interests, which are dangerous for good or evil. (1936/1942: 383–384)

5. These figures are intended to diagram the primary relationships of boomerang politics. For this reason one way arrows have been used to indicate the most important paths of influence even though this may not completely reflect the multiplicity of relations and all the paths of influence in a complex political environment.

3 Transnational Civil Society and the Campaign for the Cancellation of Third World Debt

1. A role later complemented by the Millennium Development Goals.
2. In the 1970s Oxfam UK had gone so far as to try and remove the rights to the name "Oxfam" from Oxfam Canada because it believed the Canadian group was too overtly political and policy oriented (Tomlinson 2008).
3. In 1989 the book was adapted as a BBC documentary and was broadcast on December 28, 1989 (TNI 2006).
4. These images had been produced by a CBC news team while covering the Ethiopian famine in the fall of 1984 (God's Tears 2005).
5. In 1995 the proliferation of NGOs and CSOs continued. The Bretton Woods Project (BWP) was established by the Development and Environment Group, a network of UK-based NGOs, to facilitate the monitoring of the social and environmental impacts of WB and IMF policies and projects (BWP 2006). The BWP also received funding from the Mott Foundation (Smithey 2008).
6. In 1999 the crisis in the Long Term Capital Management hedge fund further added to concerns regarding the stability and sustainability of the international financial system.
7. Also known as HIPC 2.
8. They had also delivered it to the Secretary General of the United Nations, Kofi Annan, at the Millennium summit earlier in September.

9. The Group included Bill Ferguson of Jubilee USA; Jennifer Henry and Kristen Mercer of Kairos, Canada; Pam Foster of the Halifax Initiative; Denise Comanne and Eric Toussaint of CADTM, Belgium.
10. In 2005 Oxfam went so far as to use a feature film "The Girl in the Café" as a lobbying tool and ensured that copies of the film got to ministers' aides (Fried 2008). This film was a romantic and inspirational story about how "the girl in the café" convinced one British diplomat to abandon his cynicism and "make a difference" at a fictitious international conference.
11. The meeting was organized with the support of the UNCTAD Secretariat; NGLS; Focus on the Global south, a Thai-based NGO; and the Thai NGO Coordinating Committee on Development (NGO-COD).
12. Halving extreme poverty and hunger
    Achieving universal primary education
    Achieving gender equality
    Reducing child mortality by two-thirds
    Reducing maternal mortality by three-quarters
    Reversing the spread of HIV/AIDS, malaria and other major diseases
    Ensuring environmental sustainability
    Creating a global partnership for development
    (Millennium Project 2006).
13. This was called Toronto terms. This percentage later increased to 67% under Naples terms and in 1996, when the HIPC initiative was adopted, this was increased to 80% (Paris Club 2006).
14. Polanyi's theory was originally based at the level of the state but the same dynamic can be seen at the global level. In Polanyi's work the countermovement is regressive and authoritarian – the rise of Nazi Germany – but arguably countermovements can be either regressive or progressive.

4 The World Economic Forum as a Site of Contestation

1. In 1989 one series of the World Link covers unselfconsciously featured the image of a youthful, clean-cut, Caucasian businessman as the ideal face of the WEF but by 1993 the male-dominated image of the WEF had come under scrutiny (Herald 1993). The profoundly gendered tone of the WEF can also be seen in the use of the term "Davos Man." Samuel Huntington had originally written about "Davos culture" but in 1997, the *Economist* (1997) transformed this phrase to "Davos Man." The catchy phrase, including its gendered implications, was adopted without comment perhaps because "Davos Man" seemed to represent the majority of participants at the WEF perfectly.
2. For example, participants at Davos warned that a dangerous cocktail of aggressive traders, speculative investors and complex financial instruments had emerged (Cohen 1995). Andrew Crockett, General Manager of the BIS, warned of dangers of senior managers not understanding derivatives (Norman 1995b). In 1996 various means to ensure financial stability were discussed (Seiberg 1996; Isaac 1996; Schwab and Smadja 1997a). In 1997 Howard Davies, Deputy Governor of the Bank of England, and Andrew Crockett of the BIS participated in a seminar on global measures to safeguard against instability (Warner 1997).

3. For example, in 1998 there were sessions on searching for deeper meaning in life (Cooperstone 1998) and a particularly well-received session "On Death and Dying" (WEF 1998c: 10). In 1999 there were sessions on "Globalisation with a Human Face", "You Can't Take It With You: Making Philanthropy more Effective" and "Five Things Wrong with the World and What Business Can Do to Help" (WEF 1999i; Saporta 1999). In the closing session Nadine Gordimer, UNDP Goodwill Ambassador, spoke out about eradicating global poverty, and Princess Anne held business responsible for the negative impacts of globalization on the world's children (WEF 1999k).
4. Just how much Gates' public image has evolved over the past decade can be seen by comparing his present contributions to this view of him in 1998: "Davos Man is most publicly embodied in Bill Gates, the ubiquitous chairman of the Microsoft Corporation.... To most of the executives he is a heroic figure, and not just because he built a huge business from scratch. He is the very epitome of a flexible magnate, as shown most recently when he discovered that he had not foreseen the internet. Gates turned his immense operations around on a dime, reorganising his business in pursuit of the new market opportunity.... By all accounts he is a ruthless competitor, and the evidence of his greed is a matter of public record; he has devoted only a miniscule portion of his billions to charity or to the public good" (Barber and Jonquieres 2000).
5. This interaction resulted in the establishment of the Global Compact, a business organization committed to "upholding human rights, labour, environmental and anticorruption standards" around the world. By 2009 it had grown to 7,700 corporate members (United Nations Global Compact 2009).
6. In the panel "Is Global Capitalism delivering the goods?" Jean Chrétien, the Prime Minister of Canada, Lee Kuan Yew former Prime Minister and, at the time, Senior Minister of Singapore, and the President of Poland were all critical of financial markets while Jon Corzine of Goldman Sachs defended them. In the panel "Preventing and Managing Future Financial Crises" Robert E Rubin, US Treasury Secretary, defended a market-based economic system while Joseph Stiglitz talked about market failure in finance (WEF 1999o).
7. Although Sachs (2000a), one of the early proponents of the benefits of liberalization, remained fairly pro-market he expressed scepticism of the free markets as the answer to development, especially in Africa. US President Clinton, UK Prime Minister Blair, Louis Schweitzer, CEO of Renault, George Soros and Joseph Stiglitz all presented views highlighting the limitations of the free market mechanism (WEF 2000e; Crane 2000a; Crane 2000b). Others such as Ernesto Zedillo, President of Mexico, and Vaclav Klaus, former Czech Minister of Finance, maintained their belief in market processes as the solution (WEF 2000f; Czech News Agency 2000a; Freeman 2000b; Barbur and Jonquieres 2000a).
8. This panel included Bono, Desmond Tutu, Her Majesty Queen Rania, Gloria Macapagal Arroyo, President of the Philippines, and Elie Wiesel, with Charlie Rose as moderator.
9. For example in 2000 there were a number of panels on financial liberalization and what regulatory or supervisory systems might be most appropriate (WEF 2000a). Concerns were expressed with respect to the difficulties involved in calculating risk in the increasingly complex global financial

markets (WEF 2000o). There were sessions on avoiding financial crises and the progress in establishing the G20 (Martin 2000a). In 2001 there were sessions on microfinance and the usual ones on stability. In the 2002 breakfast session on global financial markets there was no mention of Africa or the possible human impact of the concern that foreign investment funds might be drying up in Latin America (de Souza 2002; see also WEF 2002h). In 2003 panels were devoted to managing the technical challenges of finance and the difficult-to-balance relationship between regulation, trust and financial innovation. While there were some critical voices decrying the lack of corporate ethics and the "new breed of businessman [who] has gone out into the world intent on making a fast buck", the human impact of financial crisis was absent (WEF 2003g).

10. Although, in the end, Bono was unable to attend in 2001, this was the beginning of an important relationship (WEF 2001h).
11. Parson Weems was the author of the apocryphal story about George Washington and the cherry tree. In this quote "Parson Weems" stands for an exaggerated and outdated moral code of proper behaviour.

5 Conclusion

1. It is worth recalling that while market logic is an effective way of maximizing benefit for those goods and services included in its calculus, it is notoriously blind to others which have been defined as external to its logic. These externalities typically include environmental and social "goods" which are difficult to quantify and therefore do not lend themselves to the forms of calculation available by means of market processes.
2. There were often connections between these campaigns and the campaign for debt cancellation that would be fascinating to explore but this would be well beyond the scope of a single book.
3. This discussion draws on Keck and Sikkink (1999).
4. It is striking however, that although the benefits of strict market discipline were discredited with respect to financial liberalization in the case of international trade the discourse did not change in the same way. If anything the commitment to free trade as the preferred remedy to economic inequality and as a means of achieving economic development appears to have grown during this period.

Selected References and Interviews

Selected references

Abdelal, Rawi. 2007. *Capital Rules*. Cambridge and London: Harvard University Press.

Abdelal, Rawi, Mark Blyth and Craig Parsons eds 2010. *Constructing the International Economy*. Ithaca, NY: Cornell University Press.

Act Up. 2006, at www.actup.org, June 30, 2006.

Aggarwal, Vinod and Horst Schulman. 1991a. "Debt Forgiveness: Dangerous Trend or Absolute Necessity?" *World Link*, 5: 37–39.

Annan, Kofi. 2002. "Special Message from Kofi Annan, Secretary General of the United Nations 04.02.2002." *Session Summaries* at http://www2.weforum.org/site/knowledgenavigator.nsf/Content/, January 21, 2009.

Annan, Kofi. 1998. "Kofi Annan." *World Link*, March/April: 13–14.

Annan, Kofi.1997. "Partnership for Prosperity and Justice." *World Link*, March/April: 17.

Anonymous International Public Servant. 2008. See Interview list.

Anonymous Transnational Activist. 2005. See Interview list.

Anthony, Debra and José Silva. 2005. "'GROUP OF 19': THE CONSENSUS OF PORTO ALEGRE?" at http://www.ipsterraviva.net/tv/wsf2005/print.asp?idnews=153, November 30, 2008.

Anti-capitalist Convergence. 2006. "About the ACC," at abolishthebank.org/about the acc.shtml May 16, 2006.

Arnold, Tom. 2004. "You Want Markets to Sell into, You Need to Help Africa." *Business and Finance*, February 12, 2004.

Arrighi, Giovanni. 1994. *The Long Twentieth Century*. London: Verso.

Ash, Timothy Garton. 2001. "Money See, Money Do." *The Globe and Mail* (Canada), February 2: A15.

Associated Press. 2002. "Terror Haunts Forum." *Herald Sun* (Melbourne), January 29: Business 45.

Atkinson, Mark. 2000. "Those Other Bug Killers That Could Rescue the World from Disaster." *The Guardian* (London), January 31: City 23.

ATTAC. 2003, at attac.org.uk/attac/html/about.um, December 17, 2003.

ATTAC. 2002. "NGO Statement: the Public Eye on Davos." at http://www.attac.de/archive/010125wefstatement.php, June 13, 2007.

Avant, Deborah D., Martha Finnemore and Susan K. Sell. 2010a. *Who Governs the Globe?* Cambridge: Cambridge University Press.

Avant, Deborah D., Martha Finnemore and Susan K. Sell. 2010b. "Conclusion: Authority, Legitimacy and Accountability in Global Politics" in *Who Governs the Globe?*" Avant, Finnemore and Sell eds, Cambridge: Cambridge University Press.

Ayres, Jeffrey M. 2003. "Global Civil Society and International Protest: No Swan Song Yet for the State" in *Global Civil Society and Its Limits*, ed. G. Laxer and S. Halpern. New York: Palgrave Macmillan, 25–42.

Bakker, Isabella, ed. 1994. *The Strategic Silence: Gender and Economic Policy.* London: Zed.

Bandy, Joe and Jackie Smith. 2005. "Factors Affecting Conflict and Cooperation in Transnational Movement Networks" In *Coalitions across Borders,* ed. Joe Bandy and Jackie Smith. New York: Rowman and Littlefield, 231–252.

Bank for International Settlements (BIS). 1999. "Comments on the Reports on the International Financial Architecture August 1999." at http://www.bis.org/publ/othp03.pdf, November 12, 2002.

Bank Information Center (BIC). 2006. at http://bicusa.org, May 16, 2006.

Barber, Lionel and Guy de Jonquieres. 2000. "Comment and Analysis: That's Snowbiz: Is Davos Losing Its Purpose? Despite All the Glitz and Commercialism the World's Power Elite Would Not Miss the Chance to Brainstorm Together." *Financial Times,* January 29: 14.

Barlow, Maude and Tony Clarke. 2001. *Global Showdown How the New Activists Are Fighting Global Corporate Rule.* Toronto: Stoddart.

Barrett, Jennifer. 2002. "World Economic Forum: A Post Mortem." *Newsweek Web Exclusive,* February 5, at http://www.lexisnexis.com.proxy.library.carleton.ca/lnacui2api/api/version1/getDocCui?lni=45TJ-V8X0-00KP-N4KF&csi=5774&hl=t&hv=t&hnsd=f&hns=t&hgn=t&oc=00240&perma=true, April 17, 2007.

BBC Worldwide Monitoring. 2003a. "Tanzania's Mkapa on Globalization at Economic Forum in Davos, Switzerland." *BBC Monitoring Africa – Political The Guardian web site, Dares Salaam,* January 27 at http://www.lexisnexis.com.proxy.library.carleton.ca/us/lnacademic/delivery/PrintDoc.do?fromCart=fals..., December 27, 2007.

BBC Worldwide Monitoring. 2003b. "Swiss Ready to Shoot Down Unauthorized Aircraft Over Davos." *Swiss Info Website BBC Monitoring Europe – Political* January 15 at http://www.lexisnexis.com.proxy.library.carleton.ca/us/lnacademic/frame.do?tokenKey=rsh-20.68767.1..., December 27, 2007.

Beattie, Alan. 2006. "Data Show Real-Term Aid Fell in 'Year of Africa.'" *Financial Times,* December 6.

Beattie, Alan. 2004. "G7 Meeting Urged to Seek Currency Market Calm." *Financial Times* (London), January 26: International Economy 8.

Bello, Walden. 2001. "When Davos Meets Porto Alegre: A Memoir." *zNet,* February 1 at http://www.zcommunications.org/when-davos-meets-porto-alegre-a-memoir-by-walden-bello, November 8, 2011.

Best, Jacqueline. 2006. "Co-opting Cosmopolitanism? The International Monetary Fund's New Global Ethics." *Global Society,* 20(3): 307–327.

Best, Jacqueline. 2005. *The Limits of Transparency.* Ithaca, NY: Cornell University Press.

Bevanger, Lars. 2001. "Who Are the Genoa Protestors?" at http://news.bbc.co.uk/2/hi/europe/1450323.stm, August 19, 2009.

Bhagwati, Jagdish. 2001. "Corporate Conduct." *World Link,* March/April: 29.

Bienefeld, Manfred. 1996. "Is a Strong National Economy a Utopian Goal at the End of the Twentieth Century?" In *States Against Markets,* ed. Robert Boyer and Daniel Drache. London and New York: Routledge.

Birchfield, Vicki. 1999. "Contesting the Hegemony of Market Ideology," *Review of International Political Economy* 1: 27–54.

Birchfield, Vicki and Annette Freyberg-Inan. 2005. "The Case of Attac." in *Critical Theories, International Relations and 'the Anti-Globalisation Movement:*

The Politics of Global Resistance, ed. Catherine Eschle and Bice Maiguashca. London and New York: Routledge: 154–173.

Blyth, Mark. 2002. *Great Transformations: Economic Ideas and Institutional Change in the Twentieth Century*. Cambridge: Cambridge University Press.

Bono. 1999. "World debt Angers Me." *Guardian*, Tuesday February 16. www.guardian.co.uk/print/0,3858,3822490-103677,00.html, November 8, 2011.

Boorman, Jack. 1998. "Devils in the Detail of Debt Relief." *Guardian*, Monday November 9.

Bott, Martin. 2004. "Swiss Fear Violence at Davos Summit." *The Independent* (London), January 20: Foreign News 10.

Brasset, James and Richard Higgott. 2003. "Building the Normative Dimensions of a Global Polity." *Review of International Studies* 29: 29–55.

Braudel, Fernand. 1979/1992. *Civilization and Capitalism, Vol. III, The Perspective of the World*. Trans Sian Reynolds. Berkeley: University of California Press.

Braudel, Fernand. 1979/1982. *Civilization and Capitalism, Vol. II, The Wheels of Commerce*. Trans Sian Reynolds. New York: Harper and Row.

Braudel, Fernand. 1979/1981. *Civilization and Capitalism, Vol. I, The Structures of Everyday Life*. Trans Sian Reynolds. New York: Harper and Row.

Bretton Woods Project (BWP). 2006. at http://brettonwoodsproject.org/, May 29, 2006.

British Broadcasting Corporation (BBC). 2006. at http://news.bbc.co.uk/onthisday/hi/dates/stories/july/13/newsid_2502000/2502735.stm, November 8, 2011.

British Broadcasting Corporation (BBC) 2000. "Debt Pressure on Richest Countries." BBC Thursday, 20 July at http://news.bbc.co.uk/2/hi/asia-pacific/843185.stm, August 19, 2009.

Brittan, Samuel. 1995a. "Davos Notebook: Mexico Will Not Be the Last Shock." *Financial Times* (London), February 2: 22.

Brittain, Victoria. 1999a. "The Economics Page; Comment/Rousseau revisited by Alternative Davos; Victoria Brittain on Impetus of Another Global Agenda." *Guardian* (London), February 1: 19.

Brittain, Victoria. 1999b. "Environment: High Pressure; As the World's Political and Economic Powers Met in the Swiss Alps Last Weekend, the Tenets of Their Elitist Faith Were Met with a Serious Challenge." *Guardian* (London), February 3: 4.

Brown, Gordon. 2005. "Striking a New Deal between Rich and Poor." *Global Agenda*, January: 90–91.

Brysk, Alison. 2009. *Global Good Samaritans: Human Rights as Foreign Policy*. Oxford: Oxford University Press.

Bunting, Madeline. 1999. "Why the Debt Campaign Is So Important," *Guardian Unlimited*, Wednesday June 16, at http://www.guardian.co.uk/world/1999/jun/16/debtrelief.development, November 8, 2011.

Busby, Joshua William. 2007. "Bono Made Jesse Helms Cry: Jubilee 2000, Debt Relief, and Moral Action in International Politics." *International Studies Quarterly*, 51: 247–275.

The Business. 2005. "Drivel in Davos." *The Business*, January 30: 13.

Canadian Conference of Catholic Bishops (CCCB). 1999. "Letter to PM Chrétien re: Third World Debt Cancellation and Upcoming G-8 Meeting in Cologne" at http://www.cccb.ca/site/eng/media-room/archives/public-statements/1999/800-letter-to-pm-chren-re-third-world-debt-cancellation-and-upcoming-g-8-meeting-in-cologne, November 8, 2011.

Canadian Security and Intelligence Service (CSIS). 2000. "Anti-Globalization – a Spreading Phenomenon," Perspectives Report #2000/08 August 22, at http://www.csis.gc.ca/pblctns/prspctvs/200008-eng.asp, November 8, 2011.

Carnegy, Hugh. 2002. "Davos Man Takes to the Streets of New York." *Financial Times* (London), February 1: International Economy 11.

Carnegy, Hugh. 2001. "Guilt Stings West to Rush of Fine Intent" *Financial Times*, January 30 at http://specials.ft.com/davos2001/FT32SBTJLIC.html, December 12, 2007.

Carnegy, Hugh and Lionel Barber. 2001. "Davos 2001 – Day Four – News and Analysis Fox Points Out the Dangers of Globalisation." *FT.com – Special reports/ Davos 2001*. at http://specials.ft.com/davos2001/FT351H45KIC.html, December 17, 2007.

Carpenter, R. Charli 2010 "Governing the Global Agenda: 'Gatekeepers' and 'Issue Adoption' in Transnational Advocacy Networks." in *Who Governs the Globe?* Avant, Finnemore and Sell eds, Cambridge: Cambridge University Press.

Carr, Jonathan. 1986. "Salvation Glimpsed from High on Swiss Alp." *Financial Times* (London), February 5: I 2.

Carr, Jonathan. 1985. "Europe's Wise Men Bow Down to the U.S. Boom." *Financial Times* (London), February 5: I 16.

Carr, Jonathan. 1984a. "World Bank Chief Seeks End to 'Negative Transfers'." *Financial Times* (London) January 27: European News 2.

Carr, Jonathan. 1984b. "Big Deals and Small Talk in Davos's High-Class Bazaar." *Financial Times*, February 2: I 2.

Carter, Jimmy. 2004. "The Human Right to Peace." *Global Agenda*, January: 60–61.

Castells, Manuel. 1996. *The Information Age: Economy, Society and Culture Volume I The Rise of Network Society*. Oxford: Blackwell.

Castells, Manuel. 1997. *The Information Age: Economy, Society and Culture Volume II The Power of Identity*. Oxford: Blackwell.

The Catholic Agency for Overseas Development (CAFOD). at cafod.org.uk, November 10, 2006.

The Catholic Institute for International Relations (CIIR) 2007 at www.ciir.org, January 30, 2007.

Caulkin, Simon. 2005. "Business: Management: Time for a Commercial Break: Markets Are All Very Well, But Using Them Internally Or in the Public Sector Can Be Dangerous." *Observer*, March 6: 11.

Center of Concern (CoC) 2006. at www.coc.org/, October 16, 2006.

Centre for Economic Policy Research (CEPR UK). 2006. "Global Economic Institutions (GEI) Research Programme." www.cepr.org/gei/moregei.htm, October 31, 2006.

Centre de Recherche et d'information pour le Développement (CRID) 2006 at http://www.globenet.org/ifi/, June 08, 2006.

Cernetig, Miro. 2002. "Enron's Fall Darkens Summit: Leaders at Global Forum Fear Effects of Giant's Collapse." *Globe and Mail* (Canada), February 1: B1.

Cerny, Philip G. 2009. "Multi-Nodal Politics: Globalisation Is What Actors Make of It." *Review of International Studies*. 35: 421–449.

Cherian, George. 1994a. "Welfare State Comes Under Attack." *Straits Times*, January 31: 10.

Cherian, George. 1994b. "Rao: Reforms to Continue But with Measure of Humaneness." *Straits Times*, February 3: 2.

Chernow Ron. 1990. *The House of Morgan*. New York: Grove Press.
Chirac, Jacques. 2005. "Speech to Davos World Economic Forum January 26, 2005." at www.currencytax.org/governments_respond/resolutions_motions_bills.php#182, June 22, 2006.
Chirac, Jacques. 2003. "Bring Fairness to Globalization; the Group of Eight." *International Herald Tribune* January 25: Opinion 8.
Christian Aid. 2006. at Christian-aid,org.uk, October 16, 2006.
Chweiroth, Jeffrey. 2010. *Capital Ideas: The IMF and the Rise of Financial Liberalization*. Princeton: Princeton University Press.
Chweiroth, Jeffrey. 2008. "Organizational Change from within: Exploring the World Bank's Early Lending Practices." *Review of International Political Economy* 15(4): 481–505.
Clarke, Tony and Maude Barlow. 2001. *Global Showdown: How the New Activists are Fighting Global Corporate Rule*. Toronto: Stoddart.
Clarke, Tony and Maude Barlow. 1997. *MAI the Multilateral Agreement in Investment and the Threat to Canadian Sovereignty*. Toronto: Stoddart.
Clinton, Bill. 2004. "Session Summary Opening Lunch 21.01.2004." at www.weforum.org/node/98058, November 23, 2011.
Clinton, William J. 2000. "Address to the Annual Meeting 2000, Davos Switzerland, 29 January 2000." *Documents*. Geneva: WEF at http://archive.bibalex.org/web/20000816041526/weforum.org/davos.nsf/Documents/Home+-+Annual+Meeting+-+Address+by+US+President+Clinton, April 04, 2006.
Cohen, Andrew. 2001. "Davos Report: Keeping the Faith" *World Link* March/April: 40.
Cohen, Barry. 1995. "Soros: Leaving Mount Olympus." *World Link*, January/February: 113–116.
Cohen, Benjamin J. 1998. *The Geography of Money*. Ithaca, NY: Cornell.
Cohen, Benjamin J. 1996. "Phoenix Risen The Resurrection of Global Finance." *World Politics*, 48 January: 268–296.
Cohen, Benjamin J. 1977. *Organizing the World's Money*. New York: Basic Books.
Colitt, Raymond and Ed Crooks. 2003. "Business Audience Hails Lula Speech." *Financial Times* (London), January 27: World News 6.
Collins, Carole J L, Zie Gariyo and Tony Burdon. 2001. "Jubilee 2000: Citizen Action Across the North South Divide." In *Global Citizen Action*, eds M. Edwards and J. Gaventa. Boulder: Lynne Rienner.
Commission for Africa. 2005. *Our Common Interest: Report of the Commission for Africa*. March at http://assets.mediaglobal.org/documents/Our_Common_Interest_Commission_For_Africa.pdf, December 15, 2009.
Comité pour l'annulation de la Dette du Tiers Monde (CADTM). 2006. at www.cadtm.org/, June 08, 2006.
Comité pour l'annulation de la Dette du Tiers Monde (CADTM) 2003. "About the CADTM?" at www.cadtm.org/imprimer.php3?id_article=246, June 08, 2006.
Cook, Peter. 1992. "The Triumph of Capitalism." *Globe and Mail*, February 15: B21.
Cookson, Clive. 2001. "INTERNATIONAL ECONOMY: Gates Boosts Aids Research with Dollars 100m." *Financial Times* (London), January 29: 7.
Cooper, Andrew F. 2008. *Celebrity Diplomacy*. Boulder, CO and London: Paradigm.
Cooper, Marc. 2002. "50,000 Celebrate Official Opening of the World Social Forum." *The Nation* February 1 at http://www.thenation.com/article/letter-p%C3%B4rto-alegre-2, November 8, 2011.

Cooperstone, Cynthia. 1998a. "And What about my Soul? Searching for a Deeper Meaning in Life." *1998 Annual Meeting Report*. Geneva: WEF at web.archive.org/web/19990224134315/www.weforum.org/activities/annual_meeting/last_year_re... April 19, 2007.

Copetas, A. Craig, 2008 "Warnings Ignored, Forum Says." *National Post*. October 25: FP20.

Cowell, Alan. 2005. "In Davos, Spotlight Turns to Africa." *International Herald Tribune*, January 28: News 1.

Cowell, Alan. 2004a. "Davos Forum Faces Host of Economic Uncertainties." *International Herald Tribune*, January 21: News 1.

Cowell, Alan. 2004c. "Economic Talks Draw Elite to Davos, But Have No Salient Issue." *The New York Times*, January 21: A5.

Cowell, Alan. 2003b. "Tear Gas Keeps Away Protestors at Davos." *The International Herald Tribune*, January 27: News 3.

Cowell, Alan. 1999. "Annan Fears Backlash over Global Crisis." *The New York Times*, February 1: A14.

Cox, Robert. 1986. "Social Forces States and World Orders." in *Neoliberalism and Its Critics*, ed.. Robert Keohane. New York: Columbia University Press.

Cox, Robert. 1983/1993. "Gramsci, Hegemony, and International Relations." in *Gramsci, Historical Materialism and International Relations*, ed. Stephen Gill. Cambridge: Cambridge University Press.

Crane, David. 2002a. "Economic Forum Visits Big Apple." *The Toronto Star*, January 31: Sports 3.

Crane, David. 2002b. "Enron Casts Dark Cloud Over Forum." *The Toronto Star*, February 4: A2.

Crane, David. 2001. "Summit's Hot Button is Globalization." *The Toronto Star*, January 28: NEWS.

Crane, David. 2000a. "The Battle of Seattle Echoes at Davos Forum." *The Toronto Star*, January 29: Business.

Crane, David. 2000b. "China Marches on Despite Huge Obstacles." *The Toronto Star*, February 3: Business.

Crane, David. 1999a. "Learning to live with Global Volatility." *The Toronto Star*, February 6: Business.

Crane, David. 1999b. "No Easy Way to Curb Currency Speculation." *The Toronto Star*, February 13: Business.

Crane, David. 1997a. "Beware of Globalization Backlash." *The Toronto Star*, February 1: E2.

Crane, David. 1997b. "U.N. Chief Issues Poverty Challenge Says Big Business Has Obligation to Poor Countries." *The Toronto Star*, February 2: A13.

Crane, David. 1996a. "Harris on Investment Trail Says World Business Leaders Have Wrong Idea about Ontario." *The Toronto Star*, February 5: D6.

Crane, David. 1992. "Aid Plan Crucial to New Soviet States." *The Toronto Star*, February 2: H4.

Crane, David. 1990. "Foreign Aid Easy Target for Budget-Cutters But It Keeps Third World from Growing." *The Toronto Star*, February 5: C4.

Crane, David. 1989a. "Plan to Slash Third World Debt a Priority for U.S. and Europe." *The Toronto Star*, January 29: A1.

Crane, David. 1989b. "Promise of Better, More United World Depends on Political Will, Forum Told." *The Toronto Star*, February 4: C2.

Crane, David. 1989c. "Problems in the Global Village Need a New Form of Diplomacy." *The Toronto Star*, February 4: D2.
Crane, David. 1988a. "We Could Play An Important Role with Innovative Foreign Policy." *The Toronto Star*, February 6: C2.
Culpeper, Roy. 2008. See Roy Culpeper interview.
Czech News Agency. 2000a. "Klaus Warns Against Third Way at Economic Forum." *Czech News Agency*, January 29 at lexisnexis.com.proxy.library.carleton.ca/universe/document?_m=82c160e43b865ff4cfef8488...June 14, 2007.
Davies, Howard. 1999. "The Davos Menu." *World Link*, March/April: 14.
Dávila, Francisco Suárez. 1999. "The Developing Countries and the International Financial System." In *G-24: The Developing Countries in the International System*, ed. Eduardo Mayobre. Boulder, CO: Lynne Rienner.
Davis, Bob and David Wessell. 1998. "World Bank, IMF Art Odds Over Asian Austerity." *Wall Street Journal*, January 8.
Davis, Steven. 2004. See Steven Davis interview.
Days of dissent. 2006. "We Will Disrupt This Conference" at www.daysofdissent.org.uk/berlin.htm, May 8, 2011.
Dean, Mitchell. 1999. *Governmentality: Power and Rule in Modern Society*. London: Sage.
de Goede, Marieke. 2005. *Virtue, Fortune and Faith*. Minneapolis: University of Minnesota Press.
de Goede, Marieke. 2003. "Beyond Economism in International Political Economy." *Review of International Studies* 29: 79–97.
de Rato, Rodrigo. 2005. "Is the IMF's mandate still relevant?" *Global Agenda*, January: 103–105.
Debt AIDS Trade Africa (DATA). 2006. "What is Data" at www.data.org/whydata/, June 01, 2006
della Porta, Donatella, and Mario Diani. 1999. *Social Movements: An Introduction*. Oxford: Blackwell.
Dette et Développement (Dette). 2006. at www.dette2000.org/, June 08, 2006.
Development Group for Alternative Policies (Development GAP). 2009. at www.developmentgap.org August 5, 2009.
Dillon, John. 2005. "Analysis of the Gleneagles 2005 G8 Summit." *Kairos*, July 1, at http://www.kairoscanada.org/en/rights-and-trade/news-list/news/archive/2005/07/browse/10/article/reflections-on-the-gleneagles-2005-g8-summit/?tx_ttnews%5BbackPid%5D=142&cHash=eb466f4232, November 06, 2009.
Dillon, John. 2008. See John Dillon interview.
Dissent. 2006. at dissent.org.uk, May 12, 2006.
Downic, Andrew. 2003. "Brazil's New Leader Takes on An Unlikely Global Role." *Christian Science Monitor* (Boston), January 27: World 07.
Drohan, Madelaine. 1996. "Economic Forum a Clamour for Cash." *Globe and Mail* (Canada), February 5.
Drohan, Madelaine. 1995. "Davos Notebook Russian Team Fails to Put Up United Front at Forum." *Globe and Mail* (Canada), January 31.
Dugger, Celia W. 2005. "Commission on Poverty in Africa Seeks a Doubling of Aid." *The New York Times*, March 12: A3.
Dullforce, William. 1990. "Sun Fails to Dispel Overcast Global View." *Financial Times* (London), February 7: 2.

Dullforce, William. 1988. "Clouded Views From a Swiss Alp." *Financial Times* (London), February 3: 13.
Duncan Gary. 2005. "Stars Show Their Stripes in Battle for the Lost Continent." *The Times* (London) January 28: 41.
The Economist. 2001. "The Third Way (An Encore)." *The Economist* (US Edition), May 19.
The Economist. 2000. "Angry and Effective." *The Economist* (US Edition), September 23.
The Economist. 1998. "Keeping the Hot Money Out." *The Economist* (US Edition), January 24: 69.
The Economist. 1997. "In Praise of Davos Man." *The Economist* (US Edition), February 1: 18.
The Economist. 1996. "Networking Off-Piste in Davos." *The Economist* (US Edition), February 10: 75.
The Economist. 1987. "Magic Mountains for the Mind; Davos the Symposium as Industry." *The Economist,* December 26: 20.
The Economist. 1985. "Management; Apple-Pie Acumen Replaces Sake Savvy." *The Economist,* February 9: 54.
The Economist. 1980. "Buy Tomorrow Like Japan." *The Economist,* February 14: 18.
Eichengreen, Barry. 1999. "The Future of the International Financial Architecture, a Council on Foreign Relations Task Force." *Foreign Affairs* 6: 169–184.
Eichengreen, Barry. 1995. *Golden Fetters*. New York: Oxford.
Elkington, John. 2004. "It's the System, Stupid!" at http://www.opendemocracy.net/node/1711, November 18, 2008.
Elkington, John. 2003. "The Road to Davos." *Open Democracy,* January 16. at http://www.opendemocracy.net/globalization-institutions_government/article_899.jsp, November 8, 2011.
Elliot, Larry. 2005a. "Elephant in the Room Can't Leave It All Up to Sharon: Skating on Thin Ice." *Guardian* (London), January 31: City 23.
Elliot, Larry. 2005b. "CBI Chief Claims Davos Hijacked" by NGOs." *Guardian* (London) January 31: Home 2.
Elliot, Larry. 2004a. "Business and Media: UN Secretary Warns of World Ruled by Law of the Jungle." *Guardian* (London), January 24: City 23.
Elliot, Larry. 2004b. "Clinton Doctrine: No Way Back on Globalisation, Ex-President Tells Davos." *Guardian* (London), January 22: City 20.
Elliot, Larry. 2001a. "World Economic Forum: the South Rises as Bush Fails to Show: behind the Cordon, a Confession. Globalisation Is Not Delivering." *Guardian* (London), January 27: City 28.
Elliott, Larry. 2001b. "Economics: Opening Gambit without Strategy." *Guardian* (London), January 29: City 23.
Elliot, Larry. 1999. "G7 Look at Plans for Debt Relief." *Guardian* (London), February 19: 2.
Elliot, Larry. 1998a. "Flat Earth Gurus Convert." *Guardian* (London), February 2: 19.
Elliot, Larry. 1998b. "Davos Notebook: No Asylum from World's Sickness." *Guardian* (London), January 31: 24.
Elliot, Larry. 1997. "Davos Notebook: New Labour Lets the Chance Slip" *Guardian* (London), February 1: 22.

Elliot, Larry. 1996a. "Davos Notebook: Infantry Loses Out in Battle of Dole." *Guardian* (London), February 3: 31.
Elliot, Larry. 1996b. "Mexico's Woes Dwarfed by Those Facing Russia." *Guardian* (London), February 5: 15.
Engler, Mark. 2005a. "John Paul II's Economic Ethics." *Foreign Policy in Focus*, April 5 at http://www.fpif.org/articles/john_paul_iis_economic_ethics, November 8, 2011.
Engler, Mark. 2005b. "Historic Victories, New Challenges." *Foreign Policy in Focus*, May 17 at http://www.fpif.org/reports/historic_victories_new_challenges, November 8, 2011.
Engler, Mark. 2005c. "The last Porto Alegre." *Foreign Policy in Focus*, February 24 at http://www.fpif.org/reports/the_last_porto_alegre, November 8, 2011.
Epstein, Charlotte. 2010. "Moby Dick or Moby Doll? Discourse, or How to Study the "Social Construction of' All the Way Down." in *Constructing the International Economy*. Abdelal, Blythe, and Parsons eds Ithaca, NY: Cornell University Press.
The Equator Principles. 2009. at http://equator-principles.com/resources/equator_principles.pdf, November 8, 2011.
Escobar, Arturo. 1995. *Encountering Development*. Princeton: Princeton University Press.
European Network on Debt and Development (EURODAD). 2006a. eurodad.org, May 29, 2006.
Ferguson, Jonathan. 1988. "Sony Chief's Criticism Offends Executives." *The Toronto Star*, February 4: A2.
50 Years is Enough. 2004. "50 years is enough." at http://www.50years.org/pdf/10thAnniversary/history.pdf, August 17, 2009.
50 Years is Enough. 2002. "Network Platform and Demands to the World Bank." at 50years.org, November 13, 2003.
50 Years is Enough. 2000. "World Social Forum: Porto Alegre, Brazil." *Economic Justice News*, 3 September at www.50years.org/ejn/v3n/brazil.html, November 13, 2003.
50 Years is Enough. 1994. "Original Platform of 1994." at http://www.50years.org/about/94platform.html#top, August 17, 2009.
Finance Canada. 2005a. "Helping the Poorest – An Update on Canada's Debt Relief Efforts." at http://www.fin.gc.ca/toc/2005/cdre0105_-eng.asp, November 8, 2011.
Finance Canada. 2005b. at fin.gc.ca/news01/01-105e.html, November 11, 2005.
The Financial Times. 2001. "Over 30 Years of Schmooze!" at http://specials.ft.com/davos2001/FT31N8TMEIC.html, November 9, 2011.
The Financial Times. 1983. "Slippery Slopes." *Financial Times* (London), February 2: I12.
Fleck, Fiona. 2004a. "World Forum Protest Staged From a Distance." *The New York Times*, January 25: 1–10.
Fleck, Fiona. 2004b. "Antiglobalization Forces Shift to Pragmatic Tactics; Global Economic Outlook." *International Herald Tribune*, January 21: Special Report 17.
Focus on the Global South (Focus). 1999. "Focus on the Global South Annual Report 1999." at www.focusweb.org/publications/Annual%20Report/anrep99.pdf, June 08, 2006.
Foster, Pam. 2008. See Pam Foster interview.

Foucault, Michel. 1983. "Afterword The Subject and Power." in *Michel Foucault: Beyond Structuralism and Hermeneutics* second edn, ed. Herbert Dreyfus and Paul Rabinow. second edn. Chicago: University of Chicago Press: 208–226.

Foucault, Michel. 1977. *Discipline and Punish: The Birth of the Prison.* trans. Alan Sheridan. New York: Pantheon Books.

Foucault, Michel. 1976/1980. "Lecture Two: 14 January 1976." in *Power/Knowledge selected Interviews and Other Writings 1972 – 1977,* ed. Colin Gordon. trans. Colin Gordon, Leo Marshall, John Mepham, Kate Soper. New York, London: Harvester Wheatsheaf.

Fraser, Barbara and Paul Jeffrey. 2004. "Looking Ahead: Church Groups Seek New Models of Solidarity." *National Catholic Reporter,* November 26: 14.

Fréchette, Louise. 2008. "Reflections on the Role and Future of the UN." Presentation February 29 at the Center on Values and Ethics, Carleton University, Ottawa.

Freeman, Alan. 2000a. "Economic Activists Set Their Sights on Davos Get-Together." *Globe and Mail,* January 27: A10.

Freeman, Alan. 2000b. "Blair Urges Fresh Round of Trade Talks; But WTO Debacle in Seattle Has Cast Pall Over Annual Gathering of Business Elite." *Globe and Mail,* January 29: A10.

Freeman, Alan. 1999. "Elite gets together for schmooze-fest. The mix of business and political leaders is at the heart of the World Economic Forum." *Globe and Mail,* January 29: A17.

Freeman, Alan. 1998. "Oracle chairman fumes of Microsoft the View from Davos: Ellison takes his spat with Gates to the World Economic Forum." *The Globe and Mail Report on Business,* February 3: B15.

Fried, Mark. 2008. See Mark Fried interview.

Frieden, Jeffrey. 1991. "Invested Interests: the Politics of National Economic Policies in a World of Global Finance." *International Organization,* Autumn: 425–451.

Friedman, Milton. 1999. "Confirmed Convictions." *World Economic Affairs,* Winter: 50–56.

G7. 2002. "Statement of G7 Finance Ministers, June 2002." at http://www.g-7.ca/final_halifax_e.html, November 12, 2002.

G7 Finance Ministers. 1998. "Strengthening the Architecture of the Global Financial System: Report of G7 Financial Ministers to G7 Heads of State or Government for their meeting in Birmingham in 1998" at http://www.g7.utoronto.ca/finance/, December 17, 2009.

G20. 2001. "News release, Meeting of the G20 Finance Ministers and Central Bank Governors Nov 16–17, 2001." at http://www.g20.org/news/003-e.html, November 12, 2002.

Galbraith, John Kenneth. 1983. *The Anatomy of Power.* Boston: Houghton Mifflin.

Gale, Fred and Marcus Haward. 2011. *Global Commodity Governance.* Basingstoke: Palgrave Macmillan.

Gates, Bill. 2008. "Making Capitalism more Creative." *Time.com,* July 31 at http://www.time.com/time/magazine/article/0,9171,1828417,00.html, November 9, 2011.

GATT-Fly. 1985. *Debt Bondage or Self Reliance, A Popular Perspective on the Global Debt Crisis.* Toronto: GATT-fly.

Geller, Andy. 2001. "Gates Pledges $100M to fight AIDS. *The New York Post,* January 28: O28.
George, Jim. 1994. *Discourses of Global Politics.* Boulder, CO: Lynne Rienner.
George, Susan. 2007. See Susan George interview.
George, Susan. 1992a. "Uses and Abuses of African Debt the International Squeeze on poor Countries" published in Dissent (summer 1992), reprinted in *TNI Ideas,* November at tni.org June 15, 2006.
George Susan. 1992b. "The Debt Boomerang." at IPS-dc.org, June 15, 2006.
George, Susan. 1988. *A Fate Worse than Debt.* London:Penguin.
Germain, Randall. 2010. *Global Politics and Financial Governance.* Basingstoke: Palgrave Macmillan.
Germain, Randall. 2005. "Global Modalities of Financial Governance: the Public Sphere and Civil Society" in *The Idea of Global Civil Society: Politics and Ethics in a Globalizing Era.* Germain and Kenny eds London: Routledge.
Germain, Randall. 1997. *The International Organization of Credit.* Cambridge: Cambridge University Press.
Germain, Randall and Michael Kenny eds 2005a. *The Idea of Global Civil Society: Politics and Ethics in a Globalizing Era* London: Routledge.
Germain, Randall and Michael Kenny. 2005b. "Understanding Global civil society: contestation, citizenship governance." in *The Idea of Global Civil Society: Politics and Ethics in a Globalizing Era.* Germain and Kenny eds London: Routledge.
Geske, Mary. 2000. "Globalization is What States Make of It: Constructivism, US Foreign Economic Policy and the Peso Crisis." *International Politics,* 37(September): 301–322.
Getz, Arlene. 2004. "Business as Usual?" *Newsweek Web Exclusive,* January 16 at www.lexisnexis.com.proxy.library.carleton.ca/us/inacademic/delivery/PrintDoc.do?fromCart=fals…, December 27, 2007.
Getz, Arlene. 2003. "Seeking Common Ground." *Newsweek Web Exclusive,* January 24 at www.lexisnexis.com.proxy.library.carleton.ca/us/inacademic/delivery/PrintDoc.do?fromCart=fals…, December 27, 2007.
Gibson-Graham, J. K. 1996. *The End of Capitalism (As We Knew It): A Feminist Critique of Political Economy.* Oxford: Blackwell.
Gill, Stephen. 1995. "Globalisation, Market Civilisation, and Disciplinary Neoliberalism." *Millennium* 3: 399–423.
Gill, Stephen. 1990. *American Hegemony and the Trilateral Commission.* Cambridge: Cambridge University Press.
Globe and Mail. 1995. "Getting It Wrong on Mexico." *The Globe and Mail* (Canada), February 3.
Globe and Mail. 1993. "News Bulletins Russian Debt Deal Urged." *The Globe and Mail* (Canada), February 1.
Global Policy Forum (Global Policy). 2006. at globalpolicy.org, October 23, 2006.
God's Tears. 2005. *God's Tears.* Alliance Atlantis Communications.
Gramsci, Antonio. 1971. *Selections from the Prison Notebooks.* New York: International Publishers.
Graz, Jean-Christophe. 2003. "How Powerful are Transnational Elite Clubs? The Social Myth of the World Economic Forum." *New Political Economy* 8(3): 321–340.

Greenberg, Susan. 1996. "Life after History." *World Link,* January/ February: 48–53.
Greenhouse, Steven. 1991. "Poland Asks West to Cancel Most of Its Big Foreign Debt." *The New York Times,* February 4: D1.
Gumbel, Andrew. 2003. "On one Side of the World 2,000 Capitalists, on the Other 100,000 Social Activists; Porto Alegre Which of Them Will Inherit this Earth?" *Independent* (London). January 24: News 3.
Haas, Peter M. 1992. "Introduction: Epistemic Communities and International Policy Coordination." *Knowledge, Power and International Policy Coordination,* special issue of *International Organization* 46(1): 1–35.
Halifax Initiative. 2006. at http://www.halifaxinitiative.org, June 19, 2006.
Halifax Initiative. 2002. at http://www.halifaxinitiative.org, December 12, 2002.
Hall, Peter A. 1989. *The Political Power of Economic Ideas: Keynesianism across Nations.* Princeton, NJ: Princeton University Press.
Hallinan, Conn. 2006. "The Devil's Brew of Poverty Relief," July 19 at fpif. orgfpiftxt/3374, September 20, 2006.
Harris, Francis. 1996. "Democracy and Reform." *World Link,* March/April: 22–23.
Hayek, F. A. 1976. *Law, Legislation and Liberty. Volume 2: The Mirage of Social Justice.* Chicago: University of Chicago Press.
Heilbroner, R. L. 1996. *Teachings from the Worldly Philosophy.* New York: W. W. Norton.
Held, David. 2005. "Washington Gets It Wrong." *Global Agenda,* January: 100–101.
Held, David. 2004. *Global Covenant.* Cambridge: Polity.
Helleiner, Eric. 1994a. *States and the Reemergence of Global Finance.* Ithaca, NY: Cornell University Press.
Helleiner, 1994b. "From Bretton Woods to Global Finance." in *Political Economy and the Changing Global Order,* eds R. Stubbs and G. Underhill. Toronto: McClelland and Stewart.
Helleiner, Eric and Geoffrey Cameron. 2006. "Another World Order? the Bush Administration and HIPC Debt Cancellation." *New Political Economy* 11(1): 125–140.
Helleiner, Eric and Stefano Pagliari. 2011. "The End of an Era in International Financial Regulation? A Postcrisis Research Agenda." *International Organization,* 65 Winter 2011: 169–200.
Herald. 1993. "If I Ruled the World... I'D Probably Be a Man." *Herald,* (Glasgow), February 2: 4.
Herald. 1988. "AIDS 'huge' cost threat." *Herald,* February 3: Herald Business 15.
Herfkens, Eveline. 2005. "Eight Reasons Why Northern NGOs Should Frame Their Campaigns in the Context of the Millennium Goal 8." at www.millen-niumcampaign.org, October 6, 2006.
Hieber, Loretta. 2001. "Globalization: for better or Worse?" *World Economic Forum Annual Meeting Report.* Geneva: World Economic Forum: 15–16.
Hoagland, Jim. 1994. "2 Victors in Russia's Reform Battle." *The Washington Post,* February 2: A19.
Hoagland, Jim. 1989. "Bury the Baker Plan." *The Washington Post,* February 2: A25.
Hogg, Sarah. 1989. "Banks Should Be Helped to Cut Debt Burden, Says US." *Independent,* January 30: Business and City 18.

Hutton, Will. 1999. "Comment: Where World Leaders Can Get in Touch with Their Anger." *The Observer*, January 31: 28.
Hutton, Will. 1998. "Kinder Capitalists in Armani Specs." *Observer*, February 1: 22.
Hutton, Will. 1995. "Crisis in Mexico Should Puncture the Conservatives' Complacency." *Guardian* (London), January 30: City 30.
Hutton, Will. 1994. "Davos Notebook: What the World Prefers May Be Bad News for Jobs." *Guardian* (London), January 29: City 28.
Hutton, Will. 1993. "New Tribalism Threatens to Infect Us All." *Guardian* (London), February 1: City 11.
Hutton, Will. 1992. "Prince tells top bosses profit is not all." *Guardian* (London), February 5: Home 18.
IFIwatchnet. 2006. at ifiwatchnet.org/about/item.shtml?x=42993, June 19, 2006.
The Independent. 2002. "Outlook: Even Corporations Are Getting a Social Conscience." *Independent,* February 9: Business 19.
Indypendent. 2002. "WEF Calendar." *Indypendent* February 2001[sic]: at www.nyc.indymedia.org, October 15, 2004.
The Institute for International Finance. 2006. "Review of Last Annual Meeting." at www.iif.com/about/index.quagga, May 1, 2006.
The Institute for Policy Studies (IPS). 2006. at www.ips-dc.org/, June 15, 2006.
International Forum on Globalization (IFG). 2009. "History." at http://www.ifg.org/about/history.htm, August 18, 2009.
International Forum on Globalization (IFG). 2006. at www.ifg.org/, June 22, 2006.
International Monetary Fund (IMF) 2006. "Poverty and Social Impact Analysis of Economic Policies." at www.at imf.org/externatl/np/exr/facts/sia.htm, April 3, 2006.
Isaac, William M. 1996. "Maybe Time Has Come For Some Regulation To Be Left to the Market." *The American Banker*, February 15: 4.
Jacobs, Andrew. 2002. "Forum in New York: DEMONSTRATORS; Simple, If Radical Agendas Lead Thousands to Protest." *The New York Times*, February 3: Section 1, 17.
Jacobsen, John K. 2003. "Duelling Constructivisms: A Post-Mortem on the Ideas Debate in Mainstream IR/IPE." *Review of International Studies*, 29: 39–60.
James, Harold. 1996. *International Monetary Cooperation since Bretton Woods*. Washington, New York and Oxford: Oxford University Press.
Jebb, Fiona. 1992. "Economies Laid Waste." *World Link* November/December: 20–25.
Jenkins, J. Craig. 1983. "Resource Mobilization Theory and the Study of Social Movements." *Annual Review of Sociology* 9: 527–553.
Jeremic, Rusa. 2002. "A report from the 2002 World Social Forum." *Kairos* at http://www.kairoscanada.org/e/resources/wsf/rtpRusaWSF02.asp, December 19, 2007.
Jerusalem Post. 1997. "Arafat, PM Not Invited to Davos Summit." *The Jerusalem Post*, December 23: Economics 13.
Jiji Press Ticker Service. 1987. "Major Industrial Powers Likely to Hold Monetary Meeting in Davos." Jiji Press Ticker Service, January 12 at web.lexis-nexis.com.proxy.library.carleton.ca/universe/printdoc, April 30, 2007.
Jim. 2002."Brief History of the World Economic Forum." *Interactivist Info Exchange* January 7 at http://interactivist.autonomedia.org/node/640, November 9, 2011.

Johnston, Hank. 2011. *States and Social Movements.* Cambridge: Polity.
Johnston, Josée. 2003. "We Are All Marcos? *Zapatismo,* Solidarity and the Politics of Scale." in *Global Civil Society and Its Limits.* eds G. Laxer and S Halpern. New York: Palgrave Macmillan, 85–104.
Jonquieres, Guy de. 2004. "Davos Delegates Prepare for Round of Talks Set on Thin Ice: Falling Dollar Fears and Rifts between US and Allies Over Iraq Could Dominate This Year's World Economic Forum Says Guy De Jonquieres." *Financial Times* (London), January 19: 18.
Jonquieres, Guy de. 2000. "World Economic Forum: US Heads for Post-Seattle Talks with EU Trade Agenda." *Financial Times* (London), January 31: 10.
Jonquieres, Guy de and John Lloyd. 2001. "Davos 2001 – Comment To Have and Have Not." *FT.com – special Reports/ Davos 2001,* January 26 at http://specials.ft.com/davos2001/FT3CONNGGIC.html, December 12, 2007.
Jonquieres, Guy de and Holly Yeager. 2002. "Davos goes West." *Financial Times* (London), January 25: Comment and Analysis, 16.
Jubilee 2000. 2006a. "Who We Are." at www.web.archive.org/web/19981111185023/http://www.jubilee2000uk.org/, May 18, 2006.
Jubilee 2000. 2006b. "Pope John Paul Calls Debt 'the Shadow of Death'." at www.web.archive.org/web/19981111185023/http://www.jubilee2000uk.org/, May 18, 2006.
Jubilee 2000. 2005. at www.jubilee2000uk.org, November 21, 2005.
Jubilee Australia. 2006. at www.jubileeaustralia.org, June 12, 2006.
Jubilee Debt Campaign. 2006. "The Multilateral Debt Relief Initiative: The Good, the Bad and the Ugly." June 26 at http://www.jubileedebtcampaign.org.uk/?lid=2098, December 19, 2009.
Jubilee Debt Campaign. 2005a. "Origins of the Debt Movement" at www.jubileedebtcampaign.org.uk, November 21, 2005.
Jubilee Debt Campaign. 2005b. "The Birth of Jubilee 2000" at www.jubileedebt-campaign.org.uk/?lid=279&tmpl=jdcmainprint, November 9, 2011.
Jubilee Movement International. 2002. at http://www.jubilee2000uk.org/jmi/main.htm, November 12, 2002.
Jubilee Research. 2007. "What Happened When." at jubileeresearch.org/jubilee2000/final/when.html, January 30, 2007.
Jubilee Research. 2006a. "ACCRA Declaration." at www.jubileeresearch.org/jubilee2000/accra.html, June 13, 2006.
Jubilee Research. 2006b. "Jubilee 2000 Petition." at jubileeresearch.org/jubilee2000/petition.html, June 13, 2006.
Jubilee Research. 2006c. "Jubilee 2000 International Campaigning Statement." at jubileeresearch.org/jubilee2000/policy_papers/statement.html, June 13, 2006.
Jubilee Research. 2006d. "Latin America Campaign Says Cap Debt Service at 3% of Budget." at jubileeresearch.org/jubilee2000/news/latin1202.htm, June 13, 2006.
Jubilee Research. 2006e. "Nobel Peace Prize Winner Says Debt Is 'Massive Violation of Human Rights'." at jubileeresearch.org/jubliee2000news/nobel12901.html, June 13, 2006.
Jubilee Research. 2006f. "10,000 Jubilee Campaigners Expected to Form Human Chain Outside Opening Reception of World Trade Organisation." at jubileeresearch.org/jubilee2000/news/wto2911.html, October 6, 2006.

Jubilee Research 2006g. "What Happens Next: Campaigning on Debt beyond the Millennium Year." At jubileereserch.org/jubilee2000/whatnext/debt.html, June 13, 2006.
Jubilee Research. 2005. "Havana Conference Southern and Northern Civil Society Unite against the Injustice of Debt." at jubileeresearch.org/latest/havanna010005.htm, November 25, 2005.
Jubilee South. 2006. "Welcome to the Jubilee South Website." at Jubileesouth.org, 08/06/2006.
Jubilee South. 2004. "Jubilee South Newsletter January 2004." at www.jubileesouth.org/news/EpyyuVkVVuCJICfHGU.shtml, June 8, 2006.
Jubilee South. 2003. "Jubilee South e-bulletin" Vol.1 No. 1 Posted on March 29 2003." at www.jubileesouth.org/news/EpyyuVkVVuCJICfHGU.shtml, June 8, 2006.
Jubilee South. 2002. "The International Peoples' Tribunal on Debt Verdict." at www.jubileesouth.org/tribunal/index.htm, June 8, 2006.
Jubilee South. 2001. "Jubilee South Newsletter Vol. 1 No. 2." December at www.jubileesouth.org, June 8, 2006.
Jubilee USA. 2006. at www.jubileeusa.org, October 11, 2006.
Juniper, Tony. 2002. "Society; Environment: It's Your Shout: World Heavyweights Are Beginning to Listen to Dissent." *Guardian* (London), February 13: Society 9.
Juniper, Tony. 2000. "Profits of Doom." *Guardian* (London), February 9: Society 4.
Juniper, Tony and Hilary Wainwright. 2001. "Society: Environment: Worlds Apart: Tony Juniper in Davos and Hilary Wainwright in Porto Alegre Report on Two Forums on Globalisation That Symbolise the Widening Gap between Rich and Poor." *Guardian* (London), January 29: Society 8.
Kairos. 2006a. "Kairos: Another Kind of Time." kairoscanada.org, June 13, 2006.
Kairos. 2006b. at www.kairoscanada.org, 03/10/2006.
Kairos. 2003a. "Who we are." at www.kairoscanada.org/english/who.htm, November 13, 2003.
Kairos. 2003b. "KAIROS Background Paper Briefing Note on International Debt Updated: January 2003." at www.kairoscanada.org/english/debt/background(030109).htm, November 13, 2003.
KAIROS: Canadian Ecumenical Justice Initiatives and the Halifax Initiative Coalition. 2005. "Analysis of June 11, 2005 G8 Debt Proposal." at http://www.halifaxinitiative.org/updir/Analysis_of_June_11_Formatted.pdf, November 9, 2011.
Kahn, Joseph. 2000. "Economic View: Globalization: If You Can't Beat It, Reshape It." *The New York Times*, February 6: Section 3 page 4.
Kaletsky, Anatole. 2004. "A Right Merry-Go-Round in Davos." *The Times* (London) January 27: Business 28.
Kane, Molly. 2008. See Molly Kane interview.
Kapstein, Ethan B. 2006. "Architects of Stability: International Cooperation among Financial Supervisors." *BIS Working Paper199*. Basel: Bank for International Settlements.
Kapstein, Ethan B. 1994. *Governing the Global Economy*. Cambridge: Harvard.
Kaufman, Henry. 1990. "The Legacy of Debt." *World Link*, March/April: 92–93.

Kaur, Hardev. 2001. "Scandals and Failed Promises of Globalisation." *Business Times* (Malaysia), January 29: 6.

Keck, Margaret and Kathryn Sikkink. 1999. "Transnational Advocacy Networks in International and Regional Politics." *International Science Journal*,. March: 89–101.

Keck, Margaret and Kathryn Sikkink. 1998. *Activists Beyond Borders*. Ithaca, NY: Cornell University Press.

Keegan, William. 2004. "Business & Media: Davos View: Downhill Race Is Main Event." *Observer*, January 25: Business 8.

Keegan, William. 2000. "Clashes as Clinton Makes Trade Plea; Ghost of Seattle Returns as Police Fire Warning Shots to Quell Masked Protesters." *Observer*, January 30: 22.

Kenen, Peter B. 2001. "The International Financial Architecture: What's New What's Missing" at iie.com, May 30, 2006.

Kenny, Michael and Randall Germain. 2005. "The Idea(l) of Global Civil Society." in *The Idea of Global Civil Society: Politics and Ethics in a Globalizing Era*. Germain and Kenny eds London: Routledge.

Keohane, Robert and Joseph Nye. 1977. *Power and Independence: World Politics in Transition*. Boston: Little Brown.

Keynes, John Maynard. 1936/1942. *The General Theory of Employment, Interest and Money*. London: Macmillan and Co. Ltd.

Keynes, John Maynard. 1920/2004. *The Economic Consequences of the Peace*. Mineola, NY: Dover Publications.

Kiely, Kathy. 1994. "Larry Summers Mind Over Matter." *World Link* January/February: pp. 46–50.

Kindleberger, Charles P. 1996. *Manias Panics Crashes*, 3rd edn. New York: John Wiley and Sons.

King, Stephen. 2005. "Like Comic Relief But with Bigger Chequebooks." *Independent*, January 31: Business 37.

Kirton, John, Ella Kokotsis, Vanessa Corlazzoli, Mike Varey, Aaron Raths, Laura Sunderland and the G8 Research Group. 2006. *Debt Relief: Africa 2005 Gleneagles Final Compliance Report*. at http://www.g8.utoronto.ca/evaluations/2005compliance_final/2005-07-g8-f-comp-afdebt.pdf, 12/06/2006.

Klein, Naomi. 2001. "The Battle of the Global Gatherings." *The Globe and Mail* (Canada), January 24: A15.

Knobel, Lance. 2000. "Overview of the Annual Meeting 2000." *New Beginnings: Making a Difference. Report on the Annual Meeting 2000 of the World Economic Forum:* 10–12.

Kohli, Sheel. 1999. "Fischer Strikes Back at 'Lying' IMF Critics." *South China Morning Post*, February 2: 6.

Kuhn, Thomas. 1970. *The Structure of Scientific Revolutions*. ed 2. Chicago: University of Chicago Press.

Lapham, Lewis. 1998. *The Agony of Mammon*. London and New York: Verso.

Larner, Wendy. 2000. "Neo-liberalism: Policy, Ideology, Governmentality." *Studies in Political Economy*. 63: 5–25.

Larner, Wendy. 1997. " 'A Means to an End': Neoliberalism and State Processes in New Zealand." *Studies in Political Economy* 52: 7–38.

Lasswell, Harold. 1936. *Politics; Who Gets What, when, How*. New York: Smith.

Laurance, Ben. 1999. "It's a Crisis All Right. Smug Consensus Has Fractured; Billions Are Suffering But the Big Shots Cannot Agree Why." *Observer,* February 7: 4.

Lavelle, Kathryn C. 2011. "Sovereign Debt and Sovereign Default: the International Politics of Workouts in Latin America, Africa, and Europe." Paper presented to the annual meeting of the International Studies Association. March 18, 2011. Montreal.

Lazarus, Suellen. 2004. "The Equator Principles: a Milestone Or Just Good PR?" *Global Agenda,* January: 106–107.

Lemeur, Loic. 2005 "Angelina Jolie Stands Up against Global Poverty." January 29 at http://loiclemeur.com/english/2005/01/angelina_jolie_.html, November 9, 2011.

Levinson, Macha. 1997. "The Immeasurables: Broadening the Debate." *Global Competitiveness Report 1997:* 80–83.

Lewis, Stephen. 2005. *Race Against Time.* Toronto: Anansi.

Leyshon, Andrew and Nigel Thrift.. 1997. *Money/Space.* London and New York: Routledge.

Lindblom, Charles. 1982. "The Market as Prison." in *The Political Economy,* Thomas Ferguson and Joel Rogers eds. New York: M. E. Sharpe Inc: 3–11.

Lindblom, Charles. 1977. *Politics and Markets.* New York: Basic Books.

Linklater, Andrew. 1982. *Men and Citizens in International Relations.* London: Macmillan.

Lipschutz, Ronnie D. 2010. "Corporate Social Responsibility and the Problem of Human Rights: Who Is Protecting Whom?" in *Corporate Social Responsibility Comparative Critiques.* Lipshutz and Raman eds Basingstoke: Palgrave Macmillan.

Lipschutz, Ronnie D. with James K. Rowe. 2005. *Globalization, Governmentality and Global Politics.* London: Routledge.

Lloyd, John. 2001a. "From Porto Alegre to Quebec: Brazil's Anti-Davos Summit Failed to Produce a Constructive Alternative to Capitalism But, It Made Davos Man Sweat." *The Globe and Mail* (Canada), February 14: A15.

Lloyd, John. 2001b. "Attack on Planet Davos: Global Capitalism Has a New Enemy – the World Social Forum in Brazil." *Financial Times* (London), February 24: Weekend FT, 1.

Lobe, Jim. 2004a. "Secrecy Reigns at Global Economic Forum." *Common Dreams News Center* January 21 at www.commondreams.org/cgi-bin/print.cgi?file=/headlines04/0121-09.htm, April 16, 2007.

Loewenberg, Samuel. 2005. "That Other Forum." *The American Prospect,* March: 126.

Lukes, Steven. 2005. *Power: A Radical View.* 2nd edn. Basingstoke: Palgrave Macmillan.

Lukes, Steven. 1986. *Power.* New York: New York University Press.

Lukes, Steven. 1974. *Power: A Radical View.* London: Macmillan.

MacCuish, Derek. 2008. See Derek MacCuish interview.

Macdonald, Laura. 2005. "Gendering Transnational Social Movement Analysis: Women's Groups Contest Free Trade in the Americas." in *Coalitions across Borders,* Joe Bandy and Jackie Smith eds. New York and Toronto: Rowman and Littlefield Publishers.

Macdonald, Laura. 1994." Globalising Civil Society: Interpreting International NGOs in Central America." *Millennium.* 2: 267–85.

MacKay, Kevin. 2002. "Solidarity and Symbolic Protest: Lessons from the Quebec City Summit of the America's." *Labour/Le Travail*, 50: 21–72.
MacKinnon, Mark. 2001. "Critics Shout Down World's Financial Elite." *The Globe and Mail* (Canada), January 29: B8.
Mandela, Nelson. 1997. "Partnership against the Pandemic." *World Link*, March/April: 19–20.
Manuel, Trevor. 2002. "Reducing Poverty and Improving Equity." *Annual Meeting 2002 Global Agenda Monitor New York 31 January–4 February 2002*: 22–23.
Marques, José Carlos and Peter Utting. 2010. *Business, Politics and Public Policy: Implications for Inclusive Development*. Basingstoke: Palgrave Macmillan.
Martin, Paul. 2008. See Paul Martin interview.
Martin, Paul. 2001. "Globalization, Terrorism and the World Economy, November 16 2001." at http:www.fin.gc.ca/news01/01-105e.html, November 12, 2002.
Martin, Paul. 2000. "Comment and Analysis: Contagion, Then Complacency: World Leaders at the Davos Forum Must Join the G20's Efforts to Reform the International Financial System" *The Financial Times* (London), January 27: 27.
Martin, Ron. 1994. "Stateless Monies, Global Financial Integration and National Economic Autonomy: the End of Geography?" in *Money, Power and Space*, eds. Stuart Corbridge et al. Oxford: Blackwell: 253–278.
McAdam, Doug, Sidney Tarrow and Charles Tilly. 1997. "Toward An Integrated Perspective on Social Movements and Revolution." In *Comparative Politics: Rationality, Culture, and Structure*. M Lichbach and A Zuckerman eds. Cambridge: Cambridge University Press, 142–173.
McCarthy, John and Mayer Zald. 1979. "Resource Mobilization and Social Movements: A Partial Theory." *American Journal of Sociology* 82(6): 1212–1241.
McNamar, R. Tim. 1989. "The Debt Crisis Will End." *World Link*, 11/12: 70–71.
McNamara, Kathleen R. 1998. *The Currency of Ideas*. Ithaca, NY and London: Cornell University Press.
McRae, Hamish. 1999. "A Feeling of fin de siecle." *Independent*, February 2: Comment, 5.
Mehta, Kamalakshi. 1998. "Tigers Pause." *World Link*, March/April: 28–29.
Metcalfe, Tim. 1996. "Roar of the South Pacific Tiger Now Heard at Global Level." *South China Morning Post* (Hong Kong), February 6: 22.
Micah Challenge. 2006a. "Overview of the Micah Challenge." at www.micahchallenge.org/home/overview/Default.asp?printer_friendly=true&, May 9, 2006.
Micah Challenge. 2006b. "Micah Challenge." at www.micahchallenge.org/home/intro.asp, May 9, 2006.
Mihevc, John. 2008. See John Mihevc, interview.
Millennium Campaign. 2007a. at millenniumcampaign.org/site/pp.asp?c=grKVL2NLE&b=172249, January 24, 2007.
Millennium Campaign. 2007b. at millenniumcampaign.org/site/pp.asp?c=grKVL2NLE&b=138312, January 24, 2007.
Millennium Project. 2006. at www.unmillenniumproject.org, November 10, 2006.
Millennium Promise. 2007. at www.millenniumpromise.org/site/PageServer?pagename=home, January 24, 2007.
Miller, Karen Lowry with Jason Overdorf. 2005. "The Poor Problem." *Newsweek* (Atlantic edition), January 31: Business 40.

Monbiot, George. 2005. "Bards of the Powerful." *Guardian*, June 21 at www.guardian.co.uk/print/0,3858,5220235-116859,00.html, February 2, 2006.

Montador, Bruce. 2007. See Bruce Montador interview.

Morrison, David. 2008. See David Morrison interview.

Moschella, Manuella. 2010. *Governing Risk: The IMF and Global Financial Crises*. Basingstoke: Palgrave Macmillan.

Mouffe, Chantal. 1993. *The Return of the Political*. London: Verso.

Mulvey Paul. 2005. "Debt Relief Gains Momentum; But Howard Not Convinced as World Leaders Back Plan." *The Sun Herald*, January 30: 54.

Murdoch, Adrian. 2000. "World Economic Gaps Widening, Summit Agrees." *Scotland on Sunday*, January 30: Business 4.

Naidoo, Kumi. 2005a. "Reflections on the G8 Summit." *Civicus*, July 13, at www.civicus.org/new/content/deskofthesecretarygeneral17.htm, November 28, 2008.

Naidoo, Kumi. 2005b. "The Beginnings of the Biggest Ever Mobilisation against Poverty Launched at the World Social Forum." *Civicus*, January 31, at www.civicus.org/new/content/deskofthesecretarygeneral2.htm, November 28, 2008.

Naim, Moises. 2003. "The Global Economy: Surprises, Perplexities and Risks." *Annual Meeting 2003 Building Trust Global Agenda Monitor Davos Switzerland 23–28 January*: 22–29.

Neue Zurcher Zeitung. 2005. "Police Break up anti –WEF rally in Bern." *Neue Zurcher Zeitung*, January 23 at www.nzz.ch/2005/01/23/english/page-synd5485519.html, January 25, 2005.

The New Economics Foundation (NEF). 2005. at www.neweconomics.org/gen/, November 25, 2005.

New Internationalist. 1987. New internationalist 168 February at www.newint.org, February 16, 2006.

New Rules for Global Finance (New Rules). 2006. at www.new-rules.org, 11/10/2006.

Newsweek. 1999. "An Agenda for Action: Some Concrete Ways in Which the Brahmins of Business Can Help the Developing World." *Newsweek International*, February 1 at web.lexis-nexis.com.proxy.library.carleton.ca/universe/print-doc, April 17, 2007.

The New York Times. 2003. "Forum Seeks Accommodation with Peaceful Protesters." *The New York Times*, January 3: A7.

United Nations Non governmental Liaison Service (NGLS). 2002. *NGLS Roundup* 91 May. United Nations Non governmental Liaison Service: Geneva.

United Nations Non governmental Liaison Service (NGLS). 2001a. *NGLS Roundup* 76 August. United Nations Non governmental Liaison Service:Geneva.

United Nations Non governmental Liaison Service (NGLS). 2001b. *NGLS Roundup* 65 January. United Nations Non governmental Liaison Service: Geneva.

United Nations Non governmental Liaison Service (NGLS). 2000. *NGLS Roundup* 54 May. United Nations Non governmental Liaison Service: Geneva.

United Nations Non governmental Liaison Service (NGLS). 1999a. *NGLS Roundup* December 1998- January 1999. United Nations Non governmental Liaison Service: Geneva.

United Nations Non governmental Liaison Service (NGLS). 1999b. *NGLS Roundup* 38 July. United Nations Non governmental Liaison Service: Geneva.

Nordlinger Jay. 2005. "In Davos, Part III." *National Review Online*, January 31.

Nordlinger Jay. 2004. "Davos Journal, Part II." *National Review Online*, January 23.

Norman, Peter. 1995a. "World Economic Forum: Value of World Institutions in the Balance." *Financial Times* (London), January 30: 4.

Norman, Peter. 1995b. "Top Banker Warns of Derivatives." *Financial Times* (London), January 31: 5.

North South Institute (NSI). 2006. at www.nsi-ins.ca, June 19, 2006.

Nunn, Sam. 2002. "Achieving Security and Addressing Vulnerability." *Annual Meeting 2002 Global Agenda Monitor New York 31 January–4 February 2002*: 14–21.

O'Brien, Robert, Anne Marie Goetz, Jan Aarte Scholte and Marc Williams. 2000. *Contesting Global Governance: Multilateral Economic Institutions and Global Social Movements.* Cambridge: Cambridge University Press.

O'Brien, Timothy L. 2005. "Can Angelina Jolie Really Save the World?" *The New York Times*, January 30: Section 3 page 1.

Olesen, Thomas. 2011. "Conclusion Transnational Counter-Publics and Democracy." in *Power and Transnational Activism*. Thomas Olesen ed. London: Routledge.

O'Neill, Maureen. 2008. See Maureen O'Neill interview.

Onuf, Nicholas. 1989. *World of our Making: Rules and Rule in Social Theory and International Relations.* Columbia: University of South Carolina Press.

Open Society Institute (OSI). 2006. at www.soros.org/, June 12, 2006.

Organization for Economic cooperation and Development (OECD). 2006. *DAC in Dates: The History of the OECD's Development Assistance Committee.* Paris: OECD Publications.

Osavo, Mario. 2001. "World Social Forum Ends on Positive Note." at www.commondreams.org/headlines01/0131-01.htm, 11/12/2003.

The Other Davos. 2007. at www.otherdavos.netPages_web/english/english.html, June 13, 2007.

Oxfam UK. 2006a. at www.oxfam.org.uk, June 19, 2006.

Oxfam UK. 2006b. at www.oxfam.org.uk/about_us/historyhistory4.htm, June 19, 2006.

Palan, Ronen. 1998. "Trying to Have Your Cake and Eating It: How and Why the State System Has Created Offshore." *International Studies Quarterly* 42: 625–644.

Paris Club. 2006. at www.clubdeparis.org/en/, April 27, 2006.

Pauly, Louis W. 1997. *Who Elected the Bankers? Surveillance and Control in the World Economy.* Ithaca, NY: Cornell University Press.

Payer, Cheryl. 1982. *The World Bank.* New York and London: Monthly Review Press.

Payer, Cheryl. 1974. *The Debt Trap.* New York and London: Monthly Review Press.

Peoples' Global Action (PGA). 1998. "Davos 98: The World Economic Forum Strikes Again." at www.parascope.com/mx/articles/davos98.htm, January 21, 2005.

Pettifor, Ann. 2001. "The World Will Never Be the Same Again ... Because of Jubilee 2000." at www.jubileeresearch.org/analysis/reports/world_never_same_again/intro.htm, November 21, 2005.

Pettifor, Ann. 1998. "A Personal View of the Jubilee 2000 'Human Chain' Demonstration on 16 May 1998, during the G8 Summit in Birmingham." at www.jubileedebtcampaign.org uk, November 21, 2005.

Pfanner, Eric. 2004. "Leaders in Davos Are Hoping for More Than Just a Talkfest." *The International Herald Tribune,* January 21, Finance 11.

Pigman, Geoffrey Allen. 2010. *Contemporary Diplomacy.* Cambridge: Polity Press.

Pigman, Geoffrey Allen. 2007. *The World Economic Forum.* London and New York: Routledge.

Pigman, Geoffrey Allen. 2002. "A Multifunctional Case Study for Teaching International Political Economy: The World Economic Forum as Shar-pei or Wolf in Sheep's Clothing?" *International Studies Perspectives.* 3: 291–309.

Pike, Alan. 2001. "SURVEY – DAVOS: Sensitive to Ethical Concerns: Corporate Responsibility by Alan Pike: Rioting in Seattle Has Given Both Business and Political Leaders Good Reason to Pause for Thought and Consider." *Financial Times* (London): Survey 6.

Piven, Frances Fox and Richard A. Cloward. 1995. "Collective Protest: A Critique of Resource Mobilization Theory." in *Social Movements: Critiques, Concepts Case-Studies,* ed. Stanford M. Lyman. London: MacMillan: 137–167.

Plate, Tom. 2002. "Corruption May Hit Capitalism as Hard as Terror." *The Straits Times* (Singapore), February 2: Analysis.

Polanyi, John C. 1997. "In Praise of Science's 'Idealistic Tendencies.'" *The Toronto Star,* February 13: A25.

Polanyi, Karl. 1944/1957. *The Great Transformation.* Boston: Beacon Press.

Porter, Tony. 2005. *Globalization and Finance.* Cambridge: Polity Press.

Porter, Tony. 1993. *States, Markets and Regimes in Global Finance.* New York: St Martin's Press.

Porter, Tony and Karsten Ronit eds 2010a. *The Challenges of Global Business Authority.* New York: State University of New York Press.

Porter, Tony and Karsten Ronit. 2010b. "The Complexities of Global Business Authority and the Promise of Democracy." in *The Challenges of Global Business Authority.* Porter and Ronit eds New York: State University of New York Press.

Public Broadcasting System (PBS). 2006. at www.pbs.org/wgbh/pages/frontline/aids/cron/crontext.html, May 31, 2006.

Public Citizen. 2002. "Davos World Economic Forum: Pricey Corporate Trade Association Loses Its Camouflage" *Public Citizen's Global Trade Watch* January 31, Washington DC: Public Citizen.

Public Eye on Davos. 2004. "Keynote speech by Mary Robinson (21.01.04)." *Berne Declaration,* at www.evb.ch/enp25002736.html?cms_show_printable=1, November 19, 2008.

Public Eye on Davos. 2003. "Conference Program 2003." *Berne Declaration,* at www.evb.ch/index.cfm?page_id=1772, June 13, 2007.

Public Eye on Davos. 2001a. "NGO Statement 2001. 28.01.01." *Berne Declaration,* at www.evb.ch/p25001627.html, June 13, 2007.

Public Eye on Davos. 2001b. "Conference Program 25.01.01." *Berne Declaration,* at www.evb.ch/p25001621.html, June 13, 2007.

Public Eye on Davos. 2000. "NGO Statement 2000. 25.01.00." *Berne Declaration,* at www.evb.ch/p25001707.html, June 13, 2007.

Puttnam, David. 2004. "Social Enterprise – Hearts before Pockets; Big Business Is Starting to Realise That If It Is to Adapt to a New World, It Needs the Help of Social Entrepreneurs." *New Statesman,* February 9.

Ragan, Christopher. 1999a. "The Devil's in the Details: An Interview with Jeffrey Sachs." *World Economic Affairs* Winter: 28–33.

Ragan, Christopher. 1999b. "Confirmed Convictions: An interview with Milton Friedman." *World Economic Affairs* Winter: 50–56.
Ramesh, Randeep. 2004. "Society on the Move: the World Social Forum Brings Together the Poorest People on the Planet. Randeep Ramesh in Mumbai Hears New Calls for the Environment and Social Justice." *Guardian* (London), January 28: Society 12.
Rayfuse, Bruce. 2008. See Bruce Rayfuse interview.
Réformer les Institutions Financières Internationales (RIFI). 2006. at www.globenet.org/ifi/, June 8, 2006.
Reilly-King, Fraser. 2006. "Mind the (Growing) Gap – Debt, Aid, and Trade." at http://halifaxinitiative.org/content/press-response-july-13-2006, November 9, 2011.
Reimann, Kim D. 2006. "A View from the Top: International Politic, Norms and the Worldwide Growth of NGOs." *International Studies Quarterly,* 50: 45–67.
Reinventing Bretton Woods Committee (RBWC). 2006. at http://rbwf.org/cms/index.php, April 4, 2006.
Reitan, Ruth. 2007. *Global Activism.* London and New York: Routledge.
Reuters. 2002. "Forum in N.Y. Calls on Rich to Aid Poor." *The Toronto Sun,* February 3: News 10.
Robertson, Justin. 2009. *US-Asia Economic Relations* London: Routledge.
Robinson, Fiona. 1999. *Globalizing Care.* Boulder, CO and London: Westview Press.
Robinson, Nick. 2005. "Four Brainy White Men Who Know That African Poverty Is Stupid." *The Times* (London), January 29: Features 23.
Robinson, William I. 2004. *A Theory of Global Capitalism.* Baltimore and London: Johns Hopkins UP..
Rodger, Ian. 1992. "Higher and Mightier Yet at Davos World Forum." *Financial Times* (London), February 7: I2.
Rodrik, Dani. 2008. "John Williamson and the Washington Consensus." at http://www.typepad.com/services/trackback/6a00d8341c891753ef01053589003a970c, April 23, 2009.
Rodrik, Dani. 1997. "Has Globalization Gone Too Far?" at http://rodrik.typepad.com/dani_rodriks_weblog/2008/10/john-williamson-and-the-washington-consensus.html, May 30, 2006.
Rowan, Hobart. 1989. "Camdessus Urges Support for Debtors" *The Washington Post,* January 28: D11.
Rubin, Trudy. 2001. "Shifting Attitudes on Global Economy." *The San Diego Union-Tribune,* January 27:B-10:2,7; B-6:1.
Rubin, Trudy. 1997. "Confronting Social Ills." *Journal of Commerce,* February 11: 7A.
Ruggie, John G. 1998. *Constructing the World Polity: Essays on International Institutionalization.* New York: Routledge.,
Ruggie, John G. 1982. "International Regimes, Transactions and Change: Embedded Liberalism in the Postwar Economic Order." *International Organization.* Spring 36(2): 379–415.
Russell, Jenni. 2002. "Where the Elite Preens Itself." *New Statesman,* January 28 at web.lexis-nexis.com.proxy.library.carleton.ca/universe/document?_m=66b9ed802d38d53bcfc16cf..., June 20, 2007.
Sachs, Jeffrey. 2000. "Reforming the Reformers." *World Link,* March/April: 10.

Sachs, Jeffrey. 1998. "Recipe for Disaster." *World Link*, January/February: 15–16.

Sachs, Jeffrey. 1997. "IMF is a Power unto Itself." *The Financial Times*, December 11.

Safire, William. 1994. "Russia's Bumpy Road to Reform." *Times-Picayune* (New Orleans), February 2: B7.

Sally, Razeen. 1998. *Classical Liberalism and International Economic Order*. London and New York: Routledge.

Sanger, David E. 1997. "Fat Cat Spat; Look Who's Carping Most about Capitalism." *New York Times*, April 6: Section 4 page 1.

Saporta, Maria. 1999. "Turner, Gates to Join in Philanthropic Effort." *The Atlanta Journal and Constitution*, February 10: 02F.

Structural Adjustment Participatory Review International Network (SAPRIN) 2009. "Overview." at www.saprin.org/overview.htm, August 18, 2009.

Scarboro Missions. 2006. at www.scarboromissions.ca, November 13, 2006.

Schaeffer-Duffy, Claire. 2004. "Forum Challenges Globalization." *National Catholic Reporter*, February, 12: 14.

Schmemann, Serge. 2002. "Forum in New York: The Overview; Rich and Powerful Gathering At Elite Forum on Economy." *The New York Times*, January, 31: A1.

Scholte, Jan Aart. 2002. "Civil Society and the Governance of Global Finance." in *Civil Society and Global Finance*, eds. Jan Aarte Scholte, with Albrecht Schnabel. London: Routledge, 11–32.

Scholte, Jan Aarte with Albrecht Schnabel eds. 2002. *Civil Society and Global Finance*. London: Routledge.

Schwab Foundation. 2007. "History of the Foundation." at www.schwabfound.org/history.htm, June 13, 2007.

Schwab, Klaus. 2005. "The Executive Chairman's Statement." *World Economic Forum Annual Report 2004/2005*: 2–5.

Schwab, Klaus. 2004a. "Preface." *Global Competitiveness Report 2004–2005*.

Schwab, Klaus. 2004b. "EDITORIAL The Business Community Bears a Huge Responsibility." *NEWSLETTER*, January 2004, Geneva: World Economic Forum at www.weforum.org

Schwab, Klaus. 2004c. "Welcome to the Annual Meeting 21.01.2004." at www.weforum.org/en/knowledge/Themes/Economy/FinancialMarkets/index.htm

Schwab 2004d "The Executive Chairman's Statement." *Annual Report 2004/2005*. Geneva: World Economic Forum: 2-5.

Schwab, Klaus. 2004e. "Shaping Prospects for a Dangerous World; World Economic Forum." *International Herald Tribune*, January 20: International 6.

Schwab, Klaus. 2003. "Introduction." *Annual Meeting 2003 Building Trust Global Agenda Monitor*. Geneva: World Economic Forum: 2–3.

Schwab, Klaus. 2002. "Foreword." *Annual Meeting 2002 Global Agenda Monitor*. Geneva: World Economic Forum: 2–4.

Schwab, Klaus. 2001a. 2001 GCR 2001a Preface Schwab p. 7.

Schwab, Klaus. 2001b. "Message from the President" *Annual Report 2000–2001*. Geneva: World Economic Forum.

Schwab, Klaus. 2000a. "Opening session." at http://webarchive.org/web/20000522075343/www.weforum.org/pressreleases.nsf, November 23, 07.

Schwab, Klaus. 2000b "Preface." *Global Competitiveness Report 2000*: 7.

Schwab, Klaus. 2000c. "This Did Not Work in Seattle." *UN Chronicle* 2: 15.

Schwab, Klaus. 1994. "Opening Remarks." *World Link*, March/April: 112.

Schwab, Klaus. 1993. "Rallying All the Forces for Global Recovery." *World Link*, March/April: 100.

Schwab, Klaus. 1990. "Achieving Global Relevance." *World Link* January/ February: 33.

Schwab, Klaus and Malcolm MacLaren. 1995. "Our Growing Indifference Endangers World Peace." *International Herald Tribune*, January 26 at www.iht.com/articles/1995/01/26/edklaus.php, September 30, 2008.

Schwab, Klaus and Claude Smadja. 2001. "The Work That Matters in Davos Will Be Going On Indoors." *International Herald Tribune*, January 23 at http://www.iht.com/articles/2001/01/23/edklaus.t.php, 01/09/2008.

Schwab, Klaus and Claude Smadja. 2000a. "We Need Structures to Help Steer Globalization." *International Herald Tribune*, January 27 at www.iht.com/articles/2000/01/27/edklaus.t.php, 01/09/2008.

Schwab, Klaus and Claude Smadja. 1999a. "Globalization Needs a Human Face" *International Herald Tribune*, January 28 at www.iht.com/articles/1999/01/28/edKlaus.t.php, 07/06/2007.

Schwab, Klaus and Claude Smadja. 1999b. "1999 Annual Meeting Report Can Globalization Have a Human Face? It Must." at http://webarchive.org/web/20000819013512/www.weforum.org/AM_arch.nsf/Documents/Home+-+Reports+and+Publications+-+Archives+-+1999+annual+Meeting+report+-++-+Can+Globalization+Have+a+Human+Face, June 13, 2007.

Schwab, Klaus and Claude Smadja. 1998. "We Need New Rules for the New Game." *International Herald Tribune*, January 29 at www.iht.com/articles/1998/01/29/edKlaus.t.php, 01/09/2008.

Schwab, Klaus and Claude Smadja. 1997a. "A New Ballgame for Which Players?" *International Herald Tribune*, January 30 at www.iht.com/articles/1997/01/30/edklaus.t.php, 07/06/2007.

Schwab, Klaus and Claude Smadja. 1997b. "Join Forces to Solve the Shareholder-Stakeholder Equation." *International Herald Tribune*, January 31 at www.iht.com/articles/1997/01/31/edklaus.t_0.php, 07/06/2007.

Schwab, Klaus and Claude Smadja. 1996. "Start Taking the Backlash against Globalization Seriously." *International Herald Tribune*, February 4 at www.iht.com/articles/1996/02/01/edklaus.t.php?page=2, 01/10/2008.

Schwab, Klaus and Kate Taylor. 2005. "Business Leaders and AIDS." *International Herald Tribune* January 27 at http://www.iht.com/articles/2005/01/26/opinion/edlet.php, 07/06/2007.

Seiberg, Jaret. 1996. "Kansas City Fed Chief Foresees Day When Riskiest Banks Go Without Insurance." *The American Banker*, February 5: 2.

Seidman, Gay. 2001. "Adjusting the Lens: What do Globalizations, Transnationalism, and the Anti-apartheid Movement mean for Social Movement Theory?" In *Globalization and Social Movements*, John A Guidry et al. eds Ann Arbor, MI: University of Michigan Press.

Selowsky, Marcelo. 1989. "Additional Comment from the World Bank." *World Link*, 9/10: 12.

Sennett, Richard. 1998. "The Dizzy Life of Davos Man." *Independent*, October 11: Features, 2.

Sikkink, Kathryn. 1998. "Transnational Politics, International Relations Theory and Human Rights: a New Model of International Politics Is Needed to Explain the Politics of Human Rights." *Political Science and Politics*. 31(3): 517–521.

Simmons, Beth. 1994. *Who Adjusts?* Princeton, NJ: Princeton University Press.
Sinclair, Timothy J. 1994. "Passing Judgement: Credit Rating Processes as Regulatory Mechanisms of Governance in the Emerging World Order." *Review of International Political Economy,* 1(1): 133–159.
Skidelsky, Robert. 2000. *John Maynard Keynes Volume 3 Fighting for Britain 1937–1946.* London: Papermac.
Slaughter, Anne Marie. 2004. *A New World Order.* Princeton: Princeton University Press.
Smadja, Claude. 1998. "Foreword." *1998 Annual Meeting Report, World Economic Forum* at web.archive.org/web/19990224222422/www.weforum.org/activities/annual_meeting/last_year_re…,April 19, 2007.
Smadja, Claude. 1989. "The Debt: Time for Concerted Action." *World Link* 4: 2.
Smith, Adam, 1789/1937. *The Wealth of Nations.* 5th edn. ed. Edwin Cannan. New York: The Modern Library.
Smith, Jackie and Joe Bandy. 2005. "Introduction: Cooperation and Conflict in Transnational Protest." In *Coalitions across Borders,* eds. Joe Bandy and Jackie Smith. New York: Rowman and Littlefield: 1–17.
Smith, Tony. 2003. "Brazilian Leader Vows He Will Plead for the Poor in Davos." *The New York Times* January 23: A4.
Smithey, Sandra N. 2008. See Sandra N. Smithey interview.
Sojourners. 2006. at www.sojo.net/, May 24, 2006.
Soros, George. 2001. "Lonely at the Top; the Digital Divide: Why Is It Important?" *World Link* March/April 2001 24.
Soros, George. 1998. *The Crisis of Global Capitalism.* Public Affairs: New York.
Soros, George. 1997. "The Capitalist Threat," *The Atlantic Monthly,* February: 45–58.
South China Morning Post. 1999a. "Mahatir Keeps His Cool as Opponents Turn Up the Heat." *South China Morning Post,* February 2: 6.
de Souza, Nick. 2002. "Brighter Days Ahead?" *World Link,* March/April: 44.
de Souza, Nick. 2001. "Sweet Charity." *World Link* March/April: 42.
Standing Committee on Finance. 1999. at http://www2.parl.gc.ca/HousePublications/Publication.aspx?DocId=1039908&Language=E&Mode=1&Parl=36&Ses=2, August 19, 2009.
Staunton, Denis. 2004. "UN Refocuses Global Agenda on Rights Issue." *The Irish Times,* January 24: World News 10.
Steans, Jill. 1998. *Gender and International Relations.* New Brunswick N. J.: Rutgers UP.
Steinberg, Kevin. 2003a. "Inside the World Economic Forum." *Global Agenda* January: 18.
Stevens, Geoffrey. 1987. "Democracy 'Beautiful' Danny the Red Now a Green." *The Globe and Mail* (Canada), February 2 at web.lexis.nexis.com.proxy.library.carleton.ca/universe/document?_m=f96a40c16808a478559d83c…, April 30, 2007.
Stiglitz, Joseph E. 2002. *Globalization and Its Discontents.* New York: Norton.
Stiglitz, Joseph E. 1999. *The Future of the International Financial Architecture.* World Economic Affairs Winter: 35–38.
Stiglitz, Joseph 1998. "More Instruments and Broader Goals: Moving towards the Post-Washington Consensus 1998 WIDER Annual Lecture, Helsinki." at www.globalpolicy.org/component/content/article/209/43245.html, August 18, 2009.

Stocking, Barbara. 2003. "Poverty Inequality and Development." *Global Agenda Monitor 2003*. Geneva: WEF: 30–37.

Strange, Susan. 1998. *Mad Money: When Markets Outgrow Governments*. Ann Arbour, MI: University of Michigan Press.

Strange, Susan. 1988. *States and Markets*. New York: Basil Blackwell.

Strom, Stephanie with Louis Uchitelle. 2002 "A Global Icon Retools for Meaner Streets." *New York Times*, January 27: Section 3, 1.

Strong, Maurice. 1990. "Taking Account of Eco-nomics" *World Link*, 7/8: 48.

Tax Justice Network. 2006. "Steering Committee." at www.taxjustice.net/cms/front_content.php?idcatart=13, 11/10/2006.

TEARfund. 2006. at www.tearfund.org, 01/11/2006.

The Other Economic Forum (TOES). 2005. at www.toes-usa.org, November 25, 2005.

Thomas, Bryan R. 1992. "The Other Economic Summit." *Green Left Weekly* at http://www.greenleft.org.au/node/3385, November 9, 2011.

Thorsell, William. 2008. See William Thorsell interview.

Thorsell, William. 1996. "Only a Ship of Fools Would Ignore the Shrinking Passenger List." The *Globe and Mail*, February 17.

Thorsell, William. 1995. "Mercurial Power." *Globe and Mail*, February 11: D5.

Thrift, Nigel and Andrew Leyshon. 1999. "Moral Geographies of Money." in *Nation States and Money*, eds Eric Helleiner and Emily Gilbert. London: Routledge.

Tomlinson, Brian. 2008. See Brian Tomlinson interview.

Transnational Institute (TNI). 2007. "TNI History." at www.tni.org/history/index.htm, January 30, 2007.

Transnational Institute (TNI). 2006. at www.tni.org, October 17, 2006.

Transnational Institute (TNI). 1998. at www.tni.org/asem-london/aepf 1998.htm, January 30, 2007.

Transnational Institute (TNI). 1996. at www.tni/asem-bangkok/aepf1996.htm, January 30, 2007.

Triffin, Robert. 1978. "Gold and the Dollar Crisis." *Princeton Essays in International Finance No. 132*. Princeton: Princeton University Press.

Uchitelle, Louis. 2000. "Economic View; From the Streets of Seattle to the Table at Davos." *The New York Times*, January 30: Section 3 page 4.

Uchitelle, Louis. 1998. "International Business; I.M.F. May Be Closer to Lending-Curb Idea." *The New York Times*, February 3: D4.

Uganda Debt Network (UDN). 2006. at www.udn.org.ug, June 13, 2006.

Underhill, Geoffrey. 1997. "Private Markets and Public responsibility in a global system: Conflict and Co-operation in Transnational Banking and Securities Regulation." in *The New World Order in International Finance*, ed. G. Underhill. New York: St Martin's Press: 17–49.

United Nations (UN). 2003. *Monterrey Consensus of the International Conference on Financing for Development*. New York: United Nations at www.un.org/esa/ffd/monterrey/MonterreyConsensus.pdf, August 20, 2009.

United Nations (UN). 1995. "Copenhagen declaration on Social Development." at http://www.un.org/documents/ga/conf166/aconf166-9.htm, November 9, 2011.

United Nations (UN). 1948. "Universal Declaration of Human Rights." Washington: World Service Authority.

United Nations Development Program (UNDP). 2009. "Origins of the Human Development Approach." at http://hdr.undp.org/en/humandev/origins/, August 21, 2009.

United Nations Global Compact. 2009. "Overview of the UN Global Compact." at www.unglobalcompact.org/AboutTheGC/, October 29, 2009.

Usborne, David. 2002. "Anti-Forum Activists March and 'Twinkle' to Little Effect." *Independent* (London), February 4: Foreign News 10.

Vanguard. 2004. "Pan Africa; Annan to Convene Summit on Development." *Africa News,* January 24.

Wadler, Joyce. 2002. "Forum in NY: the Chief Visionary Discusses His Creation" *New York Times, January* 31: A16.

War on Want. 2006. at www.waronwant.org, 08/06/2006.

Warner, Jeremy. 2004a. "US Threatens to Pull Out of Basel Bank Agreement." *Independent* (London), January 24: Business 21.

Warner, Jeremy. 2004b. "Davos Casts Its Usual, Worrisome Forecast." *Sunday Tribune* January 25: 6.

Warner, Jeremy. 2002. "Outlook: Even Corporations Are Getting a Social Conscience." *Independent* (London), February 9: 19.

Warner, Jeremy. 1998. "So You Want to Meet the Men Who Run the World?" *Independent,* February 1: News17.

Warner, Jeremy. 1997. "Davies Tells Banks to 'Stress Test' Portfolios; World Economic Forum: Bank of England Deputy Governor Calls for Global Measures to Safeguard against Risk. Beware of Globalization Backlash." *Independent,* February 1: 17.

Watson, Matthew. 2005. *Foundations of International Political Economy.* Hampshire and New York: Palgrave MacMillan.

Weaver, Catherine. 2010. "The Meaning of Development: Constructing the World Bank's Good Governance Agenda." in Abdelal et al. eds *Constructing the International Economy* Ithaca, NY: Cornell University Press.

Wendt, Alexander. 1992. "Anarchy Is What States Make of It: the Social Construction of Power Politics." *International Organization.* 46(2): 391–425.

Whiteband. 2006. at www.whiteband.org 04/10/2006

Williamson, John. 2008. "Williamson versus the Washington Consensus." at www.growthcommissionblog.org/content/williamson-versus-the-washington-consensus, April 23, 2009.

Williamson, John. 2006. "Should There Be a Development Consensus?" *Global Competitiveness Report 2005–2006 Policies Underpinning Rising Prosperity.* Geneva: World Economic Forum: 155–162.

Williamson, John. 2004. "A Short History of the Washington Consensus." Paper commissioned by Fundación CIDOB for a conference "From the Washington Consensus towards a new Global Governance," Barcelona, September 24–25, 2004 at www.ild.org.pe/files/williamson0904-21.pdf, April 23, 2009.

Wiwa, Ken. 2005. "Davos and Goliath Discover Africa." *Globe and Mail,* January 29: A19.

World Bank (WB). 1999. "Canada's Chrétien Calls for More Debt Relief; Plans to Push Proposal at Cologne Summit in June." at http://web.worldbank.org/WBSITE/EXTERNAL/NEWS/0,,contentMDK:20045227~menuPK:34460~pagePK:64003015~piPK:64003012~theSitePK:4607,00.html, August 19, 2009.

World Council of Churches (WCC). 2006. at www.wcc-coe.org, October 13, 2006.

World Council of Churches (WCC). 1998. "The Debt Issue: A Jubilee Call to End the Stranglehold of Debt on Impoverished People." at http://www.oikoumene.org/en/resources/documents/wcc-programmes/public-witness-addressing-power-affirming-peace/poverty-wealth-and-ecology/neoliberal-paradigm/debt-issue-a-jubilee-call.html, November 9, 2011.

World Council of Churches (WCC). 1985. *The International Financial System: An Ecumenical Critique, Report of the Meeting of the Advisory Group on Economic Matters held in Geneva Switzerland November 1–4, 1984*. Geneva: World Council of Churches.

World Development Movement (WDM). 2006. "Campaigns." at www.wdm.org.uk/campaigns/debt/index/htm, 08/06/2006.

World Development Movement, (WDM). 2001. "The Vicious Circle: AIDS and Third World Debt." June at www.wdm.org.uk/cambriefs/Debt/vicious.pdf, 08/06/2006.

World Economic Forum (WEF). 2008a. "History and Achievements." at www.weforum.org/en/about/History%20and%20Achievements/index.atm, June 25, 2008.

World Economic Forum (WEF). 2008e. "About." at www.weforum.org/en/about/Members%20and%20Partners/index.htm, May 25, 2008.

World Economic Forum (WEF). 2005a. *Strategic Insight the Agenda Review for Global Leaders Annual Meeting 2005 Davos Switzerland*. Geneva: World Economic Forum at www.weforum.org/pdf/AM2005/AM2005_StrategicInsight.pdf, 10/01/2008.

World Economic Forum (WEF). 2005b. *Annual Report 2004/2005 Shaping the Global, Regional and Industry Agendas*. Geneva: World Economic Forum.

World Economic Forum (WEF). 2005c. *Global Agenda*, January Issue 3.

World Economic Forum (WEF). 2005d. *Global Town Hall Report*, January 26. Annual Meeting 2005, Davos Switzerland. Geneva: World Economic Forum.

World Economic Forum (WEF). 2005e. *Global Governance Initiative Report 2005* at webarchive.org/web/20050410084237/www.weforum.org/site/homepublic.nsf/Content/Global+Gov…, November 21, 2007.

World Economic Forum (WEF). 2005f. "Getting the Millennium Goals Back on Track 27/01/05." *Session Summaries* at www.weforum.org/en/knowledge/Themes/Economy/KN_SESS_SUMM_12525?url=/en/knowledge/Themes/Economy/KN_SESS_SUMM_12525, 10/11/2007.

World Economic Forum (WEF). 2005g. "Funding the War on Poverty 28.01.2005." *Session Summaries* at web.archive.org/web/20051023113510/www.weforum.org/site/knowledgenavigator.nsf/Content/…, July 18, 2007.

World Economic Forum (WEF). 2005h. "Spotting the Next Bubble Before It Bursts 27.01.2005." *Session Summaries* at www.weforum.org/en/knowledge/Themes/Economy/FinancialMarkets/index.htm, 10/11/2007.

World Economic Forum (WEF). 2005k. "Hedge fund Fever Heats up 28.01.2005." *Session Summaries* at www.weforum.org/en/knowledge/Themes/Economy/Regulation/index.htm?ssUserText=&fragment12_NextRow=101 *4, 10/11/2007.

World Economic Forum (WEF). 2004a. "A New Front in the AIDS Battle." *The Davos Report*. Geneva, Switzerland and Washington, DC: Foreign Policy and World Economic Forum: 20.

World Economic Forum (WEF). 2004b. *Annual Report 2003/2004. Partnering for Security and Prosperity*. Geneva: World Economic Forum.

World Economic Forum (WEF). 2004c. *Global Agenda*. Geneva: World Economic Forum.

World Economic Forum (WEF). 2004e. "Are Financial Markets Still (Somewhat) Crazy after All These Years? 24.01.2004." *Session Summaries* at www.weforum.org/en/knowledge/Themes/Economy/FinancialMarkets/KN_SESS_SUMM_9861?url=/en/knowledge/Themes/Economy/FinancialMarkets/KN_SESS_SUMM_9861, October 21, 2007.

World Economic Forum (WEF). 2004g. "Have the Post War Global Institutions Reached the End of the Road? 23.01.2004." *Session Summaries* at www.weforum.org/en/knowledge/Themes/Humanities/History/index.htm?ssUserText=&fragment12_NextRow=..., October 21, 2007.

World Economic Forum (WEF). 2004h. "So What?" *The Davos Report*. Geneva, Switzerland and Washington, DC :Foreign Policy and World Economic Forum: 25.

World Economic Forum (WEF). 2004i. "World Economic Forum FAQs." at www.weforum.org/site/homepublic.nsf/content/98C41CC46D969FOBC1256E04 0..., 2004/02/04.

World Economic Forum (WEF). 2004j. "Davos 2004: By the Numbers." *The Davos Report*. Geneva, Switzerland and Washington, DC: Foreign Policy and World Economic Forum: 7.

World Economic Forum (WEF). 2004l. "Taking the Initiative." in *The Davos Report*. Geneva, Switzerland and Washington, DC: Foreign Policy and World Economic Forum: 18.

World Economic Forum (WEF). 2004n. "What Future for the International Financial System? A Unique Public-Private Dialogue Launched by the World Economic Forum and Reinventing Bretton Woods Committee." at www.weforum.org/site/homepublic.nsf/content/What+Future+for+the+International+Fi na..., January 20, 2005.

World Economic Forum (WEF). 2003a. *Annual Meeting 2003 Building Trust Global Agenda Monitor Davos Switzerland 23–28 January*. Geneva: World Economic Forum.

World Economic Forum (WEF). 2003b. *Annual Report 2002/2003 Building Trust, Peace and Reconciliation*. Geneva: World Economic Forum.

World Economic Forum (WEF). 2003c. *Global Agenda* January Issue 1.

World Economic Forum (WEF). 2003d. *Session Summaries* at http://www.weforum.org/en/knowledge/ 10/11/2007.

World Economic Forum (WEF). 2003e. "Open Forum." *Annual Meeting 2003 Building Trust Global Agenda Monitor* Geneva: World Economic Forum: 41.

World Economic Forum (WEF). 2003f. *Global Competitiveness Report 2002–2003*. Geneva: World Economic Forum.

World Economic Forum (WEF). 2003g. "Will Tougher Regulation Help Create Trust? 24.01.2003" at http://www.weforum.org/en/knowledge/Themes/Economy/Regulation/KN_SESS_SUMM_7619?url=/en/knowledge/Themes/Economy/Regulation/KN_SESS_SUMM_7619, July 16, 2007.

World Economic Forum (WEF). 2002a. *Annual Meeting 2002 Global Agenda Monitor*. Geneva: World Economic Forum.

World Economic Forum (WEF). 2002b. *Annual Report 2001–2002 Solidarity in a Challenging Year.* Geneva: World Economic Forum.
World Economic Forum (WEF). 2002e. "For Hope 31.01.2002." *Session summaries* at http://www2.weforum.org/site/knowledgenavigator.nsf/Content/, January 21, 2009.
World Economic Forum (WEF). 2002f. "Canadian Prime Minister Announces US $ 500 Million G-8 Partnership with Africa." February 3 at http://web.archive.org/web/20020208134140/www.weforum.org/site/homepublic.nsf/Content/Canadian... 07/01/2008.
World Economic Forum (WEF). 2002g. "Attacking Hunger and Poverty: The Other Global Campaign 01.02.2002." *Session Summaries* at http://www2.weforum.org/site/knowledgenavigator.nsf/Content/ 21/01/2009.
World Economic Forum (WEF). 2002h. "Responding to Financial Market Volatility 01.02.2002." *Session Summaries* at http://www2.weforum.org/site/knowledgenavigator.nsf/Content/, January 21, 2009.
World Economic Forum (WEF). 2001a. *World Link,* May/April.
World Economic Forum (WEF). 2001b. "Annual Meeting in Davos." *Annual Report 2000/2001.* Geneva: World Economic Forum: 4–5.
World Economic Forum (WEF). 2001c. *World Link,* March/April.
World Economic Forum (WEF). 2001h. "Debt Relief: Is It Just About Cancelling the Bill? 27.01.2001" at www.2.weforum.org/site/knowledgenavigator.nsf/Content/Debt%20Relief_%20Is%20IT%20Just%... January 21, 2009.
World Economic Forum (WEF). 2000a. *New Beginnings: Making a Difference Report on the Annual Meeting 2000.* Geneva: World Economic Forum at http://archive.bibalex.org/web/20000229211509/weforum.org/davos.nsf/Documents/Home+-+Annual+Meeting+-+About+the+Annual+Meeting+-+This+year's+Annual+Meeting 06/04/2006
World Economic Forum (WEF). 2000d. *Global Competitiveness Report 2000.* Geneva: World Economic Forum.
World Economic Forum (WEF). 2000e. "A SHARED VISION." *World Link,* March/April.
World Economic Forum (WEF). 2000f. "BRAVE NEW WORLD." *World Link,* March/April.
World Economic Forum (WEF). 2000g. *World Link,* March/April: 57.
World Economic Forum (WEF). 2000i. "Annual Meeting 2000, Selected List of Civil Society Representatives." at web.archive.org/web/20000302042723/www/weforum.org.davos.nsf/documents/Home+-+Annual..., November 23, 2007.
World Economic Forum (WEF). 2000j. "The World Economic Forum to Open 30th Annual Meeting." *Press Release* January 18 at web.archive.org/web/20000711234652/www.weforum.org/pressreleases.nsf/d25efacce8b2-cec7c125684300342f32/d6e7489beef2efe2c12568750062e76c!OpenDocument, November 23, 2007.
World Economic Forum (WEF). 2000k "Global Warning." *World Link,* March/April: 34.
World Economic Forum (WEF). 2000m. "Conference summaries." at web.archive.org/20000617155619/www.weforum.org/conferencesum.nsf/lede5-c855enc1256874003d7164/fb352abc0478d4d8c1256874005a79ce!OpenDocument. 2/12/2007.

World Economic Forum (WEF). 2000o. "Session summaries." *Knowledge Navigator,* at http://www2.weforum.org/site/knowledgenavigator.nsf/Content/ 02/12/2007.

World Economic Forum (WEF). 1999c. *World Link,* March/April.

World Economic Forum (WEF). 1999d. "Gore Announces Two Initiatives on Farm Talks and Debt Relief in Davos." *Press Release* January 29 at web.archive.org/web/19991012055047/www.weforum.org/publications/press releases/am9908 9..., November 14, 2007.

World Economic Forum (WEF). 1999e. *Global Competitiveness Report 1999.* Geneva: World Economic Forum.

World Economic Forum (WEF). 1999f. "Social issues, Science and technology at the World Economic Forum." *Press Releases* February 3 at web.archive.org/web/19991010015103/www.weforum.org/publications/pressreleases/am98 soci...November 14, 2007.

World Economic Forum (WEF). 1999h. "World Economic Forum to Open its Annual Meeting." *Press Release* January 19 at web.archive.org/web/19991011215145/www.weforum.org/publications/press releases/am9901 9..., November 14, 2007.

World Economic Forum (WEF). 1999i. "How Can We Deal with the Casino of Global Capitalism?" *World Economic Forum Knowledge Navigator* at www.weforum.org/site/knowledgenavigator.nsf/Content/5AE62729186CF02EC125..., January 28, 2004.

World Economic Forum (WEF). 1999k. "Gordimer questions value of globalization in Davos Closing Session." *Press Release,* February 2 at web.archive.org/web/19990903002911/live99.weforum.org/am9931_990202.asp, June 13, 07.

World Economic Forum (WEF). 1999o. "Session Summaries." at http://www2.weforum.org/site/knowledgenavigator.nsf/Content/Global+Issues.html 2/12/2007

World Economic Forum (WEF). 1998b. *World Link,* January/February.

World Economic Forum (WEF). 1998c. *World Link,* March/April.

World Economic Forum (WEF). 1998e. *Global Competitiveness Report 1998.* Geneva: World Economic Forum (WEF).

World Economic Forum (WEF). 1998f. "World Economic Forum to Focus on Managing Global Volatility." *Press Release* January 20 at web.archive.org/web/19991011200644/www.weforum.org/publications/press_releases/am98_vola..., November 14, 2007.

World Economic Forum (WEF). 1998g. "Economic leaders urge partnership with private sector against growing inequities." *Press Release* February 1 at web.archive.org/web/19991009211741/www.weforum.org/publications/press_releases/am98_igwe..., November 14, 2007.

World Economic Forum (WEF). 1997a. *World Link,* January/February.

World Economic Forum (WEF). 1997b. *World Link,* March/April.

World Economic Forum (WEF). 1996a. *Global Competitiveness Report 1996.* Geneva: World Economic Forum.

World Economic Forum (WEF). 1995a. *World Link,* January/February.

World Economic Forum (WEF). 1995b *World Link,* March/April.

World Economic Forum (WEF). 1994a. *World Link,* January/February.

World Economic Forum (WEF). 1993b. *World Link,* January/February.

World Economic Forum (WEF). 1993c. "Latin America Free trade revolution." *World Link,* March/April: 7.
World Economic Forum (WEF). 1992c. *World Link,* May/June.
World Economic Forum (WEF). 1991a. *World Link,* January/February.
World Economic Forum (WEF). 1990d. "George Soros: From Wall Street to Budapest."*World Link,* 5/6: 56–57.
World Economic Forum (WEF). 1989. "Forum Insights." *World Link,* 7/8: 25.
World Economic Forum and International Institute for Management Development (WEF and IMD). 1991. *World Competitiveness Report 1991.* WEF and IMD.
World Economic Forum and International Institute for Management Development (WEF and IMD). 1990. *World Competitiveness Report 1990.* Geneva: WEF and IMD.
World Economy, Ecology and Development or Welwirschaft, Okologie & Entwicklung (WEED). 2006. at www.weed-online.org, 08/06/2006.
World Social Forum (WSF). 2003a. "Point-counterpoint On the Tobin Tax." *Terra Viva* online January 28 at http://ipsnews.net/fsm2003/28.01.2003/nota8.shtml, November 9, 2011.
Wyles, John. 1987. "Davos Forum Looks to US for Lead." *Financial Times* (London), February 4: I2.
Yergin, Daniel and Joseph Stanislav. 1998. *The Commanding Heights.* New York: Simon and Schuster.
Younge, Gary. 1999. "New Beat to Saving the World from Debt." *Guardian,* February 15 at http://www.guardian.co.uk/world/1999/feb/15/debtrelief.development?INTCMP=SRCH, November 9, 2011.
Yunus, Muhammad. 2006. Interview, The Current, CBC Radio, broadcast November 14, 2006.
Zadek, Simon. 2005a. "Accountability Reflections 31-01-2005." *Open Democracy Blog 2005* at http://www.opendemocracy.net/node/18378, November 30, 2008.
Zadek, Simon. 2005b. "Millennium Development Goals 27-01-2005." *Open Democracy Blog 2005* at http://www.opendemocracy.net/node/18381, November 30, 2008.

Interviews

Anonymous International Public Servant. Telephone interview, May 27, 2008.
Anonymous Transnational Activist. Interviewed in Ottawa, June 2, 2005.
Manfred Bienefeld, Academic and activist. Interviewed in Ottawa, May 7, 2008.
Roy Culpeper, President North South Institute. Telephone Interview, April 28, 2008.
Steven Davis, Professor Emeritus of Philosophy, WEF participant. Interviewed in Ottawa, September 23, 2004.
John Dillon, Program Coordinator, Global Economic Justice, Kairos Canada. Telephone interview, May 30, 2008.
John Foster, Principle Researcher Civil Society/ Governance, North South Institute. Interviewed in Ottawa, July 6, 2007.
Pam Foster, Coordinator Halifax Initiative 1997–2005. Interviewed in Ottawa, April 17, 2008.

Mark Fried, Public Policy Coordinator Oxfam Canada. Interviewed in Ottawa, April 25, 2008.
Susan George, Academic and activist. Interviewed in Chicago, March 1, 2007.
Molly Kane, Executive Director Interpares. Interviewed in Ottawa, June 9, 2008.
Derek MacCuish, Executive Director Social Justice Committee. Telephone interview, May 2, 2008.
Paul Martin, Canadian Finance Minister 1993–2002, Canadian Prime Minister 2003–2006, WEF participant. Telephone interview, July 4, 2008.
John Mihevc, Team Leader Kairos Canada. Telephone Interview, April 18, 2008.
Bruce Montador, Canadian Public Servant, VP Multilateral Programs Branch CIDA. Gatineau, Quebec March 30, 2007.
David Morrison, Director of Communications UNDP, Director and Member of the Executive Board at the WEF 1995–1999, WEF participant. Telephone interview, June 17, 2008.
Maureen O'Neill, President International Development Research Centre 1997–2008, WEF participant. Interviewed in Ottawa, September 18, 2008.
Bruce Rayfuse, Director International Finance and Development Division, International Trade and Finance Branch, Department of Finance, Canada 2000–2005. Interviewed in Ottawa, April 30, 2008.
Sandra N. Smithey, Environment Program Officer, C.S. Mott Foundation, Telephone Interview, June 17, 2008.
William Thorsell, WEF Media Leader 1990–2000, WEF participant. Telephone interview, May 7, 2008.
Brian Tomlinson, Coordinator Policy Team the Canadian Council for International Cooperation. Interviewed in Ottawa, April 27, 2008.

Index